John Maynard Keynes

John Maynard Keynes is arguably the most important and influential economist of the twentieth century, and stands alongside Adam Smith and Karl Marx as one of the most famous economic thinkers of all time. Keynes's radical reassessment of the accepted principles of economics led to new ways of thinking about how to deal with financial crises and economic depressions, and encouraged governments to increase levels of state investment in order to encourage economic growth.

This historical biography shows how Keynes was more than an academic theorist and how his policy proposals had a significant impact on the economic and financial architecture of many Western countries from the 1920s onwards, and on the post-war international financial system. It also tells the story of his colourful private life – Keynes was an active member of the Bloomsbury group of artists and intellectuals, he entertained various 'secret' male lovers in his youth, he married a famous Russian ballerina in 1925 and he was also an astute collector of fine art and antiquarian books. Vincent Barnett emphasises the relationship between the personal and professional by presenting the book chapters in pairs, examining first the central features of Keynes's life, personal development and policy ideas over the period in question, and then the theoretical content of his major writings from the same period.

Barnett argues controversially that allowing psychology a much greater role within economics was a main but often-neglected feature of *The General Theory of Employment, Interest and Money*, and that Keynes's policy writings were more concerned with Britain's national interest than is sometimes recognised. The result is a concise new biography that is both intellectually rigorous and easily accessible to students and anyone else seeking to understand the life and work of England's foremost economist.

Vincent Barnett has been a Research Fellow on numerous economics and economic history projects at various UK universities. His previous publications include *E.E. Slutsky as Economist and Mathematician* (2011), *Marx* (2009) and *A History of Russian Economic Thought* (2005).

Routledge Historical Biographies

Series Editor: Robert Pearce

Routledge Historical Biographies provide engaging, readable and academically credible biographies written from an explicitly historical perspective. These concise and accessible accounts will bring important historical figures to life for students and general readers alike.

In the same series:

Bismarck by Edgar Feuchtwanger
Calvin by Michael A. Mullett
Oliver Cromwell by Martyn Bennett
Edward IV by Hannes Kleineke
Elizabeth I by Judith M. Richards
Gladstone by Michael Partridge
Henry V by John Matusiak
Henry VII by Sean Cunningham
Henry VIII by Lucy Wooding
Hitler by Michael Lynch
Lenin by Christopher Read
Louis XIV by Richard Wilkinson
Mao by Michael Lynch
Martin Luther King Jr. by
    Peter J. Ling
Martin Luther by
    Michael A. Mullet

Marx by Vincent Barnett
Mary Queen of Scots by
    Retha M. Warnicke
Mao by Michael Lynch
Mussolini by Peter Neville
Nehru by Ben Zachariah
Neville Chamberlain by Nick Smart
Emmeline Pankhurst by
    Paula Bartley
Richard III by David Hipshon
Trotsky by Ian Thatcher
Mary Tudor by Judith M. Richards

Forthcoming:

Franco by Antonio Cazorla-Sanchez
Gandhi by Benjamin Zachariah
Churchill by Robert Pearce

John Maynard Keynes

Vincent Barnett

Routledge
Taylor & Francis Group

LONDON AND NEW YORK

First published 2013
by Routledge
2 Park Square, Milton Park, Abingdon, Oxon OX14 4RN

Simultaneously published in the USA and Canada
by Routledge
711 Third Avenue, New York, NY 10017

Routledge is an imprint of the Taylor & Francis Group, an informa business

British Library Cataloguing in Publication Data
A catalogue record for this book is available from the British Library

Library of Congress Cataloging in Publication Data
Barnett, Vincent, 1967–
    John Maynard Keynes / Vincent Barnett.
    p. cm. – (Routledge historical biographies)
    1. Keynes, John Maynard, 1883–1946. 2. Keynesian economics. 3. Economists–Great
    Britain–Biography. I. Title.
    HB103.K47B29 2012
    330.15'6092–dc23
    2012026006

ISBN: 978-0-415-56769-5 (hbk)
ISBN: 978-0-415-56770-1 (pbk)
ISBN: 978-0-203-07475-6 (ebk)

Typeset in Garamond
by Saxon Graphics Ltd, Derby

Printed and bound in Great Britain by the MPG Books Group

Contents

List of plates   vii
Acknowledgements   ix

Introduction   1

1   A most indescribable and extraordinary game   14

2   Early writings   27

3   Selling economics by the hour and on the Q.T. (of M.)   37

4   Early economics   52

5   Killing Germans as cheaply as possible   63

6   The economic consequences of war   82

7   Cycling for Britain's national interest   94

8   The method of modern statesmen   116

9   The fool's gold standard and *laissez faire*   127

10 The fluctuating value of monetary reform   148

11 Organising prosperity   158

12 It all comes out in the wash   184

13 Multiplying (un)employment by expectations   198

14 Liquidising the classical theory   226

15 War finance and the post-war economic order   248

Conclusion   261
Notes   278
Index   295

List of plates

Plates (between pages 150 and 151)

1 Keynes in the early 1920s.
2 Keynes in 1925 with his wife the Russian ballet
  dancer Lydia Lopokova.
3 Keynes formulates a plan to finance the war and to
  avoid its most disastrous economic consequences.
4 Keynes in his study with his extraordinary collection
  of rare and valuable antiquarian books.

Acknowledgements

My first debt is to Keynes's previous biographers, Roy Harrod, Donald Moggridge and Robert Skidelsky, whose valuable works have been consulted throughout the writing of this book. Skidelsky's three-volume account is an especially impressive achievement, and this more modest Routledge Historical Biography on Keynes cannot hope to compete with Skidelsky's monumental effort with respect to scope. It can, however, provide a different perspective, a fresh approach and an easier point of entry for those lacking the time to devote to three long volumes. Moggridge's remarkable efforts in editing Keynes's *Collected Writings* have also proved invaluable. To save repetition, in the references the various volumes of the *Collected Writings* are listed simply as *CW*.

My second debt is to the archivists and librarians at King's College, Cambridge, who were very helpful on my visits to the Keynes Papers, and have kindly given their permission to quote directly from Keynes's personal papers. Unpublished writings of J.M. Keynes © The Provost and Scholars of King's College, Cambridge, 2013. My third debt is to Professor Robert Pearce, whose comments on draft versions of the chapters of this book as it was being composed were extremely helpful and wise, and always promptly received.

Given that much of my previous work has been devoted to Russian economists, how I came to write this book deserves to be explained. I first visited the Keynes Papers for my 1998 book on N.D. Kondratiev, who had met with Keynes at Cambridge in 1924. Having seen the historian's feast that is the Keynes Papers first hand, and realising more fully Keynes's own connection with

Russia, I began researching Keynes and Russia during the First World War, and subsequently published two journal articles on this theme. Much later, the opportunity of writing a second contribution to the Routledge Historical Biography series arose, and I selected Keynes. I hope that readers do not think this was a regrettable choice.

Introduction

Geniuses *are* very peculiar.[1]

J.M. Keynes

John Maynard Keynes was undoubtedly the most influential economist of the twentieth century. For his followers this was unquestionably a positive thing, enabling economic growth across the world by encouraging increased state investment and higher levels of employment, while for his critics this was certainly a negative thing, bringing about increased inflation and a greater susceptibility to crises through reckless government expenditure. It might even be argued that these diametrically opposite views were two sides of the same coin.

Whether Keynes was also the 'greatest' economist of the twentieth century is a more contentious question, one that usually elicits a much wider range of responses. Was he the 'greatest' economist as a pure theorist, as an applied economist, as an economic policy adviser, or even as all three? Without doubt it can be said for sure that he was one of the greatest economic innovators of the twentieth century, and (arguably) one of the three most important and influential economists of all time, alongside his illustrious predecessors Adam Smith and Karl Marx.

But, just as with these other two intellectual giants (and perhaps in some ways even more so), Keynes's legacy has proved extremely controversial and frequently disputed, but perhaps in a rather different way. If Smith was celebrated (or damned) as the philosopher-king of free market capitalism, and Marx was celebrated (or damned) as the philosopher-king of centrally planned socialism, what precisely was Keynes the philosopher-king of? This book will argue that he was the philosopher-king of pragmatic economic realism, a subtle and contradictory practicality that both Smith and Marx were often blind towards, and sometimes denied was possible, but was in truth the only way past the rigid fantasy-ideologies of political extremism.

Part of Keynes's problem as a philosopher-economist was precisely the non-messianic complexity of his approach. Unlike the over-simplified versions of both Smith ('the market solves everything') and Marx ('the plan solves everything'), even the over-simplified version of Keynes ('state intervention solves everything that the market cannot') is more restrained and less indoctrinating than either of the previous two. Pragmatic realism is hardly the most visionary of philosophies, but it should be recognised that there is no necessary connection between how inspiring particular sets of ideas are, and how accurate and useful they are. It should not be forgotten that Nazi ideology was hugely inspiring to those who believed in it, and that sceptical agnostics who doubt the efficacy of all political action in principle have never murdered their opponents on a mass scale: the worst political actions are always supremely and passionately motivated.

An indication that Keynes's legacy has sometimes been misinterpreted, even (or especially) in his country of birth, comes from a very mundane topic: the naming of English towns. As was rightly explained in 1975:

> The surname 'Keynes' is pronounced 'Kaynes' as it is in several place-names in England, such as Horsted Keynes and (hopefully) Milton Keynes.[2]

Milton Keynes was an English new town constructed in the 1970s, fifty or so miles north of London. This quotation evidently tempted fate, as its name is actually pronounced as 'Milton Keeynes', not 'Milton Kaynes', but this was perhaps an apt misinterpretation for its era: the 1970s were a time when Keynes's theories were almost universally out of fashion. For many mainstream economists, the very idea of 'fashion' is something irrelevant to economic understanding. To the historian, however, fashion can be very significant, either as something to use in order to provide explanations for things as they were, or as something to carefully avoid, as falling into the trap of following an existing historiographical trend can produce misleading history.

Biography and the individual economist

A historical biography of an economist presents many traps for the unwary author. Firstly, the right balance must be struck between a consideration of the person's theoretical contributions to economics, and their life and work outside of pure economics. Following a successful previous example (Marx), this task will be accomplished here by presenting the main chapters in pairs. The first chapter of each pair will mainly consider Keynes's life and policy work in a given time-period, while the second chapter will mainly consider his theoretical contributions in this same period.

The reason for this division is so that readers can navigate their way through the book by following only the first or only the second of each pair of chapters if they so desire, depending on whether they are more interested in Keynes the practical policy-maker or Keynes the theoretical economist. Or they can read through all the chapters in sequential order, in order to obtain a fuller understanding of both. The first chapter of each pair will contain only a limited presentation of Keynes's economic ideas, so that readers who find the theoretical aspects of his work difficult to follow can still find much of interest to tackle. In the second chapter of each pair, full compass to a presentation of Keynes's wide range of theoretical innovations will be allowed, which means that the level of discussion will inevitably be higher. A great effort will be made to explain his economic ideas in as clear and as straightforward a manner as is possible, but the subject itself necessitates that complex terms and some algebraic equations are deployed in the second chapter of each pair.

Secondly, the relationship between economics and history as subject-disciplines has not always been an amicable one. Many mainstream economists have eschewed history as irrelevant to economics, and many empiricist historians have eschewed economic theory as irrelevant to history. Thankfully, Keynes did not ignore history, as it was for him an essential element of conceptual understanding. Many of his works of pure theory included historical examples and employed arguments based on historical data. But this raises an additional problem: how far does his economic theory stand or fall on whether his historical analyses have proved enduring? This is a complex question, but some consideration must be given to it in such a biography, in order to explain more fully Keynes's own arguments and his conceptual legacy.

Thirdly, the background and experience of the ideal author should perhaps be considered. Should the biography of an economist be written by a fellow economist, a historian, or even by a specialist in biographical study? All three have their pitfalls: biographers do not usually understand economic theory that well, economists are rarely also trained in historical research, and historians more usually focus on social and political events rather than on intellectual developments. The author of this book can at least claim to have written detailed biographical studies of individual economists before (on N.D. Kondratiev and E.E. Slutsky).[3] The wilfully unjust reviewer still has an easy point of critical leverage, however, as these were 'only' Russian economists: British economists are (they might claim) a whole different ballgame.

'Keynesian revolutions'

For a short and youthful period, Keynes's dictum that 'In the long run we are all dead' made something of an impression on the author of this book, who took it to mean fatalistically that whatever human beings tried to do in whatever realms were chosen, they were all condemned to suffer the same fate in the end, so just sit back and enjoy the journey. On deeper and more mature reflection, however, an entirely opposite meaning emerged, namely, that we should treat life in the short run as especially precious and meaningful, since the long run was always out of our direct control. Such Gestalt switches are of course an important part of the focus of this book, as the subject is most famous for bringing about such a revolution in economic theory virtually single-handedly.

What many refer to bravely as 'the Keynesian revolution' is of course an essentially contested concept within a continuously disputed subject-area. If in the late 1940s, a book could simply and directly be called *The Keynesian Revolution*, by 1978 an article (without fear of derision) could conclusively be called 'After Keynesian Macroeconomics'.[4] In 1999, a highly praised book documenting the crafty and protracted processes of *Fabricating the Keynesian Revolution* was the titular order of the day, but by 2011, Keynes had boldly returned as a heroic *Capitalist Revolutionary*.[5] The 'Keynesian revolution' will certainly be considered to some extent in this book, but the method adopted by the author in the main chapters will be only to consider as reliable primary sources what Keynes and his contemporaries thought they were doing at the time (as expressed in their writings), and also how observers interpreted their ideas and actions at the time. Indeed, a radical historicist could claim that, in order to prevent later interpretations of Keynes found in the secondary literature from 'polluting' their own analysis of his work, even subconsciously, only primary source materials should be read by historians when conducting such research.

The author of this book would not go quite so far, but does aim to present a historical reconstruction of Keynes's own aims and beliefs at the time he was advocating them, not a rational reconstruction of what economists today take from Keynes as being 'correct', or by what methods Keynes's 'real' contributions were integrated into mainstream economics as it developed after the Second World War. How later commentators have analysed the various issues, and how subsequent economists have taken up Keynes's theoretical legacy in various ways, will not form a major part of the analysis. Thus, the book will focus almost exclusively on Keynes's own philosophy, politics and economics and its contemporaneous critics, not 'Keynesian economics' and its numerous later mutations. As the title of a well-known book of 1968 implied, what *On Keynesian Economics and the Economics of Keynes* actually meant could be two very different things.

An indication of how the approach taken here differs from some other approaches adopted by writers towards major thinkers such as Keynes and Marx, can be gleaned from the title of a recent book by Terry Eagleton: *Why Marx Was Right*. Now, Eagleton is a talented literary theorist, but the title of his latest book on Marx is patently ridiculous. Was Marx equally 'right' when (prior to 1844) he was a critic of communist ideas, and some time later when he had become a communist advocate? Was Marx equally 'right' when he was a full supporter of Young Hegelianism, and some time later when he had developed a sophisticated critique of this movement? Was Marx equally 'right' both when (during 1848) he advocated a political alliance between the working classes and the bourgeoisie, and some time later when he had rejected such an alliance as unreliable? It might come as something of a shock to Eagleton, but people's beliefs invariably change and develop over time. To search for a 'historian's stone' that can transmute a given thinker's base inconsistencies into golden uniformity, by interpreting the entirety of their work within the framework of a single 'key' element that retrospectively validates it all, is not the mark of an objective researcher, only of a political propagandist.

Hence, this book aims to celebrate and revel in the historical, human and emergent Keynes, not to fabricate the 'real' or 'ultimate' Keynes who was either always right (as sometimes suggested by his supporters) or always wrong (as sometimes suggested by his critics). If readers doubt that anyone could be so misguided as to claim that Keynes the economist was always right, then they should consider the following assertive passage from a book very reasonably entitled *Keynes and After* from 1967: 'the basic fact is that with the acceptance of the *General Theory*, the days of uncontrollable mass unemployment in advanced industrial countries are over'.[6] In the early twenty-first century, nobody would even think about writing such foolishness.

Keynes the historical biographer

That Keynes himself would have applauded the historical approach to understanding an individual's intellectual development is evident from his own very insightful biographical sketches, of which there are numerous instances. A key example was that on the English scientist Isaac Newton, indicatively titled 'Newton, the Man'. Here Keynes argued that:

> I believe that Newton was different from the conventional picture of him. He was less ordinary, more extraordinary, than the nineteenth century cared to make him out. Geniuses *are* very peculiar...Newton came to be thought of as the first and greatest of the modern age of scientists, a rationalist...I do not see him in this light...He was the last of the magicians...Newton was

profoundly neurotic of a not unfamiliar type, but— I should say from the records – a most extreme example…Like all his type he was wholly aloof from women…the clue to his mind is to be found in his unusual powers of continuous concentrated introspection.[7]

A number of pertinent points emerge from Keynes's analysis of Newton. Firstly, the importance of understanding the scientist as a psychological type to explaining how scientific invention has often operated. And secondly, the importance of understanding Newton's non-scientific beliefs to comprehending his overall life and work. Keynes also extended this personality type approach to politicians: the US President Woodrow Wilson, for example, was declared a theological type.[8]

By using such ideas, Keynes was (perhaps not always consciously) drawing on the emerging psychological ideas of the time. Carl Jung's work on psychological types was disseminated in English in the 1920s, while Gordon Allport's work on personality traits was being developed in the 1930s.[9] Allport was especially concerned to distinguish his own approach from that of the older faculty psychology: personality traits were dynamic patterns derived from observable streams of behaviour, and hence they were not permanently fixed in stone, but subject to ongoing interactions with external forces such as the environment.[10] The young Keynes noted the 'historical interest' of the faculty hypothesis – mental phenomena being conceived as innate potentialities – but as late as 1936, he was actively using the concept of 'sanguine temperament' to explain aspects of business investment behaviour.[11]

A partial contrast with the sanguine investor was the neurotic scientist such as Newton. Although Keynes's biographical sketch of Newton was not especially long, it is very apparent from reading it that its author would have favoured the writing of 'thick' historical reconstruction of a scientist's contributions in their true living context, taking care to consider individual character psychology in detail, not a narrow rational reconstruction of only their purely scientific pursuits divorced from an understanding of them as complex individuals. The same reasoning would also apply to biographies of economists.

Perhaps Keynes's most important biographical study was that of the economist T.R. Malthus, 'important' in the sense of indicating its author's profound sense of connection to a long and eminent line of intellectual heritage. Malthus is today most famous for suggesting that population growth might outrun the availability of the earth's resources to support it. Keynes argued that Malthus's most important book, *An Essay on the Principle of Population* of 1798, was:

> ...profoundly in the English tradition of humane science – in that tradition of Scotch and English thought, in which there has been, I think, an extraordinary continuity of *feeling*, if I may so express it, from the eighteenth century to the present time – the tradition which is suggested by the names of Locke, Hume, Adam Smith, Paley, Bentham, Darwin, and Mill, a tradition marked by a love of truth and a most notable lucidity, by a prosaic sanity free from sentiment or metaphysic, and by an immense disinterestedness and public spirit.[12]

Keynes wanted to be (and ultimately was) in this long tradition of 'prosaic sanity', but he bemoaned the 'almost total obliteration of Malthus's line of approach' that had taken place as a consequence of the dominating influence of David Ricardo, which had (he claimed) been a complete disaster for the progress of economics.[13] No doubt having in mind his own exalted academic upbringing, Keynes later characterised Malthus as the 'first of the Cambridge economists'. In emphasising the continuous development of the historical Keynes across this book, rather than only the ultimate creation of the true 'Keynesian economist' (an Aunt Sally of uncertain origin), Keynes's own methodology of writing biography is thus being accurately followed.

Keynes's work as a biographer is important to understanding his legacy as an economist in another way too. For an economist to write such biographies is not especially common. For example, Adam Smith wrote little biography as such, and his historical works were usually organised thematically rather than by individual author. Smith's contemporaneous biographer Dugald Stewart, a noted philosopher, even declared that: 'I hate biography'.[14] Karl Marx certainly did discuss individual historical figures, but only really considered them as cyphers for wider class interests.

In contrast, there is an entire large volume of Keynes's *Collected*

Writings that has been devoted to his biographical studies, which contains around forty biographical sketches of politicians, economists, statisticians, scientists and assorted other individuals, which he willingly composed in different periods of his life, some (but not all) being obituaries. They range in length from the very brief (one page or so on the statistician Wilhelm Lexis) to the substantial (sixty pages or so on the economist Alfred Marshall). Moreover, some of his more important books contain significant biographical sections, such as *The Economic Consequences of the Peace* of 1919. Evidently, Keynes was very interested in the relation between an individual's personal characteristics and life-story, and their contributions to public and/or scientific endeavour more broadly conceived.

He first published a collection of his own *Essays in Biography* in 1933, and continued actively working on this theme thereafter. He was also talented at documenting such things as, according to one of his intimate friends, the two biographical memoirs on Carl Melchior (a member of the German delegation to the Paris Peace Conference in 1919) and on his early philosophical beliefs were 'among the best things that Lord Keynes ever wrote'.[15] His biographical studies were, in addition, supremely powerful. When the British Prime Minister David Lloyd George eventually read one of Keynes's sketches of him, which had been removed from an earlier book for fear of causing offence, it resulted in a major breach of their friendship: the truth sometimes hurts. It even appears that Keynes held back on allowing his biographical interest full rein, as he was sometimes 'painfully conscious that a cloud of witnesses would rise up against me and very few in my support'.[16] In hindsight he judged his biographical studies as containing 'more understatement than overstatement', and hence he stood by them entirely.

An essential theoretical component that is often used in the study of individual biography is psychology. In his brief sketch of a memorable meeting with the novelist D.H. Lawrence in 1914, Keynes wrote a little sceptically of the ultimately bogus 'thin rationalism' that was 'skipping on the crust of the lava' of the passions of the human heart.[17] Another way to describe such 'lava passions of the heart' might be psychological or behavioural propensities. As will be seen in various parts of this book, Keynes's profound concern with the psychology of behaviour was not only limited to his biographical studies, but eventually formed a significant part of his developing economic analysis as well. It also formed a key part of his political analysis as, for example, President Wilson's failings at the Paris Peace Conference were due in part to 'elements of character and psychology'.[18]

As another example, in 1930 Keynes quoted the psychiatrist Sigmund Freud on 'the love of money, and gold in particular' as a partial explanation for why the gold standard had been so ingrained in the symbolic subconscious of many people.[19] The psychologist William James explained the miserly hoarding of gold as being the result of valuing it 'not for its own sake, but for its powers. Demonetize it, and see how quickly they will get rid of it!'.[20] Keynes had studied Freud's writings in the mid-1920s, and described him as being endowed with a scientific imagination of genius.[21] He also referenced James's work.[22] Keynes's close friends Leonard and Virginia Woolf issued the English translation of Freud's *The Ego and the Id* through their own publishing company in 1927.[23] Another of Keynes's friends (James Strachey) was actually a patient of Freud's between 1920 and 1922. Keynes even linked biology, psychology and economics together directly, writing in 1930 that: 'we have been expressly evolved by nature – with all our impulses and deepest instincts – for the purpose of solving the economic problem' of guaranteeing subsistence.[24]

Neither was the relationship between economics and psychology in the early twentieth century an entirely one-way street. Freud labelled the psychological process by which an unpleasant state of tension was relieved by the relaxation of this tension, i.e. the replacement of pain with pleasure, a mental sequence that was observed from 'the *economic* point of view'.[25] It might even be possible to argue that at its root, Keynes's most famous book *The General Theory of Employment, Interest and Money* of 1936 involved the creation of a 'radical psychologist' agenda for economics itself, but this is jumping the biographical gun.

The approach adopted

There are various existing accounts of Keynes's life and work, and hence care must be taken to delineate and explain the uniqueness of this particular volume. Its main focus is on presenting and analysing Keynes's ideas, policies and contributions to both practical affairs of state and to developing new economic theory, situated in their proper historical context. The basic question investigated is to identify, explain and evaluate the underlying ideas and goals that Keynes was trying to articulate and achieve within and across his economics and other work, and if/how they developed over time. Consequently, consideration of his private life is most notably made when this had a direct and immediate influence on his professional life, and (initially) to provide a basic background sketch for the period covered in the volume as a whole. The colourful sexual escapades of Keynes's youth (numerically tabulated by him under the headings 'c', 'a' and 'w') are (today) relatively well known amongst aficionados, but do not form a major object of investigation here.

This might sound obvious enough. But to illustrate the difficulties of entering this domain lightly, the true story will be relayed of a dogmatically anti-market post-Keynesian economist ('the market is a disequilibrium wrecking-ball'), who delighted in explaining that Keynes was able to see 'outside the box' when it came to economic theory at least in part because of his homosexuality. When it was then relayed in response that by the time of the birth of the 'Keynesian revolution' in 1936, Keynes had clearly chosen heterosexuality, whereas earlier in his life when he was predominantly homosexual he had been a staunch advocate of the orthodox quantity theory of money, no cogent reply was forthcoming. It is amazing how wilfully maintained falsehoods of cause and effect are close to the hearts of so many political radicals (of both the left and the right).

It should also be emphasised that the author is a historian of ideas rather than an economist, and hence that what is conventionally taken to be Keynes's greatest contribution to economics by far – *The General Theory of Employment, Interest and Money* – is accorded only near-equal consideration alongside his other major works. This is not because the author believes that its influence on mainstream economics has been exaggerated; rather, only that the influence of Keynes's other works on the political, social and economic thought of the time was very significant. Thus, the book aims to document Keynes's influence both within and outside of economics in equal measure, and also within and outside of the UK. This latter issue deserves some further consideration. Keynes was English, and grew up in Cambridge, which was at the time a quintessentially English university city. However, because of the pre-eminent position of the UK in the world economy in the first three or four decades of the twentieth century, Keynes's writings were frequently international in scope and influence. Indeed, his first book was about India.

Keynes's life encompassed what is now regarded as the twilight and the end (or collapse) of the British Empire. He was often dealing with issues of managing what is seen today as the decline/ overthrow/succession of British political dominance in various parts of the globe, and concomitant problems relating to assisting economic development in regions with close socio-economic ties to the UK. Hence, it has sometimes been the case that Keynes's own views specifically about the UK, and its own role in the international order, have been partially obscured by intercontinental clouds. In this book, a definite effort will be made to trace Keynes's views on this topic as much as is possible, while still giving international issues a fair and reasonable degree of coverage.

It is beyond dispute that a great deal of Keynes's writings and dealings were concerned (in one way or another) with the UK, or more accurately, with aspects of economic policy relating to specific issues of immediate concern to the UK government and its financial system. However, this is not quite the same as saying that Keynes was always predominantly concerned with the long-term progress of the UK as a whole. Indeed, he only wrote two short lectures with titles that might immediately (on a very preliminary search) be taken to indicate that he was examining the overall prospects of the UK conceived in its very widest context. They were entitled 'The Economic Position in England' and 'The Economic Transition in England', and (paradoxically) they were presented to an audience in Moscow in 1925. The latter lecture in particular situated the position of Great Britain within a long-period scheme of economic epochs that evolved over centuries.

Other publications, such as *The Economic Consequences of Mr Churchill* also from 1925 and articles like 'British Foreign Policy' from 1937, were clearly about issues of immediate concern to the UK at specific instances in time, but they did not (at least obviously) provide a coherent, detailed account of the long-run development of the UK taken as a whole in all its various dimensions. He did in 1930 publish an essay entitled 'Economic Possibilities for our Grandchildren', but even this was mostly about the world economy. Keynes's views on the best path and overall prospects for the UK, conceived as part of global economic trends operating over many decades, have thus usually to be pieced together from his more immediate concerns relating to specific issues that required his urgent attention. A deliberate attempt to accomplish this task will be made in this book, as part of the wider goals identified above.

Finally, it is necessary to recognise that in any one-volume part-biographical account, full coverage cannot be given to every single issue that the subject became involved with, and the choices that have been made here are to focus fully on Keynes's economics, his wider philosophy, his concerns with the UK economy in its wider context, and his policy roles in various different contexts: his later work on international institutions has been given somewhat less coverage. Whilst this international work was undoubtedly important from a world-historical perspective, its relevance to his evolving theoretical work on economics was (arguably) only moderate. Thus, the book is structured so that *The General Theory* of 1936 constitutes the main culmination of the economic analysis: the later impact of this book, and Keynes's own activities after it was published, are only more briefly sketched. Each biographer has his or her own particular approach, and the one employed in this volume has at least been clearly articulated.

1 A most indescribable and extraordinary game

John Maynard Keynes (henceforth simply Keynes) was born on 5 June 1883 at 6 Harvey Road, Cambridge, the first child of upper middle-class parents John Neville Keynes (henceforth J.N. Keynes) and Florence Ada Brown. Keynes's parents had only recently married (in August 1882), and they were both directly associated with Cambridge University colleges. J.N. Keynes was a Fellow of Pembroke College between 1876 and 1882, and thereafter until 1885 he continued with some teaching duties; Florence Keynes had been a student at Newnham College. Both were keen readers of literature and plays who encouraged the young Keynes to engage with intellectual and aesthetic pursuits from an early age. J.N. Keynes was also an avid collector of stamps and butterflies, and encouraged his children (of which two more followed in 1885 and 1887) to participate in his hobbies.

In 1891, J.N. Keynes became Secretary to the Local Examinations Syndicate in Cambridge, and in 1893 he was elected Secretary to the University's Council of the Senate. His most significant contributions to intellectual endeavour were the publication of two books. The first, *Studies and Exercises in Formal Logic* of 1884, quickly became a standard textbook on the principles of logical analysis that was reprinted many times, and grew directly out of his teaching duties. The second, *The Scope and Method of Political Economy* of 1891, was also a product of his lectures, but was more anomalous in its economics content, as it examined methodological issues that were not always considered by mainstream British economists of the period. Although this second book was recognised as important by some, it was not particularly influential, and soon became the sort of book that was politely mentioned in passing, rather than being avidly read, digested and debated in detail. The issues that it considered were not those that excited the imaginations of many British economists, as methodological questions were viewed as already resolved, or even as quaintly passé.

Keynes was a bright and inquisitive child, but was prone to bouts of illness; for example, he contracted rheumatic fever and then suffered from St Vitus's dance, for a time exhibiting uncontrolled blinks and twitches. He was also sure that he was physically ugly, although the surviving pictures show a perfectly normal and rather handsome young child. Keynes began attending kindergarten in 1889, where he demonstrated some skill in arithmetic, and then preparatory school in 1892. He was also home taught, and worked keenly and conscientiously at his studies; impressive intellectual talents quickly made him appear superior to many of his fellow students. School reports show he was very successful and hardworking, if not quite a child prodigy in the Mozart/Mill category. The subjects that he studied at school were of the period, namely classical languages, mathematics and poetry. Keynes excelled especially in mathematics (arithmetic and algebra), and after taking the Eton entry examinations, was elected a King's Scholar starting in 1897.

Eton

Those from very different cultures often think that English public schools are unfathomably posh, and Eton's proximity to royal Windsor undoubtedly gives it added aristocratic cachet, but there was also some limited scope for entrance on merit through competitive examination, and this was how Keynes achieved admission. The academic curriculum at Eton at the end of the nineteenth century was dominated by the classics (i.e. Greek and Latin poetry and prose) and mathematics, with the addition of some history and French language. The physical curriculum included cricket, rowing, Eton football and the Eton Wall Game.

The latter was a unique sporting recreation that is only played on the Eton college field according to arcane rules involving a very high brick wall, a garden door, a tree, 'calx', 'furking', 'bully' and 'shy', which Keynes characterised favourably as 'a most indescribable and extraordinary game'.[1] Others have described it as a 'character-building brawl'.[2] The school today describes the essence of this game as follows:

> The Eton Wall Game is exceptionally exhausting and is far more skilful than might appear to the uninitiated. The skill consists in the remorseless application of pressure and leverage as one advances inch by painful inch through a seemingly impenetrable mass of opponents. Few sports offer less to the spectator...[3]

As ample verification of this last point, a full goal in the main match (worth nine points), as opposed to what was called a 'shy' (worth only one point), was last scored in 1909. To some outsiders, the Eton Wall Game was probably seen as an antiquated vestige of the obscure customs of the English upper classes, which the American Institutionalist economist Thorstein Veblen might have described as a prime example of the pecuniary canons of conspicuous leisure.[4]

At this point it is apt to consider Keynes's social background. The author of the most detailed biography described this as upper middle class, and the general attitudes of the young Keynes as middle class (as opposed to being aristocratic or working class).[5] This was true to a large degree, but Eton was, at the end of the nineteenth century, usually seen as the privileged preserve of the very wealthy and/or the very well connected. Keynes was (in part) coached through the entrance examinations by well-educated parents and by good schooling, although this special attention would have come to nothing without his natural talents: one school report declared glowingly that 'he has a remarkable mind: full of taste and perception'.[6]

Keynes subsequently found that Eton abounded in social hierarchies, formal examinations, contested prizes, ancient traditions, conservative aspirations and stinging punishments (caning). It also abounded in obscure terminology – such as 'College Pop', 'Oppidans', 'Trials', 'First Hundred', 'Eton Fives', 'Tugs', 'Fags', and 'Aquatics', all with their own special meaning known only to the initiated.

Intellectually at least Eton was more freewheeling, and many of Keynes's surviving essays demonstrate that he was encouraged to read widely and think for himself – they will be considered in more detail in the next chapter. It is worth noting that, although classics and mathematics were often favoured, Keynes took history as an individual course in the third year, and his essays in this subject were invariably clearly written, well focused on answering the question, and demonstrated a significant degree of maturity, at least for an English schoolboy. The very end of the nineteenth century was, of course, still the Victorian era, with British forces being occupied by the Boer War beginning in 1899, and the Boxer uprisings in China in 1900. From a twenty-first century perspective, such dramatic events seem to mark the beginning of the end for European control in Africa and Asia. The issue of the Boer War briefly caught Keynes's attention, in relation to which he took an equivocal anti-war position, but there was little inkling at Eton that such political events, and the end of the Victorian era in 1901, would mark the start of a profound change of fortune for the British Empire as a whole.

Although in boarding at Eton, Keynes had entered into another social milieu from that of his parents' middle-class Cambridge origins, it is clear that, in the main, he fitted in well with the public school system of education, and in turn, it served him well in developing his natural talents. He did not really rebel against anything of great significance, with the partial exception of religion, which he looked upon as an irrational anomaly of the intellect, and against which his opposition was purely intellectual. Even the intimations of feelings and acts of homosexuality contained in some of his school letters were, at Eton at least, hardly unusual, being regarded as 'sexual experiments' that many public school boys indulged in, at least temporarily.

What was rather special about the whole Eton set-up, at least for someone from a more humble background, was how attendance at this school appeared to railroad many students on an auspicious journey to the highest echelons of English public life. At the beginning of 1902, even before Keynes had finished his Eton education, his father was planning his future progress on to King's College, Cambridge, and then to the Civil Service examinations in order to enter government service, as if all this was a totally natural sequence of human metamorphosis. The only serious question that (briefly) required resolution was King's College or Trinity. In the event, Keynes won a scholarship to attend the former, and his Etonian heritage, together with his impressive intellectual capacities, ensured that he was welcomed there with open arms.

An undergrad at Cambridge

If Eton represented Keynes's intellectual beginnings, then King's College catalysed his intellectual blossoming. The serene beauty of the College and its grounds is still very much in evidence today, and visitors may experience an atmosphere of ethereal detachment as they pass from the main road in which it sits, through to the immaculately-kept quadrangle courtyard, and then on to the restrained but still imposing architecture of the main building. Keynes had entered King's in October 1902 to study mathematics, but immediately his interests and attachments diverged outwards towards philosophy and (briefly) theology, and sometime later towards economics. He later described himself in this period as a 'nonconformist', in the sense of an unwillingness to adhere to accepted doctrine simply as a means of being conventional.[7] One of his first tutors in mathematics was E.W. Hobson, author of *The Theory of Functions of a Real Variable* of 1907 and brother of the historical economist J.A. Hobson, author of *The Evolution of Modern Capitalism* of 1894.

It is important to recognise that Cambridge in this period was the home of various early twentieth-century intellectual giants, as they are unequivocally regarded today, the concentration of which in one location has (in the UK at least) been rarely repeated since. For instance, the Cambridge Conversazione Society, or the Cambridge Apostles as they were more commonly known, had the philosophers Bertrand Russell, G.E. Moore, A.N. Whitehead and J.E. McTaggart as members, as well as writers like E.M. Forster, Lytton Strachey and Clive Bell. Teaching economics at Cambridge was Alfred Marshall, certainly the most important British economist of the period; A.C. Pigou later joined him in the economics arena. Marshall's *Principles of Economics* of 1890 was (in this subject) the defining text of the era, just as Russell's *Principles of Mathematics* of 1903 was for its own philosophical sphere of influence. Another famous economist, Ralph Hawtrey, was an older member of the Apostles. Arriving at Cambridge to find such illustrious fellow attendees and accessible teachers – Russell soon became known to Keynes affectionately as 'Bertie' – must have been akin to winning the educational jackpot. Members of the Cambridge Apostles later formed the famous Bloomsbury group of writers, artists and intellectuals, of which Keynes was to become the most influential member.

Out of all these celebrated and diverse influences, one figure stands out as having by far the greatest immediate intellectual impact on Keynes's own thinking: G.E. Moore (1873–1958). It is important to put this influence in its Cambridge context. Russell and Whitehead were philosophers known as much for their investigation of the foundations of mathematics, as for work in more conventional philosophical areas such as epistemology and morality. Indeed, Russell's first book was about the foundations of geometry, and his *magnum opus* (*Principia Mathematica*, written with Whitehead) was a key part of the 'foundations crisis' that had enveloped mathematics from 1900 onwards. McTaggart was an idealist philosopher in the spirit of G.W.F. Hegel, an approach that gave full scope to the speculative imagination, as was another Cambridge Fellow G.L. Dickinson. In the social science arena, Marshall was the *doyen* of British neoclassical economics, i.e. a theory in which subjective value was used to explain exchange proportions via want satisfaction, and prices were determined by balancing supply and demand. Pigou was one of his immediate intellectual heirs, whom Keynes would later characterise as being responsible for the basic postulates of classical economics.

Moore's work in philosophy was, however, quite distinct from these various currents. His most important book, *Principia Ethica*, was published in 1903, or in the year after Keynes had first entered King's College. Its main theme (ethics) was some way askew from the burgeoning growth in philosophical logic as represented by Russell, or the Cambridge Hegelians, or even neoclassical economics as embodied by Marshall. Keynes had attended Moore's lectures on ethics in his second term at King's, and as he later recalled about *Principia Ethica*:

...its effect on us, and the talk which preceded and followed it, dominated...Moore completely ousted McTaggart, Dickinson, Russell. The influence was not only overwhelming...it was exciting, exhilarating, the beginning of a renaissance, the opening of a new heaven on earth...[8]

Keynes had clearly experienced a philosophical revelation due to Moore's book, the nature of which will be considered in more detail in the next chapter. However, it is important to realise that Moore's dramatic impact on Keynes was not really repeated through its impact on British philosophy as a whole. *Principia Ethica* had a profound influence on members of the Bloomsbury group, but that was where its influence was greatest.[9] Moore's 'exhilarating renaissance' in philosophy was far less expansive and long lasting than that of Russell's later student, Ludwig Wittgenstein, who really did initiate a revolution in British philosophy. But Wittgenstein arrived at Cambridge a decade or so after Keynes. Thus, although the young Keynes was undoubtedly a product of Cambridge, he was also partially a nonconformist within its walls.

The other end of the stereotype of Cambridge University aloofness that sometimes appears, as opposed to the intellectual powerhouse, is more treacherous: spies. Both Anthony Blunt and Guy Burgess were Cambridge educated, although in Trinity College, and both were Cambridge Apostles, although some time after Keynes. Keynes of course found Karl Marx's dialectically droll hymn to the working classes – *Das Kapital* – unappealing and even rather incomprehensible; he similarly found McTaggart's Hegelian metaphysics ultimately unappetising. There was a large difference between the national philosophical traditions of Germany and the UK at this time, the former being idealist and speculative, the latter empiricist and pragmatic. Keynes was unequivocally in the latter camp.

At King's College, Keynes avidly participated in various discussion and debating societies; he joined the Liberal Club (where he first listened to David Lloyd George), the Moral Science Club, the Walpole Society, presented papers to the Literary Society, indulged in recreational pursuits such as golf and bridge, and became president of the Cambridge Union. He also helped to create the Baskerville Club in order to indulge his book collecting habits. This latter aspect of his character deserves further attention. Keynes was an avid book collector throughout his life, a habit that had begun at an early age. Pigou described the walls of Keynes's rooms at Cambridge as being decorated with 'hundreds of ancient and curious books'.[10] For someone not afflicted with this addiction, it is difficult to convey the pleasures of acquiring antiquarian knowledge in exquisite form, by reading beautifully printed and decorated pages bound in fragrant leather. It's a little bit like taking cerebral snuff.

The youthful Keynes was so enamoured of his book collecting habit that he composed 'A Calendar of Books of J.M. Keynes' that lovingly listed his 330 acquisitions purchased between 1 November 1901 and 14 December 1902, where details of fine bindings, editions and prices paid were preserved. Item number one listed in the calendar was the complete works of Edmund Burke in twelve volumes, which cost Keynes four pounds and four shillings, a not insignificant sum. Burke was the leading political philosopher of conservatism; his most important work was *Reflections on the Revolution in France* of 1790. As an undergraduate, Keynes would write a long paper entitled 'The Political Doctrines of Edmund Burke', in which he stressed the importance of the notion that it was unwise to sacrifice a present benefit, for a doubtful greater advantage in the future.

The first (and one of the few) economics books entered in the calendar was Henry Sidgwick's *Principles of Political Economy*, 3rd edition, 1901, edited by J.N. Keynes, which was described as being 'a present from father'.[11] Sidgwick had been Professor of Moral Philosophy at Cambridge from 1882 onwards, his other important works being *The Methods of Ethics* of 1874 and *The Elements of Politics* of 1891.[12] Sidgwick was of the generation where the composition of treatises in multiple fields was still the norm. His Utilitarian approach to ethics was in the distinguished lineage of Jeremy Bentham and J.S. Mill, and within intellectual striking distance of the later developments of Moore that Keynes found so appealing.

This book collecting habit was not something separate from Keynes's intellectual development, as an interest in collecting butterflies might have been. Keynes was one of those rare book collectors who actually learnt a great deal from his own collection, as the early paper on Burke clearly demonstrated. Instead of borrowing crumpled and tatty books from the library, the collector-intellectual purchases fine and rare copies of their objects of study, which adds unfathomably to the pleasures of learning. Keynes also turned out to be an astute collector who invariably 'bought well'; his ongoing book purchasing successes will be considered in later chapters.

If Moore had exerted the greatest intellectual influence on the young Keynes, then his closest and most significant friendship at Cambridge was with Lytton Strachey, a student at Trinity with a ferocious wit and a colourfully cultivated air of contempt: Keynes later described him as a 'Voltairean'.[13] Strachey became secretary of the Cambridge Apostles in 1904, and brought to the Society a more open attitude towards homosexuality. Strachey's most well-known book was *Eminent Victorians*, first published in 1918, and although it made something of a splash when it first appeared, its long-term influence was far less than any of Keynes's major works.

The correspondence between Keynes and Strachey was substantial and ongoing, and for a time at least they certainly were lovers, although on different occasions they also competed for the sexual attention of others. Although Strachey was a match for Keynes in terms of his artistic bent and flamboyant emotional engagements, he was not a match for Keynes's brilliant intellect in the higher realms of philosophy and mathematics. Another important member of the Cambridge Apostles was Leonard Woolf, who later married Virginia Woolf (*née* Stephen), two key members of the Bloomsbury group. It was Strachey and Woolf who had first invited Keynes to join the Apostles: there is no evidence that the young Keynes was in any way afraid of Virginia.

Keynes took his undergraduate examinations in May 1905. He did reasonably well although not outstandingly so, partly because mathematics was not his true intellectual vocation, and partly because he had applied himself very well to his studies, but not exhaustively so. Arrangements were in place to allow Keynes to continue his studies at King's, and during the summer of 1905, he began to focus his attention more on the relatively new field of economics, or political economy as it was sometimes still termed. He read Marshall's *Principles of Economics* of 1890, W.S. Jevons's *Theory of Political Economy* of 1871 and his *Investigations in Currency and Finance* of 1884, and various other well-known British and Continental economics authors such as Gustav Cassel, David Ricardo, Walter Bagehot, Augustin Cournot and F.Y. Edgeworth. The only major instance of Keynes demonstrating any significant concern with an economic issue before this time had been at the end of 1903, when the question of free trade versus protectionism became a live one in the national press. Keynes was a staunch supporter of free trade, but his reasoning in its support was purely philosophical: free trade equalled free thought, whereas protectionism equalled unwarranted restrictions. The economic arguments for either at this time had gone in the main unconsidered.

In October 1905, Keynes formally applied to attend Marshall's lectures at Cambridge, and although he declared cautiously that some of his time was still reserved for other topics such as philosophy, this period witnessed a definite shift in his main interest toward economics. During the autumn of 1905, Keynes composed various essays on topics such as purchasing power indexes, taxation, the nature of capital, and freight costs, and the comments that he received in response from Marshall were very positive and encouraging. It was at this point in his life that Keynes's decision to become an economist, or at least to work in some field where his economics knowledge was central, could reasonably be originated. It is perhaps a little surprising to realise, consequently, that Keynes had not begun to study economics in any systematic fashion until he was a post-graduate, at the age of 22, and never went on to receive formal qualifications in this subject as a major.

However, despite various words of encouragement from Marshall to the effect that Keynes would make a first-rate economist, he was still hesitating about his future direction, partly because of his parents, and partly because he was genuinely unsure about what path to take. The next step in the parental master plan was the Civil Service, not economics. He remarked towards the end of 1905 that, although he was sure that remaining in Cambridge would signify intellectual death, he was not sure that a government office in London would not mean the same. Despite such misgivings, in the winter of 1905, Keynes returned his focus back to philosophy for a brief period, and then decided to give up the formal study of economics and take the Civil Service entrance exams, which included various separate papers in mathematics, politics, logic, psychology, history and economics. These he duly took in August 1906. Of course he was successful, but did best in politics, logic and psychology, and worst of all in economics.

Whitehall

In October 1906, Keynes began work as a clerk in the India Office in Whitehall. This Office was especially important because of the prevalence of British colonial rule, being one major part of the business of governing the global Empire, of which India was still 'the jewel in the crown'. Keynes had no special interest in or prior knowledge of India, but was initially only a clerk involved in communication and transport operations, for example, arranging the delivery of supplies. Intellectually he was neither a fervent promoter of the British Empire as an international cure-all, nor a doctrinaire anti-imperialist campaigner: he was a pragmatist working within the system, as he happened to find it.

Despite his initial misgivings about potential death in London, he began to enjoy his new government post and the novel intellectual demands that it was making of him. He wrote in March 1907 that:

> I like my new department...there is an excellent system by which everything comes to me to read and I read it...Some of it is quite absorbing – Foreign Office commercial negotiations with Germany, quarrels with Russia in the Persian Gulf, the regulation of opium in Central India, the Chinese opium proposals...[14]

Although Keynes was now working full-time in Whitehall, he had by no means relinquished all of his academic interests. In the autumn of 1905, he sketched out a draft outline for a project called a 'Scheme for an Essay on the Principles of Probability'. In December 1907, he submitted as a fellowship dissertation to King's College a work entitled 'The Principles of Probability'.[15] Thus, between the end of 1905 and the end of 1907, he had continued working on intellectual concerns, partly as a means of keeping his future employment options open, and partly so as to satisfy his more academic interests.

The place of Keynes's probability theory within his overall corpus of work is controversial for various reasons. Firstly, it was only tangentially connected to the main themes of his early or 'mature' economics. Secondly, although his dissertation on probability was first submitted in 1907, the book that he would later publish on this topic did not appear until 1921, and thus had been comprehensively revised. Thirdly, various economists were actively promoting the use of probability theory in econometric modelling in the 1930s, but Keynes was not really one of them. Thus, his interest in probability theory has sometimes been seen as an anomaly, especially when it is considered alongside the parallel interest he was developing in this period of his life, that of the Indian financial system. Whether it really was anomalous will be considered in the next chapter and beyond.

Keynes's work in the India Office was not especially taxing intellectually, and it allowed him ample scope to work on his fellowship dissertation. Initially, he had started in the Military section of the Office, but later moved to the more appropriate Revenue, Statistics and Commerce section. One of his tasks was to edit a report on 'The Moral and Material Progress of India', although most of his daily duties were concerned with the latter type of progress more than the former. He was occasionally quite scathing of the system of management that he found in operation in Whitehall, describing it as 'Government by dotardy', and he characterised some of the ripe India Office staff as manifesting signs of senile decay. Now based in London during the week, he took the opportunity of attending the Economic Club at University College, and often returned to Cambridge at the weekend, thus maintaining the best of both worlds.

By the summer of 1907, Keynes was complaining that work in Whitehall was 'maddening' and quite boring, although this was only part of the story, as on other occasions he was overwhelmed and very busy, and so he made the decision to leave the India Office. The dissertation on probability theory would be his means of obtaining a fellowship at King's College, which could (if he so desired) be combined with continued work on Indian economic affairs, for which he had obtained a taste. In the event, after submitting his dissertation Keynes failed to win the desired fellowship, due to a rather lukewarm report from Whitehead as examiner, and Keynes was distraught by this setback. However, Marshall came to the rescue and tentatively offered Keynes a lectureship in economics, which was confirmed when Pigou became Marshall's replacement at Cambridge in May 1908. In June, Keynes duly resigned from the India Office, but he continued the study of the Indian economy from his new academic position, and was later asked to participate in various important government commissions on Indian affairs.

The other significant development of Keynes's life in this period was a new friendship and then a full-blown relationship with Duncan Grant, an artist and friend of Lytton Strachey, who went on to draw and paint Keynes and their Bloomsbury colleagues on various occasions. Keynes became very enamoured of Grant, and often pined over his temporary absences. As Grant had first been attached to Strachey before moving on to Keynes, this emotional defection caused something of a jealous rift between Strachey and Keynes, and led to Strachey sometimes bad-mouthing Keynes behind his back. By early 1909, however, the rift was partially repaired, although they were never again quite so close as friends as they had been previously. And as a belated semi-recognition that Whitehead had roughly treated the 1907 dissertation, Keynes was elected to a new fellowship at King's College in March 1909. He was now well established on the path to becoming a professional economist, with the additional accumulation of valuable wider experience through working in the British government.

2 Early writings

The preceding account of Keynes's early life has demonstrated clearly that he was an Eton and a Cambridge man through and through. However, how did these institutions affect his early intellectual development? To answer this question the following chapter examines Keynes's very early writings in more detail, including an account of his school essays, the influence of G.E. Moore's philosophy, some aspects of his early work on probability theory and his first economics publication on Great Britain.

School essays

Keynes's school essays written on various historical and political topics while he was at Eton provide a useful source for identifying his very early beliefs. These essays attest partially to many of the attitudes prevalent in the English public school system, but they are not irrelevant to the issues that Keynes would tackle throughout much of his adult life. In one such school essay, entitled 'The English National Character', from March 1901, he identified five keywords that described this character: insular, law-abiding, tolerant, conscientious and practical. He then declared proudly that:

> There is in England a widespread feeling of stability, that is not exactly paralleled in any continental country; it is the outcome of a great continuity of history and institutions, and it breeds the tolerance which only safety can give, and the conservative self satisfaction which is the result of long established customs.[1]

According to Keynes, the political outlook of an Englishman (his own term) was permeated by a sense that his institutions had earned the sanction of time. Although these institutions required adaptation as time progressed, they would not easily be abolished. Consequently, an Englishman was characteristically:

> ...liberal but not radical, adverse to sudden change, but reconciled to it when he is once satisfied of the necessity for it. England owes her safe political position to this moderation; her typical citizen is neither reactionary nor radical.[2]

Keynes was not saying that all Englishmen were exclusively liberal, but that the 'typical citizen' was so. It is possible, of course, to question whether there was ever such a thing as the 'typical Englishman'; but conversely, it might be possible to mount a defence along the lines of 'common aspects of belief'. Opponents of Keynes's conception of Englishness might declare that this was a form of national stereotyping, but common cultural traditions are to be distinguished from allegations of 'racial characteristics'. Keynes was only 17 years old when he wrote this essay, and was clearly alluding to common social and political customs, not racial traits. A more pertinent criticism might be that Keynes did not appear to consider the 'typical Englishwoman' in any way.

Another school essay from November 1900 was provocatively entitled 'The Differences Between East and West: Will They Ever Disappear?' and made a good contrast with the previous essay. In his East/West essay Keynes argued that:

> The counter-influences of the East and the West...first came into contact in the struggle between Persia and Greece, and in this contest we see embodied one of the root distinctions that has preserved unchanged to our own times. In the West it is the individual that is all important, in the East the masses...[3]

The national conflict referred to here was the Persian Wars (490 to 449 BC), in which the Greek forces eventually defeated the Persian army and the independence of the Greek cities was recognised. This meant that, in Keynes's analysis, struggles taking place millennia ago and over long periods of time were considered as relevant to contemporary affairs.

Keynes then contrasted what he called the noble but restrictive ideology of Islam with the freedoms of Christianity, suggesting that it was the former that had caused the 'stagnation' that was characteristic of Eastern affairs. Continuing this line of thought further, he declared that:

> ...from this we see the reason why the East formed the great civilisations of the past...It could arrive at great dogmas which are true for the mass and organise great empires that further welded the mass together, but it is altogether lacking in that initiative and invention which can emanate only from individuals and without which further progress is impossible.[4]

It only takes a moment's contemplation to question how the Spanish inquisition at the end of the fifteenth century, or the English witch-hunts of the seventeenth century, could be characterised as expressions of 'Christian freedoms', and to provide counter-examples of individual initiative from within the important tradition of Islamic science. But Keynes was (again) alluding to overall trends and characteristic features, not to every specific instance.

The last of Keynes's school essays that will be considered here was entitled 'What are the Prospects of European Peace at the Present Time?', written some time in 1901. Here the various nation-states of Europe were considered vis-à-vis their attitudes to international peace and to the UK. The German Kaiser, for example, was a 'very good friend to England', and Keynes believed that the Kaiser's 'genuine attachment to the English Royal Family must be of great value in keeping the peace'.[5] After considering this and various other arguments to the effect that the prospects for peace in Europe were very good, Keynes then warned presciently that:

> Such items of the world as Central America, waling stations in the Persian gulf and in the Pacific, and sundry islands are easily coveted by the Powers; and there is consequently at the present day a greatly increased scope for international jealousy and rivalry.[6]

Although both sides of the argument relating to the prospects for peace were thus considered in the essay, perhaps in hindsight undue weight was attached to the importance of personal inter-governmental relations in affecting the outcome of the international war/peace equation.

From Keynes's three school history essays it is possible to extract a common guiding thread: the importance of nations and Empires to the long-term development of human civilisation. Robert Skidelsky characterised the young Keynes as a 'thinking patriot', as opposed to the two extremes of the obtrusive 'flag flapper' on the right and the anti-Empire 'patrophobist' on the left.[7] Indeed, the element of history that the young Keynes identified most clearly as being determinate was national-political in nature rather than economic or social, which is one of the reasons why his essay on the prospects for European war conveyed the impression in hindsight of giving too much credence to purely political interactions. In the same essay, Keynes had considered the influence of economic conditions on recent developments in Russia, explaining that this country had, over the preceding thirty years, 'taken tremendous strides Eastward' by annexing and reorganising the 'great bulk of northern Asia', but he then declared (rather inconsistently) that the Russian Tsar was an 'ardent lover of peace'.[8]

It can, therefore, be deduced from an analysis of his school essays that the very young Keynes, as a liberal individualist, placed too much faith in the power of individual action to overcome the entrenched national, military and strategic forces that he acknowledged operated on international relations. It was this individual action that he hoped could protect and preserve the 'great continuity of history and institutions' that he proudly declared had existed in the UK for centuries, but which in the end failed to prevent the outbreak of war in 1914. The individualist approach also had its complement in the more abstract field of philosophy, to which attention is now turned.

The influence of Moore

As explained in the previous chapter, the immediate influence of G.E. Moore's 1903 book *Principia Ethica* on Keynes's thinking was profound: but exactly how and in what capacity? Moore's novel philosophical argument was that ethics was concerned with the predicate 'good', and that 'goodness' was actually an indefinable simple notion like 'yellow'. Just as you could not explain to anyone what 'yellow' was solely by means of words, you had to refer to the colour visually, so it was the same with the notion of 'good': both were basic notions that contained no further divisible parts. This meant in turn that 'goodness' could not be defined in ulterior terms, i.e. as some other quality like 'pleasure' or 'natural' or 'useful'. Instead, according to Moore the most valuable ('good') things were certain states of consciousness deriving from activities such as the pleasures of human intercourse and the enjoyment of beautiful things.

However, in a later chapter of the book, entitled 'Ethics in Relation to Conduct', Moore considered practical ethics, i.e. how to decide what actions were morally right, concluding that it was possible to show which, among a range of actions, would produce the best results, or the greatest sum of total good. He declared that:

> ...all that Ethics has attempted or can attempt, is to show that certain actions, possible by volition, *generally* produce better or worse total results than any probable alternative...[9]

Keynes was so taken with Moore's approach that in the summer of 1905, he outlined his own plan to write a 'Miscellanea Ethica', including a section on practical ethics with an analysis of the notions of virtue, education and politics. He only half-jokingly declared that such a work would be 'printed in Baskerville type and published in 150 volumes'.[10] Much later, Keynes acknowledged that what he took from Moore – 'that it made morals unnecessary' – was not entirely what Moore had offered.[11]

What Keynes meant by this retrospective admission of distortion was that reading the early part of the book on its own, which declared that 'good' could not be defined, might be a license for doing whatever was desired, as 'nothing mattered except states of mind'.[12] By ignoring the later part of the book, which did make an effort to define 'right actions' more definitely, an individualistic emphasis on states of being could be obtained, states which were only defined as important in relation to a closed circle of intimate acquaintances. Keynes outlined the sort of discussions that he had undertaken while at King's College, believing them to be the result of applying Moore's ideas:

> If A was in love with B and believed that B reciprocated his feelings, whereas in fact B did not, but was in love with C, the state of affairs was certainly not so good as it would have been if A had been right, but was it worse or better than it would become if A discovered his mistake?[13]

Here the later Keynes might have had in mind the state of his own youthful affair with Duncan Grant, in which Keynes effervesced the greater degree of emotion than Grant. However, Keynes's later analysis of his early use of Moore does not really hold water, except perhaps for a brief period in 1903. This is apparent from the fact that a key element of Moore's book that Keynes did employ in the earlier period of his life was the idea of 'probable alternatives'. According to Moore, in order to judge practical 'right actions', individuals generated in their minds a set of future states of affairs that were the projected outcome of different actions, and used these future alternatives to judge what to do in the present.

It is not necessary to look very far to find an area of study that the young Keynes undertook which was linked to this approach: probability theory. Chapter XVI of Keynes's 1907 dissertation on 'The Principles of Probability' was entitled 'The Relation of Probability to Ethics, and the Doctrine of Mathematical Expectation'.[14] This was directly connectable to the chapter in Moore's book entitled 'Ethics in Relation to Conduct'. The mathematical content of Keynes's work on probability theory will be considered in a later chapter, but his early interest in probability was linked to his early interest in ethics. Indeed, Moore made a direct appearance in the dissertation and in the book, although by 1907, Keynes was critical of Moore's notion that the effects of an action over an infinite future had to be known for 'good actions' to be judged.[15] The only assumptions that Keynes the probability theorist believed were relevant to the discussion were that good was additive, and that the goodness of a part was favourably related to the goodness of the whole.[16]

Keynes's position was that the idea of one course of action being 'better' or 'morally superior' or 'our duty' compared to another course, depended on the assumption that greater goodness in any single part of the world made greater goodness in the whole world more probable. If total goodness was what Keynes called 'organic', i.e. was interconnected and interdependent on the whole, then the idea of comparing courses of action in an atomic or linear manner was questionable. In the end he supported the idea that total goodness was partially organic and partially atomic, and hence that some degree of comparison of outcomes was possible, but suggested that the complicating factor of interdependence always had to be considered.[17] If 'doing good' was not always additive and atomic, then in certain instances improving one situation might inevitably worsen others.

Keynes's solution to this potential 'compounding' problem was that 'intuitive judgement' directed at the situation as a whole should be used when evaluating right actions. He also suggested that a course of action should be seen as preferable when it involved the least risk, and when the results were estimable with the greatest certain knowledge.[18] Moral actions still had to be judged by the greater good, but in association with judgements about how the results might affect the goodness of all other situations, and with weights attached to more certain outcomes than less certain. Thus Keynes was, by 1907, still utilising many of the themes of Moore's ethical theory, but had adduced his own more advanced analysis of how moral actions should be determined. This was by using concepts from probability theory together with support for Edmund Burke's belief in the superiority of the known over the unknown (or better the devil you know).

Moore's ethical philosophy was initially attractive to the young Keynes partly because it provided a way of delineating moral issues in a logical and precise manner, rather like applying Russell's concern with philosophical logic to morality, and partly because it seemed to illuminate a median way between the unattractive extremes of J.E. McTaggart's purely abstract metaphysics, and the entirely practical precepts of the Utilitarianism tradition that had been represented at Cambridge by Henry Sidgwick. This adoption of a pragmatic middle way in philosophy had a parallel in Keynes's political concern to remain a middle-of-the-road Liberal, rather than a Reactionary or a Radical.

First publication on Great Britain

By the end of the 1900s, Keynes had taken major steps on the path to becoming an economist, apparently retiring his youthful interests in politics, history and philosophy. His first published articles in the *Economic Journal* were on 'Board of Trade Index Numbers of Real Wages' (1908) and 'Recent Economic Events in India' (1909). These topics will be considered in more detail in later chapters, where their themes are more central to the analysis. However, one of Keynes's early articles entitled 'Great Britain's Foreign Investments', which was published in *The New Quarterly* in February 1910, does connect much better with the preceding account of Keynes's very early beliefs.

Although the detail of the analysis in 'Great Britain's Foreign Investments' was clearly economics, its underlying purpose was unquestionably political, as it was a response to contemporary debates. People who Keynes referred to as Tariff Reformers, i.e. those who were calling for raised customs tariff barriers in order to protect British industry, had been arguing that free trade was drawing capital investment out of Great Britain, which was pre-eminent as a lending country, to the long-term detriment of British industry. Keynes believed that this argument was wrong, and he sought to demonstrate so in the article.

Keynes began by admitting that circumstances could conceivably exist in which 'increasing export of capital *might* be a symptom of a decaying polity', i.e. it could in certain circumstances serve to weaken British enterprise and national strength. Whether it did or did not in any instance depended on the facts of the case under review. In the period under consideration, Keynes argued that 'the yield on investments in new countries with great unexploited natural resources must tend to be greater than in old countries' with more developed economies.[19] For example, Canadian railway development was more profitable than equivalent British investments, simply because the former system was much less developed than the latter. Keynes argued that it was natural, from the profitability angle, for British capital to 'tend in the course of time' to find investment abroad in a larger absolute amount. There were some checks operating in the opposite direction, such as the greater risk and difficulty of recovery from overseas investments, but he believed that such factors had tended to decline in the recent past.

Turning his attention to specific countries, he identified India, Argentina and Canada as three major recipients of British overseas investment, these being countries 'from whence she obtains her food and the raw materials of manufacture'.[20] Out of a total of approximately £2,700 million of aggregate foreign investment, £1,312 was supplied to India and the colonies. Keynes reasoned that:

> The development of these countries is in a stage when we must put more money into them, and not, for the present, take much out, if we are to gain the full fruit of our enterprise...If we were to withdraw this credit...it would involve the slow decline of London as the financial centre of the world...[21]

Regarding the type of enterprises selected for investment, out of the total £2,700 million, £1,700 million was invested in railway construction in various countries, which was not an area that could compete with indigenous British industry, as it was location-specific. Keynes also referred to other advantages of overseas investment, such as greater variety of income sources and heightened ability to draw on non-domestic enterprises in times of emergency. In this latter case, Keynes mentioned the example of the Boer War, when wealth drawn from overseas 'was almost sufficient in itself to defray the whole cost of the war'.[22]

Keynes concluded therefore that the existing complaints regarding the volume of Britain's foreign investment were baseless. Thus, Keynes was defending free trade against the arguments of the protectionists, and, as correctly described, the 1910 article was also a 'defence of unlimited capital mobility'.[23] Robert Skidelsky consequently declared that there were 'no new paths of thought here'. This judgement is true if no new paths of economic thought was meant, but Keynes was framing the argument politically, as a means of helping to strengthen Britain's own economic position internationally. His underlying assumption was that British investment overseas must be evaluated on how favourable it was for Great Britain's national interest. Thus, the 1910 article was a defence of unlimited capital mobility in those circumstances in which it was in British interests to support it. This was something so obvious and natural for Keynes to accept in 1910, that it formed the implicit guiding thread of the entire article. It also meant that, if specific circumstances turned against such capital mobility operating in British interests, he would then change his attitude and oppose it.

Conclusion

For the very young Keynes, the British Empire was certainly seen as a mainly positive force across the globe, assisting in introducing the 'civilising' forces of economic progress and scientific enlightenment. However, it could be argued that there was an essential tension between Keynes's explicit claim to be (in his terms) a social Liberal rather than a Reactionary or a Radical, and his underlying support for Burke-type political conservatism (with a small 'c'), which runs through much of his early work.

If the rational side of his mind and his early education had made him a Liberal, supporting free thought and the right of the individual to act in their own interests both politically and economically, then there was an element of his subconscious mind that warned of the potential dangers of rationalism. This partially submerged conservatism was apparent in Keynes's very early admiration for Burke and for the long-standing institutional continuities of British history, and in his attempt to modify Moore's ethical philosophy with certain precepts of prognostic caution. How this tautly strung (yet judicious) liberal–conservatism fared as it began to encounter the dramatically unprecedented social and political upheavals of the first half of the twentieth century, is a subject of the rest of this book.

3 Selling economics by the hour and on the Q.T. (of M.)

Having secured a fellowship at King's College, Keynes began his teaching duties in the 1908–9 academic year. He first taught courses on 'Money, Credit and Prices' and 'The Stock Exchange and the Money Market', before expanding his lecturing programme to include courses on 'Company Finance', 'Currency and Banking' and 'The Monetary Affairs of India'.[1] In addition to lecturing duties, he also provided one-to-one tuition for fee-paying students as a way of supplementing his academic income. He was then awarded a permanent lectureship in economics at King's College in the summer of 1911. An awe-struck student described attending his selective but intensive tutorial classes as follows:

> ...according to custom, supervision took place in his rooms in King's College where we would sit in easy chairs around the fireplace. In these periods he never talked above our heads. He would discourse, with twinkling eyes and infectious semi-stammer, about the subject for the day. It was like a kaleidoscope: at every twist there was a pattern, neat, clear, and scintillating.[2]

This phase of concentrated teaching and research on economics and probability theory at Cambridge lasted from 1908 until the outbreak of the First World War in 1914, and this period will form the focus of this and the following chapter as an integrated pair.

Although Keynes spent much of his working effort at this time in Cambridge, he also travelled frequently, taking holidays in France, Italy, Greece, Egypt, Scotland and Constantinople. His companions for many of these trips were either Duncan Grant or the Strachey brothers (James and Lytton).[3] Other non-intellectual matters of immediate importance included Keynes's appointment to the King's College Estate Committee in 1911, and his taking on a fellowship elector role the following year, a job that involved reading and judging numerous fellowship dissertations. One visitor to Cambridge described Keynes vividly as a:

> ...picture of the young teacher of spare frame, ascetic countenance, flashing eyes, intent and tremendously serious, vibrating with... suppressed impatience, a formidable controversialist whom nobody could overlook, everybody respected, and some liked.[4]

In parallel with this academic life in Cambridge, the central hub of many of the social activities of the Bloomsbury group was 46 Gordon Square in London. Here Keynes occasionally lodged in 1911 and thereafter, and it continued to attract him as a key focus of his unconventional private life. Other addresses located in Bloomsbury – Brunswick Square, Gower Street, Fitzroy Square – also temporarily filled his need for a London base from 1909 onwards.

Keynes's London social life in this period was often closely linked with various divisions of the arts. A keen collector of paintings and sculpture – he purchased an Augustus John in 1908 and an Eric Gill in 1911 – his Bloomsbury links recurrently assisted in oiling the wheels of purchase. Another early artistic interest was in the ballet. Before the outbreak of the First World War, ballet as an art form was at the height of its international prestige, and works were produced in association with world-famous *avant-garde* composers such as Igor Stravinsky and Maurice Ravel. Keynes attended productions by Serge Diaghilev in 1911 and 1912, frequented parties given for Vaslav Nijinsky, and was lucky enough to attend the premiere of *Petrushka*. This particular interest in the Russian Ballet Company would grow in the 1920s and later enabled him to meet his first and only wife.

A number of Keynes's lecture notes from the early 1910s still survive today, and they show that he undertook his teaching duties with lucidity, insight and dedication. Another of Keynes's students from this period further confirmed that his lectures invariably showed 'clarity of argument, breadth of comprehension and wealth of historical illustration'.[5] Perhaps the most notable intellectual aspect of their content was that they demonstrated that the young Keynes believed wholeheartedly in the quantity theory of money, or what he referred to affectionately as 'the Q.T. of M.'.[6] The theoretical intricacies of this issue will be explored in the following chapter: suffice to state that the basic exchange equation that constituted the essence of this theory formed the underlying framework of what was seen as the orthodox approach to monetary economics. There was, however, one very important difference between monetary theory as it was pursued by economists in the UK at the beginning of the twentieth century, and monetary theory as it was later to develop after the Second World War.

This difference was the prevalence of the gold standard in the former period, and its gradual abandonment in the latter. All of Keynes's early theories and discussions relating to highlighting factors of importance to international monetary developments were framed in relation to gold as the ultimate anchor of value. Consequently, the question of changes in the supply and demand for gold, and its industrial and cultural employment, were in the early decades of the twentieth century of much greater significance to economic issues than they are today. This difference was important to understanding how the quantity theory of money was viewed by the young Keynes as an element of economic theory, but it was also crucial to another aspect of his early life that now deserves attention: Indian finances and trade.

Indian currency affairs

Throughout the nineteenth century, the gold standard was not the only precious metal standard in existence. There was the silver standard and also bimetallism, where both gold and silver were used to maintain the par value of currency units. However, the general trend in the second half of the nineteenth century was towards adopting the gold standard alone, and the demonetisation of silver had proceeded apace after 1876. The Indian economy had employed the silver standard until 1893, when international factors had led to its suspension. As the 1890s progressed, a *de facto* sterling exchange standard came into operation in which the Indian government sold or bought rupees (token silver coins that cost less than their face value to mint) in exchange for sterling, in order to keep the rupee's value within fixed bands against gold.[7] In order to do this, the Indian government had to keep a significant level of sterling on account in London, where the international currency exchange market was traditionally located.

Owing to these ongoing currency issues, in 1898 an Indian Currency Committee was created (conventionally referred to as the Fowler Committee), which after its deliberations, eventually came out in favour of India adopting a full gold standard system. However, some brief attempts to introduce gold as a circulating medium within India failed, as it quickly disappeared from circulation. Consequently the Indian government turned to the halfway house of holding some of their currency and gold reserves in London as a means of proximate supply for their currency interventions, directed towards supporting the rupee, in any instances of significant fluctuations of the Indian currency against foreign currencies like sterling.

This system was conventionally called a gold-exchange standard, as opposed to the full gold standard. The central difference was that in the former system, citizens could not exchange their local currency for gold at a fixed rate, nor did any officially-minted gold coins circulate domestically; instead, the government intervened on the currency markets in order to maintain a *de facto* fixed exchange rate for the rupee against gold. One of the most controversial consequences of this system was that India had to keep some definite proportion of its gold reserves outside of India, as the main centres of international currency exchange were located elsewhere, primarily in London.

All of Keynes's work on Indian finance was conducted against the backdrop of this long-standing question of the best path of currency reform for less developed countries. The question of maintaining a stable currency for India was important because sharp fluctuations or devaluations of the rupee against gold would mean that international investors would worry that investments they had made in India were at risk from currency instability, and consequently it would be harder for them to extract profits. Such instability would mean in the medium term that investors would be less likely to choose India as a location for their investments in the first place. It was also important because it would assist in preserving price stability within India.

Keynes had already been teaching a course at Cambridge on 'The Currency and Finances of India' in 1910–11, and had then continued with a course on 'The Monetary Affairs of India' in 1912–13. In one of his 1912 lectures, he noted in a section on 'hoarding' the very significant levels of absorption of bullion by the East, and provided some data on the transfer of gold and silver specifically to India. For example, in the three years ending in 1907, imports of silver into India had amounted to 71.4 per cent of total world production. Yet on average, only around a half of silver imports had been used as currency: this was partly because jewellery was of special importance in Indian culture.[8]

In March 1909, Keynes published his first full academic article on 'Recent Economic Events in India' in the *Economic Journal*. In July 1909, he submitted an article on 'India During 1907–8' to *The Economist*, and in May 1911, he presented a paper on 'Recent Developments of the India Currency Question' to the Royal Economic Society. He then took the expansive decision in November 1912 to write a book on Indian currency affairs, the reasons for which will be considered below. A contract was quickly signed with the publishing company Macmillan in December, Daniel Macmillan being an old friend and fellow Etonian, and by March 1913, proofs of the book were being checked. This was writing at a very fast pace, although Keynes had been studying Indian finances and researching the book for many years previously, and hence it was really just writing-up his long-considered findings.[9]

So far, the presentation of Keynes's interest in the Indian economy has given the impression that it was overwhelmingly linked to his wider interest in abstract monetary theory. This was partly true, and the theoretical aspect in relation to banks will be examined in more detail in the next chapter, but there was an additional element to Keynes's interest in Indian financial affairs that deserves further consideration: the political component. This angle to the debate was apparent from articles published in *The Times* in the early 1910s.

For example, on 1 November 1912, a long and prominent article by a 'well-informed Anglo-Indian Correspondent' entitled 'Indian Financial Management', argued that the Indian currency system was operated for the good and interests of London bankers and bullion dealers, rather than for the good of the Indian economy as a whole. The Secretary of State for India was brazenly accused of 'a tender susceptibility for the London bankers…who have exclusive access to his ear', and it was suggested that 'the Government of India are not free agents in this matter, for the reins are tightly held at Whitehall'.[10] It was further declared that no basic exposition of the principles of the Indian currency system existed, which was taken as evidence that either no such principles existed, or that they were deliberately being hidden, because they did not benefit India. These were serious charges being made against the British government. It was being suggested that the Indian gold-exchange standard was a system designed to operate in the interests of the London financial markets, rather than Indian economic needs.

Responding to these incendiary anti-British charges was Keynes's basic political motivation in much of his published work on Indian economics, especially his major 1913 book that was eventually entitled *Indian Currency and Finance*. Far from being only a dry treatise on the abstruse byways of monetary theory, it was partly a deliberate answer to charges that Great Britain ran colonial affairs in India solely in the interests of Britain. There was a personnel element to such charges as well, which Keynes would have understood due to his previous work in the India Office. The Under-Secretary of State for India between 1910 and 1914 was Edwin Montagu; the large bullion-brokerage company that frequently acted to buy silver for the Indian government was Samuel Montagu and Company: the two Montagu individuals were related as father and son.[11] Thus, according to critics, not only did Great Britain as a whole benefit from holding Indian reserves, but also relatives of individual British citizens working in the India Office benefited from how these reserves were purchased.

In order to counter these damaging allegations, Keynes responded to the so-called 'well-informed Anglo-Indian Correspondent' in a letter to *The Times* published on 14 November 1912. He argued that all that this correspondent had actually demonstrated was that the character of the Indian currency system was easily misrepresented, and that the basic arguments made against it were misplaced. This was because, in order to be effective, gold reserves had to be centralised, rather than be dissipated across the country as circulating coins. Keynes explained that in many countries, such as France, Russia, Austria-Hungary, Holland and Japan:

The trend of currency policy, therefore, in recent times has been to encourage the use of some relatively cheap material, cheques or notes or token silver, as the actual medium of exchange; and to ensure stability by centralizing the reserve of gold to the utmost degree, so that the local currency can be immediately exchanged for gold, when gold is needed for foreign obligations.[12]

Furthermore, holding some part of Indian precious metal reserves in London, as well as reserves partly as sterling and Treasury bills, added an extra degree of flexibility to currency arrangements, enabling the Indian government to respond to the demands of the Indian economy more easily and quickly. The reason that parts of the Indian reserve were held in sterling and UK Treasury bills was that it was far easier to transfer cash and paper bills across continents than precious metals, not (as had been suggested) that the low rate of discount offered on Treasury bills favoured the British Chancellor of the Exchequer. Keynes also explained that it was a fallacy that every increase in the proportion of gold that was held in local circulation – an increase that was desired by those wanting a full gold standard for India – would necessarily increase the stability of the domestic currency system. This was because the more troubled were the times, the more such circulating gold would be hoarded, which in turn meant that it was not available to support the domestic currency by means of central government interventions on the international exchange markets.

Keynes also referred to the charges of alleged India Office corruption more obliquely in *Indian Currency and Finance*. Here he explained that Samuel Montagu had given evidence to the original 1898 Fowler Committee on India's monetary system, a Committee that had recommended a full gold standard with an internal gold currency. Samuel Montagu had actually argued that 'any system without a visible gold currency would be looked on with distrust'.[13] Thus, Montagu had argued against the gold-exchange standard system, and consequently against the idea of Indian gold being kept in London, which had provided ammunition for the charges of corruption that were being made. Much later, Keynes described Edwin Montagu as exhibiting towards India 'an instinctive, mutual sympathy between him and its peoples'.[14] This does not suggest that India's currency system was being recommended only because it benefited British citizens and bullion traders.

Keynes then explained the real reason why Samuel Montagu and Company's involvement in the Indian government's precious metals brokerage deals had initially been kept secret, another factor that had generated controversy. It was actually because:

> A ring of speculators lay waiting to force prices up as soon as the government should appear as a buyer. Apart from the brokers who acted for the ring, there was only one firm in a position to buy large quantities of silver with the secrecy which was necessary if the speculators were to be defeated.[15]

Thus, Samuel Montagu and Company had been acting in secret in order to save the Indian government some money, not in order to line the pockets of its owners. Keynes bemoaned that, in the future, the more expensive method of the Indian government openly buying silver would have to be used, in order to counteract any possible suggestions of individual venality. He concluded the book by explaining that the Indian public would have to learn quickly that it was 'extravagant to use gold as a medium of exchange' and 'foolish to lessen the utility of their reserves through suspicion of the London money market'.[16]

Partly in response to such charges, the British government decided in 1913 to create a Royal Commission on Indian Finance and Currency. Keynes was initially offered a leadership role, but he eventually settled for a seat on the Commission, which began its work in May. The chairman was Austen Chamberlain, a former British Chancellor of the Exchequer. Keynes took an active role in cross-examining those giving evidence, and his questioning stance demonstrated his support for the continuation of the gold-exchange standard, as all his writings on India had consistently advocated. The basic additional feature that Keynes came to recommend during the Commission was the creation of an official Indian State Bank, something that had not previously existed.

Keynes's interest in Indian affairs in this period of his life was not solely professional and financial. There is some evidence that he had ongoing passionate liaisons with B.K. Sarkar, an Indian student who had arrived in Britain in 1910, and remained until 1920.

What many of the male Cambridge Apostles referred to as 'the passionate love of comrades', or more sordidly as 'the higher sodomy', was still Keynes's default setting at this time. Keynes initially assisted Sarkar in obtaining a place to study at Clare College, but financial irregularities grew until Sarkar was heavily in debt, and Keynes was forced to provide occasional letters in his support. In parallel, one 'B.K.S.' was recorded as an entry for 1912, 1913 and 1914 in Keynes's own handwritten list of sexual partners from 1915. Another separate list of his sexual activities between 1906 and 1915 provided data on the precise numbers of 'c', 'a' and 'w' that had been engaged in, abbreviations the meanings of which can only be guessed at (they were probably the most obvious ones). However, it is not possible to cross-reference the two tables and thereby deduce what variety of sexual engagement a specific individual was charged with sharing.

The intimate records for 'B.K.S.' between 1912 and 1914 followed alongside, as more notably disdained list entries, 'liftboy of Vauxhall' for 1911 and 'stable boy of Park Lane' for 1909; a more romantic entry for 1911 was described as 'Auburn haired of Marble Arch'. Even more condescendingly catalogued was an entry listed simply as 'Jewboy' (all one word) for 1912.[17] 'StG' or St George Nelson, a cockney conquest listed variously for 1909, 1910, 1911, 1913 and 1914, had annoyingly caught the clap in 1910. Gerald Shove, a close friend and fellow Apostle, described Keynes in this period as exhibiting a definite 'passion for low life'.[18] Keynes also remarked in a letter to Duncan Grant specifically about B.K. Sarkar that: 'I have had all to-day the most violent sexual feelings towards him'.[19] Evidently, Indian affairs were never so exciting as when they encompassed the full range of human experiences.

India and British investment

According to Donald Moggridge, Keynes's writings on India 'reflected what might be called the India Office view of the world'.[20] By implication, such a view was one-sided, and reflected the underlying assumptions of British Empire rule. In fact, as was indicated above, Keynes had gone out of his way to explain why his favoured gold-exchange standard system was in the best interests of India. The wider background of this debate was the political question of British rule in India. From today's perspective, the lines of distinction between the anti-imperialist ideology of those who argued that British influence was overwhelmingly negative for India and constituted a violent form of colonial exploitation, and those who took a more measured view that there were both negative and positive aspects of the British Empire for both Britain and its colonies, are very starkly drawn.

In terms of the type of analyses that were prevalent at the time, this polarity of interpretation of the economic aspect of British rule was expressed in terms of whether there was a unidirectional 'drain' of financial resources flowing from India to Britain. This question had a long and controversial history, as even Karl Marx had commented upon it in the late 1850s. After studying the relevant figures, Marx had come to the conclusion that there was actually a deficit of financial receipts from India reaching Britain, compared to British expenditure on India, when viewed from the perspective of the British Treasury.[21] However, some newspapers in the late 1900s explicitly referred to the idea of a 'drain' from India to Britain as constituting a transhipment 'of *wealth* without any adequate economic return', which (by implication) constituted a negative form of colonial exploitation.[22]

Keynes was well aware of such politically volatile charges, but he believed that they were in the main misplaced, declaring prior to the outbreak of the First World War that the overall material conditions of countries like India and Egypt had been 'somewhat improved' by British occupation.[23] Instead, he argued regarding the alleged 'drain' from India to Britain, and its supposedly damaging effect on rising domestic prices in India, that:

> The flow of capital into India, which is admittedly of the first importance for the country's economic development, is always likely to be followed by rising prices...the Secretary of State's need for remittances tends to keep prices low, and it is the influx of capital, the 'drain' from England to India, which dries them up.[24]

Here Keynes was inverting the terminology of the anti-imperialistic accusation that a 'drain' of resources from India to Britain was causing rising domestic prices in India. Instead, it was the reverse 'drain' from Britain to India of investment capital that benefited India through generating increased economic activity, and consequently caused rising domestic prices within India. The capital invested in India by Britain quite naturally and deservedly required a return on its employment, as it would wherever it was invested, but this return was not a unidirectional 'drain' of resources from India to Britain, as the capital that generated it helped to develop and advance the Indian economy itself.

Not everyone would have agreed with Keynes's positive analysis of the importance of British investment to Indian economic development. By the early part of the twentieth century, a great deal of resentment had accumulated in some quarters of India regarding British influence, which much preferred that Indians themselves should be responsible for Indian economic development. But if much greater indigenous controls were desired, together with a much-reduced role for British investments, then an alternative source would need to be provided for the capital to maintain future Indian development.

The *Economic Journal*

Another key development in this period of Keynes's life was his appointment to the editorship of the *Economic Journal* in October 1911. The *Economic Journal* was (and arguably still is) the most prestigious mainstream economics journal in the English-speaking world. It had first been issued in 1890 and was initially edited by F.Y. Edgeworth, until Keynes assumed control two decades later: his long and influential reign as editor would last until 1945. However, Keynes was hardly the most experienced editor ever to be appointed to such a role, as he had published only a few short articles, comments and notes in the *Economic Journal*, plus some letters and assorted pieces in other outlets prior to his appointment. His first book did not appear until 1913, although he had previously gained some notable experience in handling economic statistics while at the India Office. Another candidate had been initially considered for the job, W.J. Ashley, but he was not able to make enough time to conduct the substantial workload of evaluating and editing submissions, so at a meeting chaired by Alfred Marshall, Keynes was elected without challenge.

Much later, following Edgeworth's death in 1926, Keynes wrote a pen portrait of the first editor of the *Economic Journal*, praising his contributions to economic analysis and to developing the subject. He wrote that Edgeworth:

> ...established and was always anxious to maintain the international sympathies and affiliations of the *Journal*...He added to this what must have been the widest personal acquaintance in the world with economists of all nations...He had a strong feeling for the solidarity of economic science throughout the world...[25]

Keynes noted only semi-humorously that Edgeworth believed in what he called 'the law of diminishing returns in the remuneration of articles', where the rate of payment declined after ten pages and reached zero after twenty. After 1911, Edgeworth initially assisted Keynes with preparing the lesser parts of the journal (such as reviews and reports) up until 1926, a function that was later fulfilled by other editorial colleagues.

Various particularities about Keynes's editorship can be highlighted. First of all, he published many of his own articles in the *Economic Journal*, with only a few being issued in other journals. He was also not afraid of allowing his own books notable prominence: J.R. Hicks's 1936 review of *The General Theory of Employment, Interest and Money* was a whopping sixteen pages long.[26] Although this book's retrospective importance justified a lengthy review, a less confident editor would not have been quite so bold in agreeing such an expansive spatial allocation with his editorial review colleague. Keynes clearly did not share a belief in Edgeworth's law of diminishing returns as applied to the length of review articles. Secondly, most commentators agree that he functioned as an excellent editor who responded quickly and accurately to submissions, and who successfully assisted in commissioning useful content on various occasions.

His editorship was not without its controversies. He rejected some articles on economic history as 'hogwash', revealing a bias at this time in favour of *a priori* theory based on abstract concepts that had been intuitively deduced. He also only infrequently used external referees for evaluating articles, assuming much of the decision-making tasks alone. His judgement was usually correct, but occasionally a howler made its way through (or was blocked): for example, he rejected one notable submission that later contributed to the author being awarded a Nobel Prize.[27]

Keynes's private investments

Alongside Keynes's passion for book collecting, the other private activity not human-related that had the greatest impact upon his economic views was undoubtedly his private investment activities in shares, currencies and commodities. Like his book collecting habit, Keyes's investment activities started when he was young, in 1905, and continued throughout his adult life, growing in scale along the way. Obviously, unless shares are chosen at random, in deciding upon which investments to purchase and when to sell, some form of reasoning has to be used that is at least partially linked to economic understanding. Keynes was no different in this respect, and he provided various ongoing accounts of such investment principles. These will be considered at various points throughout the book. However, as no individual person is as stupid as their own theory, an interesting question is, whether Keynes's investment activities were conducted in line with his more general economic theory of the time, or against it.

Keynes's very first investment was the purchase of around £160 worth of shares in the Marine Insurance Company in July 1905, followed by around £50 worth of shares in Mather and Platt, an engineering company, six months later, a total outlay of around £210. He then held these two investments for around four years, during which their combined value fluctuated between a low point of £195 in 1907, and a high point of £218 in 1909.[28] Thus, Keynes's very first investments were hardly bountiful successes, although neither can they be considered as abject failures. From this time on his total investments increased notably, from around £539 in 1910 to around £1,691 in 1913, with various purchases including shares in Horden Collieries, Eastern Bank and U.S. Steel. The relative size of these private investments becomes clearer by pointing out that a King's Fellowship was worth £120 per annum in 1909,[29] and that his total earned income in 1910–11 was £595.

Keynes was financially able to make such relatively large

investments for someone so young through his father's earlier creation of a 'special fund' for him, made up of assorted contributions such as prize awards and birthday money. There is little surviving evidence to indicate why he chose the particular shares that he did in this period of his life, except to point out that investing in the shares of a small number of individual companies is a more risky venture than investing in (say) the shares of an investment company, which is an umbrella holding company for a wider range of securities. He had proved himself not to be risk-adverse in his youth, which was confirmed by his penchant for off-the-cuff sexual encounters when homosexual acts were still a crime: arrests by the police were nothing unusual.

Early political activities

As outlined previously, Keynes considered himself a Liberal rather than a Radical or a Conservative. In this early period of his life, he assisted with various political campaigns and participated in some politics-related issues, although his heart was never fully 'in' such humdrum organisational activities, except to the extent they added extra colour to his intellectual skills. For example, he wrote a newspaper article in December 1909 recommending that people should vote Liberal in the coming general election, and campaigned personally against Austen Chamberlain's election in East Worcester and for Edwin Montagu's election in Histon.[30] He was even asked to stand as a candidate for election on various different occasions, but always politely refused.

Consequently, the impression often given by Keynes about political activities was that he enjoyed these forays into practical affairs at least as much for their opportunity to enliven his debating experiences, as for their capacity to improve the average lot of the human condition. He certainly believed sincerely in the ideas that were espoused, but some significant degree of fun was to be had in espousing them. Gerald Shove, a fellow economist at King's College, wrote to Keynes in September 1910 expressing his shared puzzlement at the religious fervour of many political Radicals:

> It *is* extraordinary to see how even the most apostolic of socialists gets hot and dishonest as soon as one dares criticise his views...

they seem *determined* to believe it at all costs – just as the Christians are determined to cling to the cross...A good many people, I suppose, hold *all* their important beliefs in a religious way: but they're mostly quite stupid: they form, of course, the bulk of the socialist party.[31]

Keynes certainly understood and even shared this type of bewilderment at politico-religious fervour. His own early belief in Moore's philosophy was sometimes described in messianic terms, but the underlying impression given was that Keynes's 'philosophical-religious fervour' was something of an exuberant game to him, as it was to his fellow Apostles.

The other obviously political issue that Keynes engaged with in this early period of his life was supporting free trade policies against the protectionists. For example, he participated in a meeting in support of free trade in Cambridge in April 1909, and his *New Quarterly* article on British overseas investment considered in the previous chapter was written along similar lines. He was thus fully consistent in his early political engagements, as Liberals were against imposing restrictions on free thought and on free commerce.

Conclusion

The above account of Keynes's early life at Cambridge, and some of the main personal and political issues that were a part of it, might leave the erroneous impression that the development of theoretical ideas was not at the heart of his intellectual endeavours in this period. The following chapter will demonstrate that this impression is at least partially misplaced.

4 Early economics

Keynes's early economics was part of a wider period of the near-exponential growth and greater sophistication of economic ideas across many parts of Europe and America. The first two decades of the twentieth century witnessed a number of 'great debates' in topics such as monetary theory, business cycle analysis, engendering growth and the conceptual foundations of value theory. However, Keynes's most famous contributions to economic theory did not occur until the 1930s. This was a very different context to that of the 1910s and 1920s, given the onset of the Great Depression in 1929. In order to fully understand Keynes's novel later contributions, and the legacies of the older approaches to the subject, an account of the development of his early economic ideas is necessary. It is also required in order to trace any connections that exist between Keynes's work in economic theory and his policy-making efforts in areas such as Indian finance and banking policy. Consequently, this chapter introduces some of the basic elements of Keynes's economics as it had developed before the outbreak of the First World War.

The quantity theory of money

One of the earliest guides to Keynes's youthful economics is his surviving lecture notes; for example, those that were prepared for courses on 'The Theory of Money' and 'The Principles of Economics' from the early 1910s. There is not much within these notes that was not standard fare of the period, although they are clearly organised and demonstrate a detailed knowledge of the authorities of the day, as revealed by the extensive lists of further reading provided for each topic.

Many of these lectures were organised around the presentation and discussion of 'the Q.T. of M.', which Keynes certainly did not invent: he credited his predecessor at Cambridge, Alfred Marshall, with providing the definitive account. Keynes described the quantity theory of money as 'the theory of the value of money' or 'the theory of value as applied to money'. As the value of everything depended on its quantity, the quantity theory of money was often taken as a theory of the influence of the supply of money on prices, but Keynes warned that demand factors should not be ignored. He consequently declared that:

> ...*given* the value of the demand for purchasing power in the form of money, *given* that the commodity used as money is useful for no other purpose, and *given* that the average number of times each coin is used suffers no change; then the value of each unit of currency is inversely proportional to the number of units. In this form the Q.T. of M. is *absolutely valid*.[1]

Keynes was outlining the conditions in which the quantity theory of money could be asserted as true; conversely, he accepted that there were conditions in which it was not true. His early belief in the quantity theory was thus conditional: if were known: a) the total demand for money; b) the number of currency units; and c) the rapidity of currency circulation; then the value of each unit of money could be inferred.

The following equation was, in the early twentieth century, the identity most commonly used to express a standard version of the quantity theory of money:

$$MV = PT$$

M was the quantity of money in circulation, V the speed of its circulation, P the level of prices and T the volume of trading transactions. Strictly speaking, this identity was really only 'the equation of exchange': the quantity theory of money asserted that the price level (P) changed in direct proportion to the quantity of money in circulation (M). Thus, the quantity theory was usually expressed by means of the equation of exchange, but the latter was not identical with the former. This difference becomes clear when it is considered that a balancing re-equilibrium across the equation, after a hypothesised increase in the money supply, could be regained either by a rise in prices, or a rise in the volume of transactions.

In his lecture notes, Keynes explained that the quantity theory of money assumed that the level of prices depended on three basic factors: the demand for money, the supply of money and the velocity of its circulation.[2] Once the situation was posited in this stark manner, the difference between a gold-backed currency system, and one based on paper money, becomes clear. In the latter system, all three factors (the supply of, demand for and turnover velocity of money) were subject to human will, i.e. were the result of socio-economic factors within human control. In the former system, one factor, the supply of money (gold and/or silver), was the result of vagaries in the discovery of precious metals, i.e. was the result (at least in part) of factors outside of human control. It was this arbitrary element of the gold standard that the young Keynes found unsatisfactory, as he believed it would be more rational for the financial system to be entirely under human control. If it was not, then accidental new discoveries in precious metals could temporarily upset monetary equilibrium. Moreover, there was no reason to assume that the supply of precious metals would, by accident, equate to the amount that was actually necessary in order to maintain stable currencies internationally.

Keynes outlined in his lecture notes how, in a practical case, an increase in the money supply produced a concomitant increase in prices. In Great Britain, any new supply of gold did not go directly into the pockets of consumers, but instead swelled the currency reserves of the Bank of England. This tended to decrease the interest rate and increased the willingness of the Bank to lend. This greater volume of loans tended to increase the demand for existing goods and services, which finally began to influence prices in an upward direction. Keynes concluded that:

> ...there is no reason why the supply of goods should be any greater than before at the old level of price, prices rise until at the new level of price the additional supply of funds is absorbed in purchasing practically the same volume of actual goods as before.[3]

Hence, no new increase of trading activity had resulted from the increase in the money supply, which was the orthodox presentation of the quantity theory of money.

Indian banking

Despite Keynes's snuggling-up with the Q.T. of M. in theoretical terms, it might be surprising to learn that there was hardly any discussion framed around the quantity theory in his 1913 book *Indian Currency and Finance*. It did not even have its own entry in the index. *Indian Currency and Finance* was more an account of the historical development of financial institutions, rather than an exercise in abstract monetary economics. Reviewers of the book were in general favourable, *The Economist* for example praising the author's 'shrewdness of judgement and the moderate and scholarly manner in which he has handled opposing views'.[4] However, there was one element of the book that was not considered in the previous chapter: Keynes's concern to support the creation of an Indian State Bank.

It might seem extraordinary today, but India at the beginning of the twentieth century lacked a central State Bank equivalent to the Bank of England. Instead, it had various regional Presidency Banks (e.g. the Bank of Bengal, of Bombay, and of Madras), various Indian joint-stock banks, private banks, plus some European exchange banks. Although this system had functioned adequately for some period of time, Keynes believed it was flawed for various reasons, and might be exposed as inadequate in a crisis situation. His arguments were that: 1) the existing divorce of responsibility for note issue and for banking generally was a source of potential weakness; 2) there were two distinct sets of reserves (government and bankers) with no clear relation between them; 3) the absence of a State Bank led to the absence of central direction in banking policy and to difficulties for the government in using its liquid funds to best advantage. Keynes recommended that the proper model for India should be the State Banks of Europe (e.g. Germany, Holland or Russia), not the Bank of England.[5]

As previously explained, Keynes had participated in the Royal Commission on Indian Finance and Currency. As part of this process, in October 1913, he prepared a detailed 'Memorandum on

Proposals for the Establishment of a State Bank in India'. Keynes had been requested to prepare this document by other members of the Commission, who could not initially agree on whether a State Bank was necessary for India. In it he declared that:

> I attach great importance to the increased stability which a State Bank would introduce into the Indian banking system. India is not well placed at present to meet a banking crisis. The Presidency Banks are already Banker's Banks to an important extent, but they are not strong enough to support the whole burden. In effect the Government keeps a part of the banking reserves, but there is no machinery for bringing its reserves into normal connection with banking.[6]

Keynes warned that with no formal central State Bank reserve, hardly a bank rate policy, the growth of various small but daring banks, and a community un-habituated to banking, there were many components of weakness and few of strength. He proposed therefore that the existing Presidency Banks should form regional parts of a federated system, with a central board of management ruling over them based in Delhi.

Again, Keynes was concerned with designing economic policy to strengthen the Indian financial system, and with providing the Indian government with greater control over its own economy, and hence charges of imperial mismanagement were misplaced. In the end, Keynes's State Bank Memorandum was annexed to the final Commission Report, rather than being incorporated fully into it. A Reserve Bank of India was not finally created until 1935, as the outbreak of war in 1914 meant that all the Commission's recommendations were not immediately implemented. But Keynes's very specific interest in improving Indian banking structures had some wider relevance to his burgeoning pre-war economic theory in key areas, to which attention is now turned.

First thoughts on trade cycles

Keynes's first developed paper devoted to those areas of economic theory that he would devote the main part of his life to exploring was entitled 'How Far are Bankers Responsible for the Alternation of Crisis and Depression?', and it was presented to a meeting of the Political Economy Club in December 1913. At this time, Keynes had accumulated first-hand knowledge of the Indian financial system through his work in the India Office, together with an understanding of the principles of economic theory through his lecturing duties. The 1913 paper on the responsibility of bankers attempted to bring these two areas together, and aimed to provide 'a general explanation of fluctuations which is to some extent novel'.[7] What was novel was that Keynes attempted to demonstrate how rational and sensible investment decisions by bankers could still produce over-investment, which in turn could lead to financial crisis and economic depression.

Keynes divided the total resources of the community into three basic components: savings, spending and resources held 'in suspense', i.e. resources the ultimate allocation of which had yet to be determined. Financial institutions like banks held long-term savings, but they also held short-term resources deemed 'in suspense'. This meant that the value of funds invested by banks could exceed the amount actually set aside as savings, as banks might also invest part of the 'in suspense' fund if the profitable opportunity arose. But, if the holders of the 'in suspense' funds decided ultimately not to save these funds, then the total amount invested by the community could exceed the total amount saved. It was this potential non-equilibrium that could lead to financial crisis, as periods of over-investment in fixed capital led to the cash reserves of banks gradually falling, eventually reaching a lower ratio than was deemed safe. This then produced a sharp contraction of credit and a crisis, followed sometimes by a depression.[8] As he similarly declared in his lecture notes, booms of trade due to monetary factors were caused by expansions in the volume of credit, which became available for investment as banking deposits (or savings + funds 'in suspense') increased.[9]

Keynes stressed that it was genuinely difficult for bankers to detect when such periods of over-investment were occurring, due in part to the complexity of the modern system of banking. It was not necessarily that bankers were making bad investment decisions, but that the amount of sound investment opportunities were outstripping the level of savings that were available to invest, for example due to new discoveries in technology or geography.

Consequently, there was no cure for this situation until the level of savings had sufficient time to catch up with the investments that had already been made. Of course, some banks might make some bad investment decisions, and other causes of excess investment such as increased military spending and the extension of capital spending facilities were also deemed as possibilities. But for Keynes in 1913, the alternation of crisis and depression could be a 'natural' by-product of the way that the financial system operated *even when it functioned correctly* in terms of its own parameters.

This might seem a rather pessimistic explanation of trade cycles, as there was (apparently) no possibility of finding a permanent cure, or of predicting when such over-investment conditions were developing. The only glimmer of hope that Keynes allowed in his 1913 paper was that perhaps 'the necessary reaction may be taken slowly and spread over so long a period that the effect in general prosperity' might not be excessively marked.[10] In his lecture notes, he had also emphasised the importance of maintaining stability in the general price level, to help to reduce any miscalculations in business investments to a minimum.[11] Even so, the early Keynes's economic theory was clearly some considerable distance away from the active intervention in trade cycles through government investment, which he is usually taken to have advocated in the 1930s. This mix of pessimism and partial optimism was also found in his early approach to population issues.

Early views on population

Keynes's first substantive writing on population was composed sometime in 1913–14 (the exact date is contentious), and consists (as it survives today) of thirty-five roughly drafted pages that were not prepared for publication by the author as they stood at the time. Keynes used this rough composition entitled 'Population' as background work for a lecture he gave in Oxford in May 1914 entitled 'Is the Problem of Population a Pressing and Important One Now?', and (much later) as background for a short biographical study of T.R. Malthus ('the first of the Cambridge economists') that was published in 1933. He had also made some lecture notes on this topic in 1912 as one part of his undergraduate course on 'The Principles of Economics'.

Malthus was (and still is) a controversial figure within the history of economics, especially amongst left-leaning thinkers, as he had raised the danger of what has become known as the 'Malthusian devil': uncontrolled population growth. Karl Marx in particular despised him. The young Keynes, however, was more sympathetic to Malthus, although not uncritically so, in part because of his Cambridge heritage, and partly because he believed that Marx-type criticisms were misplaced.

Keynes began his draft essay on 'Population' with a consideration of Malthus's basic ideas on population change, and rebuking him for unfounded assumptions such as the inevitability of diminishing returns in agriculture and a geometric rate of population growth. However, for Keynes, Malthus was correct in so far as various natural checks on population growth (famines and wars) did occur, and right that they sometimes exerted an equilibriating effect on the tendency of the human race to propagate above what were taken as sustainable increases in subsistence supplies. Moreover, Keynes believed that the increased internationalisation of trade relations that had taken place since the end of the nineteenth century meant that food costs were now subject to global trends of population and demand, which made the economic situation for the UK more precarious. This was because food was previously produced mostly in the UK, but was increasingly being imported from overseas.

This latter issue was a very significant one for Keynes. In a note published in 1912 on the estimated value of the UK's exports and imports, he had outlined that:

> ...we are obtaining for our exports almost exactly the same prices as in 1900, but are paying for our imports appreciably higher prices than in 1900. We are, in fact, £37,000,000 a year worse off than we should be if all prices had moved equally...The deterioration...is due to the operation of the law of diminishing returns for raw products...[12]

Economists now call the relation between exports and imports of a country 'the terms of trade', which in this instance referred to the raw materials against manufactures terms of trade. Keynes warned more generally that the comparative advantage in trade was moving sharply against industrial countries. The implication of this trend was that, if it continued, it would have a profound effect on living standards across the UK. Although at the time of its first publication, Keynes's 1912 note went almost unnoticed, the issues that it had raised would later become very controversial.

The possibility of countries experiencing declining terms of trade, and changes to the relative rates of population growth that had greater national impact as international connections became more extensive, meant that nationalistic tensions had recently found the opportunity to fester and grow. Keynes anticipated portentously that:

> Racial and military feeling now runs high, and every patriot urges his country forward on a course of action in the widest sense anti-social. And the patriot has something on his side...
> The problem, therefore, is made much worse and far harder of solution by having become, since Malthus's time, cosmopolitan.[13]

What Keynes meant was that recourse to nationalistic discourse was a consequence of the loss of control that some groups were beginning to feel had taken place, due in part to early twentieth-century globalisation trends. Keynes seemed at some points in the text to have concerns for what he variously described as 'the best stock', 'decent people', and 'the population of our own country', warning that 'cosmopolitan humanitarianism' should be employed only very modestly 'in order to protect our standard of life from injury at the hands of more prolific races'.[14] In his lecture notes, however, he declared himself to be in partial sympathy with the cosmopolitans who were 'pleased by the existence of varied civilisations' and who felt 'sympathy for the aspirations of others', suggesting that he was ambiguous about the importance of nationalistic ideas.[15] It is evident that there were nationalist elements to Keynes's discussion of population in 1913–14, but there was more to it than this alone.

Underlying the discussion was a genuine concern for understanding the place of the UK in the fast-moving international trends of the period. This was so that in the future, it would be possible 'to act with our attention chiefly directed towards the economic wellbeing of the population of our own country'.[16] Keynes was a British economist, and it was natural for a British economist to be concerned with British issues. Keynes did occasionally use stereotypical language in order to describe different cultures, but in other instances he wrote as if he was deliberately negating any attempt at linking racial factors with population growth. For example, in his 1912 lecture notes on population, he declared forcefully that:

> Differences of creed, race, occupation or domicile, which are advanced to account for differences in the rate of fertility appear on closer inspection to reduce themselves to differences and changes in material prosperity.[17]

In the draft essay on 'Population', Keynes also rejected 'the fear of what is called race-suicide', as might be generated by the declining birth rates of European countries compared to India and China: national and military advantages were as likely to be diminished as increased by the tendency towards overpopulation. He did warn that 'restrictive measures' with respect to immigration and international trade might in the future be required, but he concluded that 'one can feel some hope' that Western countries would reach a population density equilibrium that was the best available. In his lecture notes he raised the issue of whether increasing population must inevitably reduce the average level of prosperity, inclining ('with some compromise') towards preferring a higher level of prosperity than higher numbers, but he also acknowledged the problem of 'national prejudice' as part of a primitive instinct for the preservation of one's own race.

Keynes's early views on population were not of much significance for his economics at this time, nor were they of great significance for his pre-war policy efforts on issues like Indian financial development, which raises the question of why they have been discussed. The answer is that they would become much more important to various issues that would develop in the following decade, when the calamitous consequences of the war in Europe would place in stark relief the need to continuously re-assert the best interests of Great Britain in a rapidly changing trans-European and international environment. In order to understand Keynes's reaction to the events of the second half of the 1910s and the early 1920s, his pre-existing beliefs have to be considered as starting-points.

Conclusion

On the eve of the outbreak of the First World War, Keynes had cemented his position as a successful and respected, if rather conventional, Cambridge economist, with his biggest departure from intellectual orthodoxy being his unenthusiastic attitude towards the British version of the gold standard, rather than any opposition to the tenets of mainstream economic theory. His most notable rebellions prior to 1914 were found in his social attitudes; he mocked religion, condoned the free expression of all types of sexuality, and expressed a healthy scepticism towards any political ideas that were held in a rigid, doctrinaire fashion. These social attitudes were of course the quintessence of Bloomsbury, and hence it might reasonably appear that while Cambridge ruled his intellect, Bloomsbury ruled his heart. However, the personal amorality of the Bloomsbury interpretation of G.E. Moore's philosophy would very soon be sorely tested by the defining event of the era, the war of 1914–18. And Keynes's own very active participation in the British war effort would lead to a break with Bloomsbury that would consign the halcyon days of pre-war London to a mere wistful evocative memory.

5   Killing Germans as cheaply as possible

Although nobody knew it at the time, the outbreak of war in the summer of 1914 marked the beginning of the end for British economic dominance in the Western world. Many took a long time to realise its full significance, but by the end of the war Keynes had no illusions as to its real meaning and its calamitous consequences for the UK economy. As will be documented in this chapter and the next, he was powerless to prevent UK financial power draining (almost literally) week-by-week across the Atlantic Ocean; indeed, his own wartime employment forced him to be an active and efficient organiser of this debilitating drain in the most intimate and excruciating way.

Keynes's role in designing Allied financial policies during the First World War was very significant, and there are enough materials for the composition of a substantial book devoted to this topic alone. Hence, only a number of key aspects of his role will be examined in some detail here. These will be: his overall strategy for financing the Allied campaign, some specific controversies over this strategy that were contested by various critics, the debates that took place over post-war reconstruction after the war was over, and the impact of the war on his personal circumstances. What will not be provided is a day-to-day guide to every specific development or correspondence he became involved with as the war progressed.

One of the most important political relationships that Keynes maintained across much of his life now requires introduction: that with David Lloyd George. Their relationship was certainly protracted but it was also often fractious and bad-tempered, yet sometimes familiar and warm. Lloyd George was Liberal Chancellor of the Exchequer from 1908 to 1915; later, he would become Liberal Prime Minister (from 1916 to 1922). As a fellow Liberal, Keynes obviously felt some affinity with Lloyd George's political beliefs, although as will be seen, these two giants of the era did not always like each other that much, and sometimes they came into direct conflict over matters of policy significance. Any attempt at evaluating Keynes's wider political significance must therefore provide some judgement regarding the veracity of his disagreements with Lloyd George.

Lloyd George also provided a useful and stark character contrast with Keynes. Keynes was rooted in Cambridge traditions, saw himself squarely as part of that tradition, and was seen by others as the same. Although he was lauded much later as a theoretical revolutionary, he took great pains to connect his new theory with Cambridge economists past: especially T.R. Malthus. By contrast, Keynes described Lloyd George at the height of their later disagreements in 1919 as follows:

> Lloyd George is rooted in nothing; he is void and without content; he lives and feeds on his immediate surroundings; he is an instrument and player at the same time which plays on the company and is played on by them too; he is a prism, as I have heard him described, which collects light and distorts it and is most brilliant if the light comes from many quarters at once; a vampire and a medium in one.[1]

Thus, Keynes the rooted intellectual looked upon Lloyd George the Janus-faced politician with a mixture of uneasy awe, disdain and bemusement. Whether the two contrasting personalities would provide an effective mix when battling for British political and military interests will be seen in what follows.

Wartime employment

In the autumn of 1914, Keynes initially returned to Cambridge to resume his lecturing duties, although overall student numbers had understandably dwindled. It was not long before he became directly involved in wartime financial issues, firstly on the question of whether the UK gold standard should be suspended because of the looming military conflict. The financial markets had been spooked by the possible outbreak of war, and at the end of July 1914, an increase in consumer demand for gold in exchange for notes resulted in the Bank of England considering whether to suspend the gold convertibility of sterling. At the time this was seen as a very considerable step, as the entire UK monetary system, and consequently the central position of London as an international financial centre, was based on the fact that sterling was freely convertible into gold.

In memoranda written expressly for the Chancellor of the Exchequer David Lloyd George, Keynes argued strongly against such a suspension, on the grounds that refusing to pay out gold at the first signs of a crisis would severely dent the reputation of the UK's financial system, and thus would detract from London's pre-eminent position as a centre for holding and transacting future gold and currency deposits. Although his position on this issue was initially designed to meet the requirements of the immediate currency crisis provoked by intimations of war, it would soon become a central peg of his entire strategy for financing the Allied military campaign.

As the war took hold, Keynes was appointed in January 1915 first as an assistant to Sir George Paish (1867–1957), who was Lloyd George's special adviser and the editor of *The Statist* magazine. In the summer of 1915, Keynes was then transferred to the Treasury Finance Division and his advisory role increased. Soon after his initial appointment, he was travelling to France for the first Inter-Allied financial conference, alongside Lloyd George, Edwin Montagu and the Governor of the Bank of England, who all became his close colleagues. The key issues discussed at this and later conferences were the precise formula for the sharing of the financial burden of the war among the Allied powers (initially the UK, France and Russia, but then Italy), and how the available military resources should best be distributed among them. Each individual nation wanted, as best it could (without being overly selfish) to minimise its own financial contribution, but simultaneously maximise its military capacity, within the limits of the collective efforts of the alliance. Keynes was in a major way responsible for negotiating and implementing the various ongoing settlements to these issues that were achieved by the Allies as the war progressed.

Within the initial alliance, the three constituent powers had different strengths and weaknesses, and also different financial and military requirements. One of the UK's major strengths was the leading capacity of London as an international financial centre, and partly because of this, it was decided that the UK should become the institutional conduit for the entire system of Allied finance. This gave Keynes an especially important role. Although he was not in ultimate political control of the UK's financial dealings, which lay with the Chancellor of the Exchequer, his knowledge of economics and the financial markets meant that his arguments carried a great deal of weight, both in the UK and within the wider Allied alliance. Both when Lloyd George was Chancellor (until May 1915), and later when Reginald McKenna took over the post (1915–16), many of the government's financial memoranda contained a significant input from Keynes. This did not mean that he always got his own way, but it did mean that he was unquestionably the most influential academic economist within the Allied system of wartime financial governance. In 1915 he was only 32 years old.

Keynes explained the essential features of Allied war finance as they developed during 1914 as follows. It was decided that a long-term strategic goal must be to maintain the convertibility of sterling into gold on international exchanges, and to maintain the purchasing power of sterling against the dollar. It was gold convertibility that would help to enable the UK to secure loans for all the Allied powers, and it was the dollar peg that would help to maintain the purchasing power of sterling in all parts of the world. If this purchasing power declined substantially, then it would be much harder for the UK to purchase the military supplies needed by all the Allies from international suppliers in order to secure victory in the war. Keynes explained in a report to the UK Chancellor of the Exchequer from October 1916 that:

Large sums are at present expended by the Treasury in maintaining the purchasing power of the £ sterling in terms of the dollar. This expenditure is the pivot of our whole financial policy and the foundation of our credit in all parts of the world. By supporting the American exchange we limit the possible depreciation of all the other neutral exchanges. And, as the exchanges of the other allies on London are also supported, the purchasing power of every member of the alliance is maintained in all parts of the world.[2]

However, as the first line of this quotation implied, there was an associated danger with this policy. Gold was limited, as were other UK financial reserves, and it was possible that a major run on sterling would exhaust the ability of the Bank of England to maintain the sterling/dollar peg and the gold standard, and that they would then collapse. In fact, this possibility was nearly realised a number of times during the period 1915–17, as major sterling crises affected the Allied system of finance at various instances.

For example, in November 1916, a major crisis was provoked by the US Federal Reserve warning private investors against taking Allied Treasury bills as security, and for the next three weeks, gold drained out of UK reserves at around $5 million per day.[3] Keynes later recalled that a continuance of this drain at a rate of between $5 and $20 million a day for only one additional week would have bankrupted the UK completely.[4] Luckily, this particular drain quickly abated. It was only the official American entry into the war in April 1917, following German submarine attacks on Atlantic sea supply routes in February 1917, which finally resolved this issue once and for all.

However, Keynes had, from early on in the war, promoted one ingenious idea to bolster the UK's own gold and financial reserves across the period 1915–17: to assume command over some of the gold of the other Allied powers. After all, it was the UK that was assuming the biggest role in securing the necessary loans for all the Allied powers; in return, it seemed fair that France and Russia should assist by transferring some of their substantial gold reserves to UK control, as partial payment for the military supplies that they were receiving through UK channels. The respective Finance Ministers initially advanced arguments as to why such transfers would be a bad idea, but eventually they agreed that necessity had forced their hands on this issue. Whether this aspect of the system of war finance had any wider consequences will be considered further on.

Personal consequences

If, before the outbreak of war, Keynes's circle of friends and acquaintances had been predominantly academic, economic and artistic, and only occasionally political, his involvement in very significant wartime financial affairs served to widen his social circle considerably. He began regular attendance at social gatherings at 10 Downing Street, became a long-serving friend of Reginald McKenna and various members of the influential Asquith family (including Margot and Herbert Henry), and a close associate of Andrew Bonar Law (the Chancellor during 1917–18 and later a Conservative Prime Minister), with whom he sometimes played bridge at 11 Downing Street. Keynes was not in any way intimidated by moving in such illustrious company, and was not concerned about disagreeing strongly with his political superiors on any particular issue, if he was convinced that he was right. One of his Bloomsbury friends even described him in 1918 as 'a bit mad on the subject of his own importance', after being informed by Keynes that he would soon be dining with the Duke of Connaught.[5] During a trip to Paris in January 1918, he had dined at the Ritz with the newspaper magnate and Minister of Information, Lord Beaverbrook.

Perhaps the most significant personal issue with wider national significance that Keynes was forced to deal with as the war unfolded was the looming necessity of military conscription, which became a real issue in the UK from June 1915 onwards. As a Treasury employee, Keynes was eventually (in February 1916) given permanent exemption from military service on the grounds that his work was of national importance. There is little doubt that his exceptionally important wartime contributions to managing Allied finances were truly of national (and even international) significance, and if anyone genuinely deserved exemption on these grounds, then it was Keynes.

However, he was ambiguous about whether he was also a conscientious objector to conscription as a matter of principle, as in February 1916 he drafted a letter claiming exemption 'to surrendering my liberty of judgement on so vital a question as undertaking military service'.[6] He also donated funds to the National Council Against Conscription. It might at first seem rather difficult to understand why someone who had very clear grounds of exemption in his Treasury duties, would also engage with arguments about exemption on grounds of conscience. However, the answer is clear: his close Bloomsbury associations.

Many of his intimate male friends such as Lytton Strachey, Duncan Grant, Clive Bell, David Garnett and Gerald Shove were at least theoretically eligible for conscription, and some were simultaneously conscientious objectors. Others, such as the poet Rupert Brooke, actively joined up – he died in April 1915. Thus, Keynes was personally concerned that the lives of some of his Bloomsbury friends would be lost if they were forcibly conscripted, and was also worried about how his personal support for the war (as revealed by his own initially welcome Treasury employment) would appear to the wider Bloomsbury circle, who were, more often than not, against the pursuit of military conflicts on moral grounds. This latter concern was not at all misplaced, as Lytton Strachey had attempted to embarrass Keynes by placing a printed copy of a very militaristic speech by Edwin Montagu on his dinner plate one evening.[7] On other occasions, Keynes testified successfully as a witness for some of his friends at official tribunals that were devoted to deciding whether an individual's objection to military service was genuinely due to conscience. Keynes certainly believed that some individuals were rightly due conscientious exemption, and perhaps partially in solidarity with them, he had flirted with claiming such an exemption in his own case as a point of principle.

The wider macro-economic components of the conscription issue were, on the one hand, the effects of withdrawing such a large quantity of labour from the domestic economy, and on the other, the strategic requirements of the UK military force in terms of size as revealed by future military planning. Both of these macro-components were controversial. There was (apparently) a trade-off between a larger army and a smaller domestic workforce, as a soldier on the front-line could not simultaneously be producing shells back at home. Consequently, in the summer and autumn of 1915, Keynes argued for definite restrictions on the size of the UK military force, as he believed that the UK economy was nearly at full capacity. This constituted a significant part of the developing conflict with Lloyd George, who, especially after becoming Minister of Munitions in 1915, argued against the restrictions on military expenditure that Keynes had continuously advanced. Here, Keynes was tacitly accepting the conventional wisdom of the Treasury position that both financial capacity, and the real resources that it represented, were fixed and given, at least in the short run. If they were pushed beyond this given capacity, then economic disaster could be the result.

For example in January 1916, Keynes defended his case in print with admirable precision. He explained that the governments of Russia, Italy, Belgium, Serbia and (partially) France were dependent on the UK for the food and military supplies that they all needed from overseas. This was because:

> ...they have mobilised with their armies so large a part of their labour supply that they cannot manufacture or raise from the soil what they require themselves...If at the beginning of the war we had immediately mobilised between 3 million and 4 million men, we could not have financed our allies without suffering by now as great an exhaustion as Germany's...[8]

Keynes believed that the UK had 'already committed our aggregate resources to the maximum of which they are capable' and that, regarding the possibility of increased supplies for the other Allies, 'our shipping resources are strained to the utmost'.[9] Thus, the essential factor for Keynes in 1916 was that any new developments could be accomplished only at the expense of what was already being done.

There were other rather extraordinary elements of Keynes's personal circumstances that emerged as the war developed. At the same time as he was negotiating crucial financial agreements on which the fate of the Western world depended, he was still assuming many of the editorial duties for the *Economic Journal*, something which is inconceivable today. And he was also allowed by his government employers to continue his own academic writing if he so desired, although he had (understandably) given up his teaching duties at Cambridge.

One characteristic aspect of Keynes's personal accomplishments during the First World War was his significant role in obtaining fine art for the British nation. In March 1918, he secured around £20,000 of UK government funds for the purchase of art at auction, ultimately destined for the National Gallery. This might appear as a frivolous waste of scarce resources at a time when British military forces were staking their lives in combat. In fact, it resulted in inspired purchases at bargain-basement prices: he obtained Cézanne's painting *Apples* for £327, and important examples of the works of esteemed masters such as Delacroix and Ingres.[10] In total, he bought four pictures for himself and over twenty for the nation. Purchasing fine art during wartime was an eminently wise decision, when many fire sales in European cities were occurring: literally. Some of his purchases are today worth many millions of pounds.

Another very personal experience that Keynes discovered during wartime was his first heterosexual relationship, which occurred towards the end of the war with Barbara Hiles. Much more significantly, in September 1918 Keynes went to see Diaghilev's new London production, in which the ballerina Lydia Lopokova was performing one of the leading roles. Keynes met Lydia for the first time after the performance, and then again soon after at social occasions. However, there was apparently no instantaneous spark of heated passion, as he described one of her ballet performances in a letter to Duncan Grant as 'poor', and on another occasion he judged rather sweepingly that: 'She is a rotten dancer'.[11] At this time Lydia was still married to Randolfo Barocchi, whom she did not attempt to leave until the summer of 1919. Lydia did not meet with Keynes again for a number of years, as she departed abruptly for the USA, but he was beginning to move away from his youthful romantic interest solely in men.

Although before 1914 he had been a rather cloistered academic, during the war Keynes was forced to weather his fair share of personal dangers. In the summer of 1915, he endured an operation for appendicitis and then developed pneumonia, from which he eventually recovered. He had been due to travel to Russia with Lord Kitchener, the Secretary of State for War, in June 1916 to continue the negotiations over the finance situation on face to face terms, but by chance was prevented from travelling at the last moment: the cruiser was sunk and most of the crew and passengers were lost. During 1917, German air raids on London resulted in Keynes making frantic dashes for cover in the basement of his lodgings. The fatefully avoided visit to Russia was an indication not only of the dangers of travel during wartime, but also of the importance of Russia to the overall Allied campaign, and to his work as a Treasury official. Russia was a crucial point of debate within the UK war effort, as will now be seen from the heated discussions that occurred in the government over the provision of Allied military supplies.

Lloyd George

Perhaps the most significantly conflicted personal relationship that Keynes was faced with as the war progressed, which had far greater national and international consequences, was with David Lloyd George. The essential points of disagreement between Keynes and Lloyd George in 1916 over war finance related to what Lloyd George believed were dangerous restrictions placed on Russian military supply orders by Keynes and the UK Treasury for primarily financial reasons. Lloyd George, as Minister of Munitions, had suggested in the summer of 1916 that Russia was being deprived of necessary war materials, namely heavy guns, heavy shells and railway materials. Keynes, in direct contrast, argued that he had made every effort to cover all reasonable Russian supply orders with Allied funds, and that anyway, physical restrictions on available freight capacity into Russia were a far greater hindrance than any financial limitations that were imposed by the UK Treasury.

In a document prepared by Keynes in association with Reginald McKenna, the Chancellor of the Exchequer in 1915–16, entitled 'Memorandum on Mr Lloyd George's Proposals' from July 1916, Keynes explained that the UK Treasury had since mid-1915 been 'engaged in enabling the Russian government to replace their former unco-ordinated and inefficient methods by a centralised and efficient machine acting in conjunction with the British war departments'.[12] The issues were at first sight clear-cut, and it might be thought possible quickly to establish who had actually been correct by consulting the relevant facts, but the issues were not quite so clear-cut as they initially appeared.

Firstly, Keynes's knowledge of finance far outweighed that of Lloyd George, which meant that he could easily out-argue him when it came to the technicalities of organising loans and operating financial instruments. Thus, when at one point in the debate, Lloyd George suggested that American companies themselves might provide the additional credit for increased orders from the Allies, Keynes demonstrated with devastating aplomb that Lloyd George's understanding of the term 'credit' in this context was faulty. If this credit were to be provided by the companies themselves or by US banks using company credit, then this would be advantageous, but if this credit was linked to British government credit or Treasury bills, then all that would be happening was that Allied finances would be covering these increased orders through an indirect path. Keynes thought (rightly) that the former source of credit was very unlikely.

Secondly, Keynes mounted a spirited defence of his treatment of Russian military orders from the time that he entered the Treasury in May 1915. Up until October 1915, the Russian government had been allowed a free hand in placing individual orders, and Keynes in turn had 'agreed to meet the whole of their commitments'.[13] After a more co-ordinated system for military ordering was established, the bulk of the new orders placed were 'just beginning to bear fruit, and will keep the Russians liberally supplied with the principal munitions of war for many months to come'.[14] As to Lloyd George's question of whether the fullest available credit from America was actively being sought, Keynes gave assurances that it was not the UK Treasury that was shying away from taking all credit that was being offered, rather it was restrictions on the US side that were the ultimate limiting factor.

Consequently, Keynes's 'Memorandum on Mr Lloyd George's Proposals' was a stinging and powerful rebuttal of Lloyd George's suggestion that the Russian side was being short-changed of military supplies. Lloyd George had no substantial public reply to offer at the time, and Keynes's demolition of his political superior's arguments would fester in Lloyd George's consciousness for years to come, making the latter politician sometimes rather unkind in his evaluation of the sharp-minded economist. On Keynes's side, the implication that parsimonious Treasury penny-pinching had been hindering the Allied military campaign was also not taken well; Keynes had thoroughly immersed himself in war finance affairs not for his own good, but because he believed his economic expertise was sorely needed. He had severely strained his relations with many of his Bloomsbury friends by doing so; some of these friends had, in effect, accused him of being a traitor to the semi-pacifist cause.

In order to evaluate to what extent Keynes and Lloyd George were right on this issue, a more detailed consideration of the facts is required. But first, some general points will be conceded. There is no doubt that both the UK and Russia initially underestimated the scale of the war as it would develop after 1914, and hence they both were caught lacking regarding obtaining the necessary long-term military supplies to prosecute the war. Consequently, the 'shells crisis', or the acute shortage of artillery munitions that developed in the spring of 1915, affected all of the main Allied nations. In addition, the Russian government bureaucracy initially demonstrated some significant deficiencies regarding the placing and organisation of its military orders, partly due to its own inefficient structure, and partly due to problems regarding the co-ordination of Russian supplies with those required by other Allies. For example, on a few occasions early on in the war, Russian military orders in the USA actually competed with similar UK orders, having the detrimental effect of increasing prices and encouraging speculation by middlemen. Hence, it was true that the establishment of a more co-ordinated joint effort in controlling Allied military orders, as was accomplished (on Keynes's watch) through the creation in September 1915 of a Russian Committee in London to approve Russian purchases funded by the Allies, was a marked improvement.

However, the question of whether physical restrictions on freight capacity really were the ultimate hindrance to Russian supplies, as Keynes suggested in 1916, was less clear-cut. In the spring and summer of 1916, the British Treasury did not support various Russian requests for additional funds specifically to purchase more rolling stock, railroad supplies and for greater road completion.[15] In fact, there were two separate issues here. Firstly, shipping capacity to Russia and the handling capacity of Russian ports, and secondly, the capacity of the internal transport system within Russia to transfer the supplies from the docks to the front lines. In reality, the latter was much more deficient than the former.

As Keynes admitted in 1919, it was the case that in Russia, 'the condition of the rolling-stock is believed to be altogether desperate, and one of the most fundamental factors in the existing economic disorder'.[16] During 1915, work was being undertaken to increase the internal transport capacity within Russia, but there were delays in completion of the railway line upgrades, perhaps partly due to insufficiencies in obtaining the necessary Allied funds and raw material supplies, and partly due to internal Russian failures in work management and organisation.[17] Moreover, in November 1916, a further Russian attempt to make additional orders of rail supplies from the US was opposed by the UK Treasury, on the grounds that, as the US was already producing railway materials at full capacity, additional Russian orders would only come at the expense of other Allied requirements.[18]

Hence, although it was true that Keynes did make every effort to meet a large portion of Russian demands for military and related orders from the summer of 1915 onwards, it would not quite be true to state that the UK Treasury had met all such requests from 1915 to Russia's unceremonious exit from the war in 1917. Lloyd George's ongoing frustrations at financial limitations on Russian supplies, which were personified in his deteriorating relationship with Keynes, had at least some basis in fact. It is worth quoting Lloyd George's stark and controversial post-war evaluation of the issue:

> I have always felt that during the War the Allies ought to have been readier to pool their resources of men and munitions of war. Had they done so Russia, Serbia and Roumania would not have collapsed.[19]

Of course, there is no way of calculating for sure whether increased Allied funding for military supplies to Russia, or for bolstering the Russian financial system more generally by transferring less gold from Russia's reserves or discouraging the printing of paper currency, could ever have prevented the revolutionary collapse in October 1917. But Lloyd George was perfectly consistent on this point during the war and then after it.[20] This must mean, in turn, that some commentators, who have taken Keynes's side on this issue against Lloyd George, could be mistaking Keynes's vastly superior armoury of economic arguments, with the solidity of his national–strategic case.

In truth, this issue was ultimately a question of overall military strategy, not merely of financial techniques. Keynes was concerned that the UK and hence the Allies could technically become bankrupt, lose the gold basis of sterling, and become embroiled in a complete financial collapse, which would in turn (he believed) lead to the war being lost. Lloyd George was concerned with the possibility of losing the war militarily whilst mistakenly attempting to retain financial solvency, which (surely) would have had the same disastrous ultimate effect on the UK economy. Keynes's opinion of Lloyd George during the war is clear from a private letter sent in April 1918. He declared in a temporarily despairing mood regarding the UK that:

> If this Govt. were to beat the Germans, I shall lose all faith for the future in the efficacy of intellectual processes...Everything is always decided for some reason other than the real merits of the case, in the sphere where I have control...I attribute all our misfortunes to [Lloyd] George. We are governed by a crook and the results are natural.[21]

Of course, Keynes was being wilfully one-sided for effect, he did not really want the UK to lose the war so that questionable decision-making processes were proved ineffectual: it was the long-standing frustrations of an academic dealing with wily politicians that were being vented.

The embers of this important conflict between Keynes and Lloyd George remained alight for many years after 1918. According to Lloyd George in his war memoirs, during the First World War Keynes was:

> ...much too mercurial and impulsive a counsellor for a great emergency. He dashed at conclusions with acrobatic ease. It made things no better that he rushed into opposite conclusions with the same agility. He is an entertaining economist whose bright but shallow dissertations of finance and political economy, when not taken seriously, always provide a source of innocent merriment to his readers. But the Chancellor of the Exchequer... sought not amusement but guidance in this rather whimsical edition of Walter Bagehot, and thus he was led astray at a critical moment...Luckily Mr. Bonar Law and I...both treated the fantastic prediction of British bankruptcy "in the spring" with the measure of respect which was due...I was still less impressed by these prophesies of evil because I knew it was part of the campaign which the Treasury were waging against my great gun programme...In his forecasts Mr. Keynes made the same mistake which had brought the late Mr. Baxter's prophecies into

disrepute. He had been too definite in the dates for the end of the world. Some of these had already passed.[22]

The latter point about Keynes's overly pessimistic predictions of bankruptcy illustrated the complexity of the wartime position very clearly. Both Keynes and Lloyd George had been partially correct on this issue. At the precise moments when Keynes had made his dire warnings of economic Armageddon, the Allied financial position really had been teetering on the edge of a precipice, with no obvious way out of the situation. But often by chance, events either turned in the UK's favour, or the financial forces abated by themselves. Lloyd George never correctly stated at the time why Keynes would turn out to be wrong, he was just throwing the dice and hoping the situation would come right by itself. But, and here is where Lloyd George was right, there was really no other option, as to risk military defeat because of internal financial restrictions would have been equally dangerous, perhaps even more so.

The USA

Underlying all the Allied debates and controversies about war finance was ultimately the position of the USA regarding both the provision of credits to the Allies as (initially) a neutral power, then, on entering the war in the spring of 1917, providing full-scale support to the Allies as their most powerful new recruit. Keynes was painfully aware that from mid-1914 onwards, the supremacy of London as the international financial centre of the Western world was gradually being eroded by the financial demands of European war, and the economic baton was slowly but surely being passed on to New York. In December 1917, he declared in rather cataclysmic terms that for Europe:

>...with the turn things have now taken, probably means the disappearance of the social order we have known hitherto...The abolition of the rich will be rather a comfort and serve them right anyhow. What frightens me more is the prospect of *general* impoverishment. In another year we shall have forfeited the claim we had staked out in the New World and in exchange this country will be mortgaged to America.[23]

In September 1917, Keynes travelled to the USA where he stayed for around a month, in order to smooth out the existing loan agreements and arrange for additional credits. However, the official US entry into the war by no means solved the various Allied financial difficulties.

When Keynes attempted to convince the USA to assume direct responsibility for the future financing of Italy and France, instead of the UK having to guarantee the loans made indirectly to France and Italy through the UK Treasury, the US made sure that the UK also relinquished its control of the non-American purchases of the Allies, a position that might have enabled to UK to gain an advantage on international markets. Keynes commented powerlessly that the US seemed to want to reduce the UK 'to a position of complete financial helplessness and dependence'.[24] The US President, Woodrow Wilson, declared privately in July 1917 regarding the Allied position, that the UK and France would soon be 'financially in our hands', although it would certainly be going too far to suggest that Wilson had deliberately timed the US entry into the war in order to maximise the transfer of economic power from the UK.[25]

Ultimately of course, all the difficulties of the UK Treasury having desperately to ration Allied financial and military resources, and the highly detrimental effect that this had on less-developed Allied countries like Russia, were the result of the US decision to remain neutral for much of the war, and its refusal to supply credit up until spring 1917 on anything other than near-commercial terms. A much earlier US entry would very probably have shortened the duration of the war, and might even have prevented some of its most negative later consequences. Lloyd George blamed Keynes-inspired Treasury rationing for the Russian socio-economic collapse in 1917, but the blame could just as easily be laid on continued US neutrality. When the USA did eventually join the war effort in the spring of 1917, it was not long before the question of the nature of the post-war order in Europe began to be seriously considered.

The negotiations over reparations

The question of German reparations for the massive physical damages wrought by the war had been first considered formally at negotiations that took place at Versailles in the autumn of 1918. Campaigning for the General Election in the UK in December 1918 and with one eye firmly focused on the anti-German feeling that was common immediately after the war, Lloyd George argued that 'we have an absolute right to demand the whole cost of the War from Germany'.[26] The sums that were soon being considered in the UK ranged from an eye-watering £25 billion, down to a relatively modest £5 billion. It is likely that Lloyd George had not fully thought through the 'whole cost' demand from an economic or an international point of view when he made this rousing statement, and partly in consequence of such jingoistic sentiments, and the unrealistic reparations figures so generated, Keynes's disillusionments with the possible terms of the peace for Europe as a whole were quickly growing.

The Paris Peace Conference beginning in January 1919 was a large-scale affair, and Keynes had little decision-making power vis-à-vis the overall terms of the reparations being negotiated. His role was as the most senior Treasury representative within the British delegation. He did, however, consistently advise and argue for reparations at the lower end of the scales being considered, while continuing to participate in drafting the various proposals under view. Keynes also revised and re-presented his own scheme for the cancellation of war debts, initially prepared at the end of 1918, which was not well received by the USA. In the relevant Memorandum on Inter-Ally Debt from March 1919, he explained that during the war the UK had exported a total of £400 million in gold, disposed of around £1,000 million of its foreign securities and had incurred an additional debt of about £1,200 million. A large portion of this gold and debt was now held by the United States. This meant in turn that:

> The United States has made a substantial financial sacrifice since she came into the war, but, inasmuch as she has not, like the rest of us, incurred foreign indebtedness, and before her entry into the war profited out of it largely, even now she is actually richer than she was in 1914.[27]

Keynes believed that, if the UK continued to owe the US Treasury the full war debt of around £1,000 million, then this would require an annual repayment of £100 million, and this burden would 'cripple our foreign development', lay the UK open to pressure from the US 'of the most objectionable description', and also 'complicate the problem of future taxation at home'.[28] The pan-European political tensions that would be generated by making all the Allies pay their debts in full would be a menace to national and financial stability everywhere. Hence, a comprehensive scheme of debt cancellation should be negotiated. Keynes admitted, however, that this proposal was unlikely to be met with much sympathy from the US side, and he was quickly proved right.

Partly in response to the failure of his debt cancellation scheme, in April 1919, Keynes then proposed a 'grand scheme for the rehabilitation of Europe'. This would have facilitated the issue of various national bonds backed by the Allied powers for use by the most devastated powers such as France and Belgium, in order to aid their economic reconstruction. US opposition again blocked this bold scheme, partly as their nationals would have constituted a large number of the bondholders. Woodrow Wilson was convinced that the US Congress would not accept US participation. In response, Keynes privately branded Wilson 'the greatest fraud on earth'.[29]

By May 1919, the final form of the Peace Treaty was beginning to appear, and Keynes did not like it at all. He mulled over his own position and decided to resign from the Treasury, partly in protest at what he passionately believed was the irresponsibility of the terms of the Treaty, which were 'outrageous and impossible and can bring nothing but misfortune', and partly out of sheer exhaustion at his inability to convince the power brokers of their errors.[30] In a reply to a request that he might reconsider his resignation and stay longer in his Treasury post, Keynes replied in the harshest terms possible:

> The Prime Minister is leading us all into a morass of destruction. The settlement which he is proposing for Europe disrupts it economically and must depopulate it by millions of persons. The new states we are setting up cannot survive in such surroundings. Nor can the peace be kept…[31]

Perhaps unsurprisingly, the initial German response to the terms of the Peace Treaty was very negative, and they threatened to refuse to sign it unless revisions were made. Some relatively minor changes were then made and the Germans eventually signed the Treaty of Versailles at the end of June 1919. Keynes was thoroughly distraught by the whole episode and took to his bed for a period of rest and recuperation. Part of his response to this highly undesirable outcome was to write a damning condemnation of the irresponsible way he believed the extremely important issue of Europe's future direction after the war had been decided, under the prophetic-sounding title of *The Economic Consequences of the Peace*. The content of this work, and to what extent its author's very negative view of the Peace Treaty was accurate, will be considered in more detail in the next chapter.

Conclusion

In just recognition of Keynes's wartime services and despite an attempt by Lloyd George to prevent it, in May 1917 Keynes was made a Companion of the Bath (C.B.), this being an order of chivalry awarded to senior military officers or senior civil servants by the British government. He was proud enough of this honour to include the letters C.B. after his name on the title page of some of his later books. However, his undoubtedly monumental efforts during and just after the First World War highlighted both the best and also the worst features of his character and experiences.

As a master of economic detail and an experienced Treasury official, Keynes assisted the Allied efforts in financial organisation in an immeasurable and positive way. But as a political–strategic novice, especially at times of acute national crisis, his flair for framing a brilliant economic argument was not always employed wisely with regards to long-term strategic aims. Thus, Lloyd George's criticisms of Keynes's rationing of military supplies during the war certainly had some basis in truth. In the next chapter, his role in deciding exactly how the total cost of the war would be covered from a financial perspective, and the longer-term strategic consequences of the terms of the peace, will be considered in greater detail.

6 The economic consequences of war

The nature of the system of controlling Allied war finance and the division of labour between the Allied powers, as was discussed in the previous chapter, were two very important things, but by what means Allied financial expenditure as a whole was to be covered was another question entirely. There were three basic methods of covering wartime expenditure: obtaining loans, increasing taxes and issuing paper currency. All three methods were used to a significant degree during the First World War, but there was significant debate about which precise constitution of the mix would be best. The most controversial of the three methods from a purely economic point of view was the inflationary issue of paper currency. As Keynes famously admitted just after the war:

> Lenin is said to have declared that the best way to destroy the capitalist system was to debauch the currency. By a continuing process of inflation, governments can confiscate...an important part of the wealth of their citizens...Lenin was certainly right. There is no subtler, no surer means of overturning the existing basis of society than to debauch the currency.[1]

Although the unprecedented scale and global nature of the First World War had made the use of inflationary financing unavoidable, at least to some degree, exactly how it would be managed and to what extent it would be employed by the various different Allies, were still open questions, at least in the early-to-middle stages of the war. Keynes considered the matter of what was the best way of financing the First World War in a number of different publications, but the most concise distillation of his (first) wartime experiences can be found in his book *A Treatise on Money* of 1930.

The best way of financing war

He explained that the issue of paper currency and the resulting price inflation had been a preferred manner of raising (some significant percentage of) wartime revenue, provided that certain other conditions were met. This was because governments had to find a way of reducing the purchasing capacity of the general population and transferring this diverted means to the war effort, in order to pay for the extra expenses of the military campaign. Allowing prices to rise more than money-wages, so that real wages were reduced, was an expedient method of diverting economic capacity from civilian use to the war effort.[2] Keynes thus favourably advocated inflationary finance during wartime for all the Allies, but only in association with other concomitant policies that will now be outlined.

The basic additional element that must be implemented was an increased tax on the profits of entrepreneurs and businessmen, who would inevitably gain from the price rises that were the consequence of increased currency issue. Since it would be entrepreneurs who would benefit from inflationary finance by being able to increase prices for the reduced level of civilian goods that were available in wartime conditions, the government must step in to 'mop up' their excess profits, and so neutralise the effects of the increased currency in circulation. For Keynes, this excess profits tax was the safest means of gathering back the additional currency that had been issued in order to finance the war effort. He wrote in 1929 on this issue that:

>...if, having allowed them to receive this additional sum, you then proceed to withdraw it from them through taxes...then this device is far and away the most efficient that exists for collecting purchasing power from the consumers and transferring it into the hands of the government.[3]

He was especially proud that the British Treasury had evolved precisely this type of tax through trial and error towards the end of the war, although he accepted that this procedure should have been implemented earlier in the UK.

Keynes evaluated the wider Inter-Ally situation on this particular issue as follows:

> The war finance of other European countries was far less "virtuous" on the above criteria of virtue…because the entrepreneurs were enabled to retain (on and in paper) a much greater proportion of their booty.[4]

The implication was that, if the 'other European countries' had been more careful in mopping up their additionally issued currency by this means, then the outcome would have been far superior. How far this evaluation was accurate is debatable, as in the Russian case it has been suggested that the authorities made nearly as good an effort in implementing Keynes's 'excess profits absorption' method as the UK authorities did.[5] Thus, in May 1916 a tax on corporate excess profits was introduced in Russia at two different levels, a basic rate of 20 per cent and a higher rate of 40 per cent. These levels were doubled in 1917, although some deductions were allowed.[6] This date of introduction was close to the date when a tax on excess profits had been introduced in the UK. Moreover, as Keynes admitted, this method had developed in the UK only *post hoc*, as an improvised necessity, as no-one had realised in the first few months of the war how long it would actually last.

It was Keynes's implicit assumption that each economy that employed his favoured method would operate in the same manner structurally, and hence that the pernicious consequences of inflation could be mitigated in the same manner in each country. But was this assumption realistic? Was the Russian economy really structurally similar to that of the UK? The former economy contained a vast semi-subsistence peasant sector that was absent from the latter.

Some analysts have pointed to the fact that the peasant sector of the Russian economy 'seceded' from the rest of the economy during the First World War as a reason for the disintegration of economic relations as the war progressed. As semi-subsistence farmers, Russian peasants preferred to eat or hoard agricultural produce rather than to sell it in exchange for money, when the supply of manufactured goods that they wanted in return dried up as a consequence of the war. Another factor in this secession was the quickly depreciating currency that peasants were forced to use in any desired market transactions, which was a result of the use of paper currency issue as a method of war finance. Ultimately it was the collapse of the Russian economy, in association with other political factors like rising worker and peasant discontent, which produced the Bolshevik victory in October 1917.

A pertinent contrast with Keynes's method of war finance is available from A.C. Pigou's 1916 book *The Economy and Finance of the War*. Pigou, Keynes's colleague at Cambridge, argued first of all that the greater burden of war finance should fall on what he called the better-to-do people, i.e. the wealthier classes. This was partly as they had more free funds available, and partly as it was more equitable for richer people to lose a significant portion of their income than poorer people. This part of the analysis might appear obvious. However, Pigou then provided a more telling stage to his argument. Regarding how to decide between financing the war by raising taxes or issuing loans, Pigou argued that the former was preferable, as government loans required future repayment out of general taxes, which meant that poorer classes would contribute as much as richer classes to relieving this future burden. Specific taxes, on the other hand, were paid directly by those on whom they were levied.[7] The third means of financing the war, overt manipulation of the currency, was according to Pigou 'ruled out of court in this country by public opinion'.[8]

What is interesting in this contrast between Keynes and Pigou is how different their respective approaches were. Keynes was less concerned with achieving a fair distribution of the burden and did not agree that inflating the currency was 'out of court'. These differences were partly conditioned by Pigou's detachment from the real situation and a lack of understanding of how serious the Allied financial position was, but it was also conditioned by Keynes's lesser concern at this time with structural issues, i.e. with differences in the social consequences of financial policies. His Treasury work necessitated that financial issues were prioritised first and foremost. However, in matters of war, such an approach might not always be the best one.

A last word of evaluation regarding the financial policies pursued by the Allies during the First World War will be left to Keynes himself. Many years later, while discussing the financing of the Second World War, he wrote that a spiral of rising prices and then wages chasing after them, as was produced by inflationary currency issue, was 'a ridiculous system' of war finance. He judged that in using it during the First World War 'the seeds of much subsequent trouble were sown'.[9] Keynes soon began to foresee some elements of this 'subsequent trouble' as early as 1919, and in consequence he penned one of his most famous, controversial and frequently debated works.

The Economic Consequences of the Peace

Keynes's 1919 book *The Economic Consequences of the Peace* was the first to bring its author international recognition (and even notoriety) outside the narrow worlds of economics and finance, and within the broader fields of politics and current affairs. It took him around four months to write and was published in December 1919. It sold very well and very quickly. It was then quickly translated into many languages, including German, French, Italian, Dutch, Spanish, Japanese and Russian, in some instances with prefaces written especially for these different audiences. Although it was brilliantly written, it was perhaps Keynes's most polemical and heart-felt book, and it was conceived in the summer of 1919 explicitly as 'a violent attack on the Peace Treaty' and the emanations of the Paris Peace Conference that was held in the first few months of 1919.[10]

Keynes's controversial argument in *The Economic Consequences of the Peace* was that 'the campaign for securing out of Germany the general costs of the war was one of the most serious acts of unwisdom for which our statesmen have ever been responsible'.[11] This was because the expectations of politicians who supported this campaign were far removed from the truth of what was actually possible, given the thoroughly bedraggled condition of the German economy. Calculating a total theoretical claim against Germany of £8,000 million on the basis of total war costs, Keynes judged judiciously that 'Germany cannot pay anything approaching this sum'.[12] Listing the numerous catastrophes that had befallen Germany during and after the war – loss of its colonies, its marine fleet, its foreign properties, cession of 10 per cent of its territory and population, loss of two million casualties, massive depreciation of its currency, outbreaks of revolution and the more general disruptions due to war – he explained that estimates of a colossal indemnity to be paid from Germany were based on the faulty assumption that it was capable of conducting greater trade after all these significant losses than prior to them.[13]

Instead of the over-inflated £8,000 million figure, Keynes estimated that the absolute maximum that Germany could afford to pay would be £2,000 million, but that in reality, even this much reduced figure could never be fully met.[14] He consequently suggested that a lump sum of £500 million should immediately be deducted from the total in respect of the surrender of German merchant ships, war materials and ceded territory, leaving a balance of £1,500 million to be paid in thirty annual instalments of £50 million each, beginning in 1923 and without accruing any interest.[15] For Keynes, the imminent danger facing Europe in 1919 was not Germany failing to make full compensation for the war, but a rapid depression of the general standard of living caused by politicians failing to provide direct provisions for the economic rehabilitation of the region. In addition, the policy of reducing Germany to a state of indebted servitude for a whole generation was abhorrent and detestable, and would 'sow the decay of the whole civilised life of Europe'.[16]

Keynes's target of attack was not only claims for exaggerated reparations payments. He also suggested, in line with his earlier rejected scheme, that all the Inter-Ally debts should be cancelled in their entirety, and that the UK should waive altogether any claims for cash payments from European Allies as 'an act of farseeing statesmanship'.[17] He explained that:

> The war has ended with everyone owing everyone else immense sums of money. Germany owes a large sum to the Allies; the Allies owe a large sum to Great Britain; and Great Britain owes a large sum to the United States. The holders of war loan in every country are owed a large sum by the state; and the state in its turn is owed a large sum by these and other taxpayers. The whole position is in the highest degree artificial, misleading and vexatious…A general bonfire is…a necessity…[18]

The United States was in a unique position in that it was a lender only, but Keynes hoped that if Europe followed the wise path of a general scheme of debt cancellation, then the US could reasonably be asked for a similar act of generosity, as its own wartime financial sacrifices had been, in proportion to its wealth, immensely less than those of Europe. However, he concluded the book on a downbeat note, as in the autumn of 1919, the reaction from the exertions, fears and sufferings of the previous five years meant that 'we are at the dead season of our fortunes'.[19]

It was true that the precise figures for feasible reparations presented in *The Economic Consequences of the Peace* were not always the ones that Keynes had advanced. For example, he presented a lower estimate of £1,000 million that could be obtained 'without crushing Germany' in October 1918, half of it to be extracted immediately and half gradually.[20] A higher figure of £2,000 million was then discussed in a Treasury Memorandum drafted, at least in part, by Keynes. The thorny issue of receiving financial reparations and simultaneously encouraging economic development was clearly articulated in this Memorandum:

> If the Allies were to 'nurse' the trade and industry of Germany for a period of (say) five years, supplying her with loans and with ample raw materials during that period, a substantially larger sum than the above could probably be extracted thereafter...[21]

The real problem here was at least partly political. How could the need to assist Germany in recovering from the economic consequences of war be sold either to the British or to the US populations, who had until very recently been baying for German blood? Wasn't it right that Germany should be made to suffer, as it bore a large portion of the blame for the European carnage? But conversely, if German was totally crippled economically in revenge for the war, then how could it pay back the large sums that it owed in reparations, and might not this generate further political tensions in the future? Keynes was one of the few participants who could understand the long-term consequences of forcing Germany into near-permanent submission, perhaps in part because he was not officially locked into any political institutions, and partly because he understood the financial intricacies of the situation.

The immediate reception of *The Economic Consequences of the Peace* amongst European reviewers and British politicians was more positive than negative, especially within the Bloomsbury group, where (for example) the poet G.H. Luce declared that nothing 'so great on politics or so profoundly moving has appeared in English' since Edmund Burke on conciliation.[22] Reviewers' reactions were frequently expressed as polarised extremes. For example, the *Quarterly Review* declared in glowing terms that:

> Few, if any writers on public finance or the dismal science of Political Economy have leaped so rapidly into fashion and celebrity as Mr. Keynes…Neither Malthus, Ricardo, Karl Marx, Bastiat, Friedrich List, Bagehot, Jevons, Henry George, nor any other economists…ever took the City and the West End by storm as Mr. Keynes has done by a single book.[23]

Others described it as a 'smashing and unanswerable indictment' of the peace settlement, as 'remarkable' for its punishing foresight, and as 'a great book…full of unforgettable phrases and of vivid portraits etched in the biting acid of a passionate moral indignation'. The negative reviews, sometimes from America, were equally extreme:

> Such superficial books as that of J.M. Keynes are the work of the most dangerous pseudo-idealists or hidebound 'liberals'…their authors are disgruntled, egotistical, clever 'mugwumps' with that tyrannous, schoolmasterish habit of mind which prefers the real or apparent enforcement of its 'cure-alls' to the attainment of plain truth and justice.[24]

What 'mugwumps' were was not explained, but it was unlikely to have been flattering. The more usual criticism of the book encountered early on was that its author was pro-German and should be awarded an Iron Cross.

However, over time a number of substantial, genuinely considered criticisms of *The Economic Consequences of the Peace* were advanced. One of these argued that Keynes had been too pessimistic as to the possibility of German economic recovery after 1918, both in terms of its gathering speed and its extent, and hence the original reparations demands were more realistic than he had allowed. Keynes was too trusting of German complaints about the consequences of reparations, and the real problem was that the Allies failed properly to enforce the actual terms that were set, given that the German side (unsurprisingly) tried to wriggle out of paying by various means.[25] Another less accurate criticism was that, by being too sympathetic to German complaints about the unfair terms of the Peace Treaty, Keynes had indirectly encouraged the growth of Nazism.

There is a degree of truth in the first contra-argument from the financial point of view, as all the combatant countries in Europe had suffered heavy losses to their economies, not just Germany, and Germany's actual industrial recovery in the 1920s was faster than many had expected. But underlying Keynes's economic case for reduced reparations was the moral/political question of not only *could* Germany pay a very large sum, but *should* Germany be made to pay a large sum, given the resentment that it would undoubtedly generate inside the country, and the wider tensions that it might produce within Europe.

Keynes was concerned ultimately not with Germany's post-war debt in isolation, but with European post-war debts in their totality, and how being forced to pay these debts in full might hinder post-war reconstruction across Europe as a whole. The key issue was always the US position. Keynes wanted Germany to pay less at least in part so that the Allies could pay less as a whole: and the ultimate direction of all Allied payments was across the Atlantic. Lloyd George was, from this perspective, shooting himself in the foot by demanding very large reparations payments from Germany, as, if the USA believed that the Allies would receive very large sums from Germany, then surely the Allies could also pay even larger sums onwards to the USA. And, given that much of the continental Allied debts (of France, Russia and Italy) had been assumed by the UK, ultimately it would be the UK that would be burdened by large debt repayments, not forgetting that Soviet Russia had repudiated responsibility for its debt entirely.

It would be naive to think that those on the US side did not see what Keynes was asking of them. But, although the full consequences of the Bolshevik revolution in October 1917 had yet to be thought-through by anyone, the threat of the spread of

Bolshevism to other European states like Germany was certainly well recognised by many of the delegates at the Paris Peace Conference. To those in the USA just after the war had ended, this nascent red threat must have seemed remote, both geographically and politically. Perhaps understandably, the USA refused to write a blank cheque for the post-war reconstruction of Europe. As portrayed in *The Economic Consequences of the Peace*, it had been the Malthusian devil of population growth that had generated Bolshevik success. But Keynes should have realised that more directly to blame was the financial anarchy of the wartime economies, for which he bore at least some medium-sized responsibility. Perhaps his ultimate failure was in not making this politico–economic connection clear enough to those that mattered in the USA. A debilitated post-war Europe would mean not only a stagnant or even a declining standard of living for many European citizens, but also the potential consequences of extremist political catastrophes as would soon be represented most dangerously by Adolf Hitler and Joseph Stalin.

Not everyone agreed with such a positive evaluation of *The Economic Consequences of the Peace* after the war, or would agree with it even a century later. In 1920, the lampooning British magazine *Punch* published the following humorous ditty, which summed up well the criticisms that were increasingly made against Keynes's opposition to the Treaty of Versailles as time passed:

> There was a superior young person called Keynes
> Who possessed an extensive equipment of brains
> And, being elected a Fellow of King's
> He taught Economics and similar things.
>
> And while we're amused by his caustic dispraise
> Of President Wilson's Chadbandian ways,
> Of the cynical Tiger laconic and grim,
> And our versatile Premier so supple and slim –
>
> Still we feel as he zealously damns the allies
> For grudging the Germans the means to arise
> That possibly some of the Ultimate Things
> May even be hidden from Fellows of King's.[26]

The 'cynical Tiger' was Georges Clemenceau, the French President at the time of the Paris Peace Conference. Keynes had argued in *The Economic Consequences of the Peace* that 'so far as the main economic lines of the treaty represent an intellectual idea, it is the idea of France and of Clemenceau': by implication, a major part of the blame for the treaty's inadequacies must lie with France.[27]

The 'supple and slim premier' was Lloyd George, the bruising negative portrait of whom in *The Economic Consequences of the Peace* was initially so caustic that Keynes experienced second thoughts, and had it removed before final publication. When it eventually appeared in print in 1933, it caused a final rupture between Keynes and its subject. In his partisan portrait, Keynes explained how, when it came to securing French reparation aims, Clemenceau's substantial political experience and superior education had gotten the better of President Wilson's naivety and Prime Minister Lloyd George's tendency to compromise:

> The French demands...were much more controversial than those of the British; and it was essential to get the British well embroiled in a Peace of selfish interests...Let [the reader] remember the Prime Minister's incurable love of a deal; his readiness to surrender the substance for a shadow; his intense desire, as the months dragged on, to get a conclusion and be back in England again. What wonder that in the eventual settlement the real victor was Clemenceau.[28]

Keynes had characterised Lloyd George in his quickly-expunged character sketch as a *femme fatale*, a 'goat-footed bard', a Welsh witch who had out-compromised himself by ostensibly taking a middle position between Wilson and Clemenceau, which in reality had meant a final submission to France. On reading a draft of the book, Keynes's mother Florence recommended that 'all the nasty hits at Lloyd George' should be eliminated. The caustic portrait itself was subsequently removed, but the overall interpretation of Lloyd George's failings in the negotiations still remained.

Conclusion

Across chapters five and six, it has been demonstrated how the axis of controversy between Keynes and Lloyd George flipped on its head. During the war itself, it was Lloyd George who demonstrated the greater long-term foresight, as he could see how short-term financial restrictions might endanger the Allied military campaign. But once the war was over, their respective positions reversed, and it was Keynes who demonstrated the greater long-term foresight, as he could see how short-term financial constraints might endanger the European economic recovery. It was the wily politician (the Welsh witch) in the immediate danger of war that had held his nerve in favour of the overall strategy better than the academic economist. But in peacetime, when the politician became subject to the more conventional interest-group restraints, Lloyd George had lost his long-term sense of strategy, and it was the economist who could see more clearly the potential medium- and long-term dangers.

One reviewer of *The Economic Consequences of the Peace* had characterised this type of conflict, perhaps a little simplistically, as a war between intellectuals and statesmen. In the 1920s, this conflict would continue unabated. The major difference, however, was that after 1919, Keynes had become a significant political figure on the international stage, as well as being a well-known academic economist from Cambridge with 'an extensive equipment of brains'.

7 Cycling for Britain's national interest

If *The Economic Consequences of the Peace* had pulled no political punches with regards to its criticisms of the ineffectiveness of the governmental debates over reparations and Inter-Ally debts, then it might be expected that Keynes should have experienced a backlash against his growing influence in government and policy-making circles from 1919 onwards. In fact, although in France and the USA there were some definite qualms about it, in the UK, the publication of this controversial book did not have the large-scale detrimental effect that it might initially have been thought to exert. Within the Bloomsbury group it was even hailed as a major part of Keynes's glorious redemption for participating in the war, as if his extended patience with the warring tribes of government had finally snapped, and he had reverted to his true home in the haughty disparagement of petty transnational politics. However, as this chapter will demonstrate, the events and controversies of the early 1920s would take Keynes even further away from the essence of the Bloomsbury ethos, rather than closer to it.

Returning to Cambridge

Having resigned from his Treasury position, precisely due to disagreements over the unfolding terms of the peace, in October 1919 Keynes went back to his lecturing duties at King's College. For almost the next two decades or so of his life he remained at King's, and divided his work time between Cambridge and London. The latter was where the intimate policy-making circles of government were located, and Keynes's principled resignation from the UK Treasury by no means symbolised any deliberate detachment or disinclination on his part from attempting to exert influence on the major economic institutions of the day. Quite the opposite in fact, as even as early as the end of 1919, the British Chancellor of the Exchequer of the day (Austin Chamberlain) was seeking advice from him on aspects of monetary policy.[1]

In the early 1920s, Keynes became more involved in providing advice to private companies, and increased his efforts to make money from investment activities. For example, he became a member of the board of National Mutual Life Assurance towards the end of 1919, and its chairman in May 1921.[2] At the beginning of 1920, Keynes created a private investment group called the Syndicate, which collected contributing funds from some friends and family members (plus his own investment share) to a total of £30,000, with the aim of speculating in foreign exchange. On first view this might seem a wise choice for an investment focus, as he had accumulated a great deal of knowledge about currency matters, first with respect to India and then internationally in relation to the war.

The strategy that was initially adopted was to venture that sterling would depreciate against the dollar and appreciate against other European currencies such as the French franc, the Italian lire and the German mark.[3] This strategy was based on Keynes's analysis of the relative strengths of these countries' economies after the war, and how the post-war financial reforms were progressing. Although initially some profits were made on this tactic, by the summer of 1920 the Syndicate's investment strategy had turned out to be disastrous, as various European currencies had begun to appreciate against sterling: Keynes was forced to cover the losses that were accumulating from his own external sources of revenue. Unperturbed by this first loss-making experience with currencies, he then re-invested additional funds in this area, and by the end of 1920 had returned to making profits.

By 1922, Keynes had widened the range of his investments to include some primary commodities such as cotton and various metals, and also securities.[4] He provided an outline of his rationale for investing in primary commodities in an article from March 1923, which also presented a more general theory of futures markets and the phenomenon of 'backwardation' of prices. Here he argued that, in purchasing forward contracts for particular crops, i.e.

buying crops on the futures market before they were harvested, the speculator provided an insurance policy for the producer against future price changes, thus supplying a useful social function. Commodity speculators (such as Keynes) were not necessarily prophets of anticipated price increases, but risk-bearers earning a fee for their services.

As the producer of a primary commodity was prepared to accept a lower price for it in advance than they thought it was likely to be worth in the future (backwardation) for the sake of certainty in the sale and price, speculators provided a valuable utility by spreading the risk of production. Self-interest was also involved, as a speculator could:

> …without paying the slightest attention to the prospects of the commodity he deals in…earn substantial remuneration merely by running risks and allowing the results of one season to average with those of another; just as an insurance company makes profits without pretending to know more about an individual's prospects of life…than he knows himself.[5]

The results of Keynes's speculation in primary commodities indicate that, across the entire 1920s, he made profits in all the individual years from 1921 to 1924 and in 1926 and 1927, but made losses in 1925, 1928 and 1929.[6] In total, the profits outweighed the losses by a ratio of approximately two to one, suggesting that his rationale for investment in commodities was a plausible one.

It was not only private individuals who trusted Keynes with designing investment strategies for them in this period. In June 1920, the King's College Estates Committee authorised him to invest £30,000 of their funds in various forms of government securities. He also became involved in other areas of University organisation such as reforming the pension retirement age and the Faculty system, and was elected as a member of the Senate Council. In 1924, he became First Bursar of King's College. However, his lecturing load was reduced from the pre-war period, allowing his efforts to be focused on the economic issues of the day, with which he was still very much involved. In the 1919/20 academic year he lectured on economic aspects of the peace and on the contemporary

European situation, and then across the first half of the 1920s, his lectures were mainly limited to topics relating to European monetary reform and problems of the international monetary system. Both of these topic areas related directly to articles and books that Keynes was working on at the time.

In terms of his own investment strategies in relation to areas other than currencies and commodities, i.e. stocks and securities, Keynes employed what he termed a 'credit cycle' investment approach across most of the 1920s. This entailed the purchase/sale of specific investments in relation to expected changes in the future conditions of the business cycle across the economy as a whole.[7] This meant that, having in mind a prediction of how the elements of the trade cycle would progress in the near future, i.e. that interest rates would rise or fall, or that demand would increase or decrease, it was then possible to predict the short-term responses of particular shares to these wider changes, and benefit from them by buying or selling these shares as was required. Much later, Keynes explained regarding this particular strategy that:

> ...I was the principal inventor of credit cycle investment... Credit cycling means in practice selling market leaders on a falling market and buying them on a rising one...By credit cycling I mean buying and selling according as you think shares cheap in relation to *money*.[8]

In one instance he even thought of forming a dedicated Credit Cycle Investment Company.[9] Such a strategy, however, required perpetual vigilance for it to be successful. As Keynes explained in an article entitled 'Investment Policy for Insurance Companies' from May 1924, the investor 'constantly revises his ideas in accordance with changing events', thus obtaining an advantage through judicious selection 'in accordance with the fluctuations which occur from time to time in relative prices', a method that he termed an 'active investment policy'.[10]

The difficulty of successfully employing this method, however, is readily apparent from a calculation comparing Keynes's own stock market investments in the 1920s, with a general market index of the period: in five of the seven years from 1922 to 1929, his own investments performed less well than the general index.[11]

Much later he admitted that, having observed five different attempts to use this particular 'credit cycle' strategy over nearly twenty years, 'I have not seen a single case of a success having been made of it' over the medium or long term.[12] As a consequence of this failure, Keynes would at the very end of the 1920s change his share investment strategy fundamentally.

It is possible to suggest that there was a connection between this specific change in investment strategy, and the development of Keynes's wider approach to economic analysis. In using the term 'credit cycling' to describe his investment strategy in the 1920s, an implicit association was being made with a specific explanation of trade cycles that was widespread at this time. Economic fluctuations, in this view, were caused by changes in the availability and application of banking credit, an approach that is conventionally characterised as a monetary explanation of cycles. Keynes had expressed some distinct sympathies with this approach at various points in the 1910s and 1920s. However, it is reasonable to argue that both the stock market crash at the end of the 1920s, and the parallel failure of his share investment strategy, provided part of the impetus for Keynes to re-think his theoretical explanation of trade cycles in a fundamental manner. This re-thinking was one part of the complex process that led to the publication of *The General Theory of Employment, Interest and Money* in 1936.

Books of the period

Credit cycling for personal gain had its definite limitations, both in terms of practical results and in terms of the intellectual stimulation that it provided. Fortunately, Keynes was at this time also engaged in more substantial literary affairs. His first two books of the early 1920s were *A Treatise on Probability* of 1921, and *A Revision of the Treaty* of 1922: the content of these works will be considered in detail in the following chapter. On first view, these two books were worlds apart in terms of both gestation and content. *A Treatise on Probability* had kept its author intermittently occupied for many years, and was a conceptual analysis of the foundations of the mathematical theory of chance. *A Revision of the Treaty* was written at a very fast pace, and was an update of recent developments in European post-war political and economic reconstruction.

Taking a deeper view, there were some definite underlying connections between the two. For example, *A Treatise on Probability* contained a chapter on the application of probability theory to practical conduct, while *A Revision of the Treaty* opened with some conceptual musings on the nature of political governance. *A Treatise on Probability* had originally been part of a larger project that Keynes had designed as early as 1905 for a theoretical analysis of human practice and ethical behaviour: *A Revision of the Treaty* (and its prequel *The Economic Consequences of the Peace*) can be seen partly as his analytical engagement with this practice of behaviour in certain specific fields of human affairs.

Taking an even wider view of all of Keynes's publications up until this time, it could be argued that he ultimately conceived of economics as that sub-division of practical behaviour that related to financial and business affairs. The underlying aim of the wise statecraft management of the economy should be to improve general wellbeing, with economic theory being conceived as the predictive power apparatus to be used in order to be able to discern the best path (in probabilistic terms) from a range of possible policy alternatives. This was a rather wide conception of economic analysis that was not always shared by contemporary British economists; but likewise, few other British economists of the period had such a wide range of professional experiences and interests as Keynes, nor of personal encounters.

Lydia Lopokova

Undoubtedly the most important new personal relationship that Keynes developed in the early 1920s was with Lydia Lopokova (1892–1981), his future wife, affectionately known as 'Loppy'. Lydia was born in the grand Imperial Russian capital of St Petersburg, attended ballet school, and then began a successful dancing career first in Russia, before travelling as a performer to Paris and the USA. Keynes had first encountered Lydia on the London stage as a ballerina in 1918, but then she left the UK for personal reasons. On her return some years later, Keynes reported at the end of 1921 that, after having lunch with her, 'I fell very much in love with her'.[13] They courted very quickly, and initially Keynes seemed afraid of his swiftly growing and passionate feelings for

Lydia, perhaps in part because he was only used to feeling such emotions for men.

The relationship certainly came as a surprise to many of his Bloomsbury friends, some of whom initially characterised Lydia as being only suitable material for an experimental affair. However by 1923, Keynes and Lydia were holidaying together, although Lydia's pre-existing estranged marriage to Randolfo Barocchi was inconveniently delaying matrimony. Divorce proceedings were under way, but were complicated by Barocchi's bigamy and various legal delays. In the meantime, Lydia continued performing in various ballets in London and Paris. Lydia and Maynard were finally married in August 1925 with a simple ceremony at St Pancras registry office, followed by a family reception in Gordon Square.

One of the most striking elements of Keynes's blossoming relationship with Lydia was how his Bloomsbury friends received both the relationship, and Lydia herself as an individual. Reactions ranged from those of benign bemusement, to tetchy annoyance, to outright hostility. Firstly, there was the question of Keynes's apparent 'defection' to monogamous heterosexuality. Keynes had experienced a few close relationships with women before Lydia, but only in the Bloomsbury experimental style, i.e. relatively short-lived and fleeting. It was, more often than not, assumed by many of his Bloomsbury friends that the default setting of Keynes's sexuality was homosexual, and that, if he were ever to get married, then it would be to a woman who was familiar with the ambidextrous web of Bloomsbury. Secondly, there was the question of Lydia herself. She had originated from a national culture very much removed from either Bloomsbury or Cambridge, and she had little experience or knowledge in common with either of them. This difference did not deter Keynes at all – in fact, it was probably part of Lydia's novel charm for him – but it did appear to concern some members of Bloomsbury.

As an indication of Lydia's reception in London circles by those at the 'hostile' end of the Bloomsbury range, in May 1922 Clive Bell reported within the circle with unabashed candour that:

Lydia has quite destroyed all conversation at Gordon Square. When it is clever she can't follow; when it is *intimate* she naturally doesn't know what we're talking about; we can't be much bawdy because she would be shocked. Her only topics are the Russian ballet, scraps of gossip...and obvious generalities. You've no notion how it bores me...[14]

One part of the problem related to living arrangements. The houses that some members of the Bloomsbury group lived in at various periods were in close proximity: in 1923, they occupied numbers 41 (Lydia), 46 (Vanessa Bell) and 50 (Clive Bell) in the same street (Gordon Square). Thus, Vanessa Bell complained at one point that it was too easy for gossiping Lydia to visit and seriously outstay her welcome. In another instance, the same source explicitly advised Keynes against the marriage, on the grounds that Lydia would be 'a very expensive wife'.[15]

Another problem was the language barrier. According to Frank Ramsey, Lydia spoke English 'so badly' that it was difficult to comprehend the real character of her mind, and thus she may have seemed less intelligent in English conversation than she actually was. To Keynes, however, this was just another part of Lydia's exotic appeal, as he reported early on in their relationship of being charmed by her 'knowing and judicious use of English words'.[16] Finally, the rather solemn Russian culture of the early twentieth century was quite different from the decadence of high Bloomsbury, even after the war was over.

Lydia's reception amongst Keynes's close family was a large degree warmer. His brother Geoffrey was interested in ballet, so they had something significant in common. And although it took some while before Lydia was formally introduced to Keynes's parents (towards the end of 1923), Florence Keynes was delighted that her son had finally 'settled down' with a woman. Neither Florence nor Neville Keynes were ever Bloomsbury aficionados, and so they did not share the common Bloomsbury hang-ups over Lydia's intellectual failings. In fact, Lydia was highly cultured in her own way, with interests across various fields of the arts, but was more reserved about the public expression of rebellions against bourgeois etiquette than were the artistically shocking mores of Bloomsbury. Lydia had, of course, more intimate experience of the consequences of real revolutionaries in her country of birth, where some of her family had stayed after 1917, and she was, in consequence, more cautious about playing with revolutionary fire than those who were far removed from these consequences in fashionably outrageous Bloomsbury.

Liberal politics

The early 1920s saw Keynes re-engage with Liberal politics in various ways. In August 1922, he lectured on reparations and war debts at the Liberal Summer School. Early in 1923, he was one of a larger group of people, including Arnold Rowntree and L.J. Cadbury, who assumed control of *The Nation and Athenaeum*, a current affairs magazine with distinct Liberal associations. The editor selected under the new ownership in the spring of 1923 was Hubert Henderson (1890–1952). He was one of Keynes's former students at Cambridge who later became an economic adviser to the British Treasury. The literary editor chosen was Leonard Woolf, husband of Virginia, and various other Bloomsbury members were frequent contributors to the magazine, including Clive Bell, Lytton Strachey and David Garnett. Keynes was also a frequent contributor of both signed articles, and anonymous contributions and pseudonymous pieces: in the period 1923 to 1931, he wrote over 150 contributions, including major articles, analytical features and descriptions of current events. Keynes was the chairman of the board of directors, and sometimes assumed editorial and other duties when those formally responsible were temporarily absent.

The context of Keynes's involvement in *The Nation and Athenaeum* is relevant to understanding his interest in it. In October 1922, Lloyd George's coalition government had finally fallen, and Andrew Bonar Law had become Conservative Prime Minister. Together with Lloyd George, the other major Liberal politician of this period was H.H. Asquith, the British Prime Minister from 1908 to 1916. Keynes was (at this time and before it) much closer personally to Asquith than to Lloyd George, and consequently the fall of Lloyd George's coalition provided the opportunity for a renewed debate over the direction of Liberal policies. An early editorial in *The Nation and Athenaeum* came out in favour of a left-leaning Liberal Party, but unequivocally rejected the class-struggle approach favoured by Labour as out-of-date dogma.

Keynes's own contributions to this magazine were partly an attempt to influence policy and public opinion on political and economic matters of contemporary importance. For example in November 1923, in relation to the forthcoming December election, Keynes proclaimed in a leader article that Liberals had something important to work for:

> Let them enter the brief fight with hope and with courage, determined if they can to restore Liberalism to its rightful task in this moderate and magnanimous country of finding a *via media* to peace abroad and contentment at home. It is on them that has now fallen the mantle of tranquility which won the last election.[17]

Keynes's view of Liberalism as 'the middle way' in politics was here clearly articulated. The overall result of this publishing enterprise was limited success, with the existing circulation level of *The Nation and Athenaeum* in the single thousands, falling by a small amount across the 1920s, but with its content being regarded by many as valuable and thought provoking. Partly due to financial problems, eventually it merged with the *New Statesman* in 1931.

Keynes also contributed to other magazines/newspapers in this period. In the USA, he published journalistic pieces in *The New Republic*. The editor of the *Manchester Guardian* commissioned Keynes to report on the proceedings of the Genoa conference held in April/May 1922, and to survey the economic prospects of Europe more generally. The Genoa conference was designed to facilitate the restoration of economic and political equilibrium across Europe, and it included for the first time on the diplomatic stage the full participation of delegates from Soviet Russia. Keynes consequently published a series of substantial *Manchester Guardian* supplements on this theme under the heading 'Reconstruction in Europe' throughout 1922 and early in 1923. Some of this material made its way into his important 1923 book *A Tract on Monetary Reform* in revised form, or was background research and analysis for it. The content and context of this book will be considered in detail in the next pair of chapters.

Debating post-war trends

Following the conclusion of the war, many of the pre-existing structural issues that had involved economists in the UK before

1914 re-appeared, if in modified form. For example, in the two-year period 1923–24, Keynes became involved in a heated and prolonged debate with Sir William Beveridge (1879–1963) on the controversial topic of population growth and its link to trends in the terms of trade facing the UK, i.e. in the terms of exchange of exports from the UK with imports into it. One element underlying this debate was Beveridge's concern that placing too much emphasis on population growth would detract attention from other causes of unemployment, but Keynes readily admitted that unemployment could be due to various different causes. Beveridge was the director of the London School of Economics, and he later authored a very important report that helped to fashion the welfare state in the UK after 1945.

In a Presidential Address to the British Association for the Advancement of Science delivered in September 1923, Beveridge had stridently criticised Keynes for comments that he had made on trends in the terms of trade between agricultural and manufacturing goods, which operated between less developed countries and the industrial states of Europe. In *The Economic Consequences of the Peace*, Keynes had written (only in passing, not as a major theme of the book) that:

> Up to about 1900 a unit of labour applied to industry yielded year by year a purchasing power over an increasing quantity of food. It is possible that about the year 1900 this process began to be reversed, and a diminishing yield of nature to man's efforts was beginning to reassert itself.[18]

This meant that the terms of trade facing some industrial countries in relation to agricultural countries were (after 1900) declining. No substantial evidence for this assertion was presented in *The Economic Consequences of the Peace*, but Keynes had based his remark on data he had discussed in a note published in the *Economic Journal* in 1912. Here he discovered from Board of Trade figures that 'we are obtaining for our exports almost exactly the same prices as in 1900, but we are paying for our imports appreciably higher prices than in 1900'.[19] Observe that the 1912 note only dealt with changes in the terms of trade for the UK, and that the statement in *The Economic*

Consequences of the Peace declared *it was possible* that such changes were affecting the wider continent of Europe.

In his 1923 Presidential Address, Beveridge disputed fundamentally that Europe after 1900 had been threatened by a falling standard of living because of diminishing returns to agriculture, which had generated the declining terms of trade for industrial goods against agricultural. Instead, Beveridge argued that the real cost of corn had been falling up to 1913, not rising. He also pointed out that it was rash to argue straight from unemployment to overpopulation, as there were many factors affecting unemployment other than population. This topic might seem only a technical question without wider consequences, but it would have very significant consequences for economic policy in both developed and less developed countries across the entire twentieth century.

The first reason for its importance was historical, as the 'Malthusian devil' (as diminishing returns in agriculture and its consequence for population growth was known) was a controversial topic politically and economically. For many on the left, the spectre of the Malthusian devil was invoked (illegitimately) in order to try to limit the growth of the 'rabble' classes, and hence the concept itself had to be defeated. The second reason for its importance was practical, as government policies had to be framed so as to get the best out of trends in the terms of trade for each country affected. This could only be done if the real trends were apparent. Dispute over the trends themselves was thus invariably connected to disputes over government policy.

Keynes's reply to Beveridge's criticisms appeared in *The Nation and Athenaeum* in October 1923, and also in the *Economic Journal* in December 1923. In relation to the empirical point about movements in the terms of trade, Keynes considered additional evidence that led him to modify his initial statements. Admitting that he had neglected to take account of the volume of trade, rather than just the terms of trade, he now declared his position was as follows:

> We [i.e. the UK – VB] are no longer able to sell a growing volume of manufactured goods (or a volume increasing in proportion to population) at a better real price in terms of food.[20]

He acknowledged that recent data had shown that the terms of trade had moved against agricultural goods, but that other changes in the pattern of the volume of trade meant that 'our manufactured exports are now buying *in the aggregate* about 12 per cent less foodstuffs than before the war'.[21] What Keynes meant was that, even though Britain's manufacturing products had benefited from improved terms of trade with agricultural goods from overseas, the volume of the UK's manufacturing exports had declined whilst its volume of food imports had grown. This produced the detrimental result that the total cost of food imports to the UK was being covered to a lesser degree than it was previously by the UK's manufacturing exports. This change would have an impact on the UK trade balance, and a significant long-term imbalance in this area would have important consequences for the UK's future economic prosperity.

Although his basic concern still remained, Keynes had modified his argument from one regarding trends in the agricultural–manufacturing terms of trade, to one regarding trends in the comparative volume of trade between manufacturing exports and agricultural imports. He warned that 'the more we have to force the volume of our trade…the worse terms do we get'.[22] If the UK was forced to increase the volume of its exports in order to cover increased agricultural imports, then this might have a downward effect on prices of manufactured goods, which in turn would negate the advantageous movement in the agricultural–manufacturing terms of trade that he accepted had occurred. Admitting that future elasticity of demand for UK manufactures was unknown, he speculated that it should not be assumed that if prices of exports were reduced, then demand would increase more than in proportion. The future was uncertain.

Beveridge published a reply to Keynes's modified position in *Economica* in February 1924. Beveridge questioned how Keynes had compiled indices from the new data (by splicing together two sets of figures), and how one of these indices was composed in terms of disaggregating 'iron and steel' products. According to Beveridge, when required changes to the data were made, the trends that Keynes claimed to have identified were mitigated, or had even disappeared. Finally, Keynes replied in a letter to Beveridge in February 1924 where he conceded some of the specific points about the new data. His main point of contention, however, was with Beveridge's wider interpretation. Keynes stressed that he had only ever highlighted the precariousness of the situation vis-à-vis trends in population and welfare, and he had not declared that there had been an actual decline in living standards across Europe before 1914. He was merely documenting one element of many complex factors that operated on the economic relationships at issue.

Many of the commentators on this debate have declared that Beveridge was the clear and outright winner, with Keynes conceding that aspects of his initial use of the data had been suspect, but in fact the real position was less clear-cut. It was apparent that the UK was Keynes's main focus when considering these population trend issues, although the wider European context was sometimes discussed. Beveridge had conceded in his original 1923 critique that for Britain alone, although not for wider Europe, the data could reasonably allow an interpretation of 'some faltering of progress' in the standard of living *for the UK* between the Victorian and Edwardian eras.[23] He accepted that, comparing the period before 1900, which showed a rising trend in UK material progress relative to population, with the period immediately after 1900, there was found:

...from 1900 to 1910 a more interesting but more dubious picture. With one exception – real wages – every index has risen, but with two exceptions – coal production and exports – the rise is slower than in previous decades, and in more than one case is barely perceptible...rapid certain growth to 1900 gives place to small and dubious improvement in the next ten years...we see a lower rate of increase, such as might, or might not, precede an actual fall...In Britain, if not in Europe as a whole, the turn of the century seems to bring a turn of fortune.[24]

It was true that Beveridge stipulated that this change might turn out to be only a transient phenomenon, but by definition this meant he was also admitting that it might not be temporary, it was just too soon to tell. He also accepted that, in the Edwardian era 'Some check to our national progress there probably was'.[25] Hence, in Beveridge's own analysis, Keynes's suggestion that there was an important turning point for the UK around 1900 had some degree of validity, even though how significant this would turn out to be in the long run was still undecided. Whether there was an absolute decline in material progress relative to population, rather than only a relative decline in the upward trend, remained in question.

Keynes had astutely understood Beveridge's concessions with respect to the UK, and explained in his letter to Beveridge from February 1924 as follows:

> ...you do not remember that the gist of my argument in *The Economic Consequences of the Peace* related to the *precariousness* of the situation, that it was full of elements of instability...you twist my statements as to the precariousness of the existing standards into a statement as to their absolute decline; and then, because no such absolute decline actually took place...you consider that you have disposed of my argument.[26]

Beveridge had created a bogus straw man, defeated this straw man in argument, and then proclaimed that Keynes had been proved wrong. Keynes had indeed revised his initial brief comments in light of later evidence, but this did not mean that his concern with future trends affecting the UK's material wellbeing was unwarranted. He was merely raising legitimate concerns for UK policy-makers to consider, in the light of trends in the factors under consideration. His basic concern was with ensuring the prosperity of the UK in a volatile world. Thus, Keynes's underlying contention was proved accurate, although some specific elements of it needed to be amended in light of Beveridge's criticisms.

Britain's national interest

If the idea of supporting British economic progress was only a partially sublimated undercurrent within the debate with Beveridge in 1923–24, then Keynes soon brought it directly to the fore in an article published in *The Nation and Athenaeum* in August 1924. This article, entitled 'Foreign Investment and National Advantage', had been first presented as a lecture in Cambridge in February 1924, and then discussed at the Liberal Summer School in Oxford, and hence was closely linked to contemporary political debates. It was also connected to changes in Keynes's economic thinking that had much wider significance for his overall intellectual development.

Keynes began the article by sketching 'the established system' of British investment, which was that investors were as willing to invest their funds overseas as in the UK, a system that had dominated across the nineteenth century. The most common form of such investments was loans to foreign governments, but other forms (such as buying foreign stocks) also existed. Accepting an earlier stage of this system in which profits from overseas investments were much higher than the domestic average, he outlined various reasons why this exceptional profitability situation would not continue in the twentieth century, and suggested that in the near future the 'motive to repudiation' of such investments by their foreign holders was likely to become much stronger. Such motives included national jealousy, the outbreak of military or revolutionary conflicts, straightforward bankruptcy and political acts against colonial powers.

Keynes then asked readers to consider two investment cases, one made at home in the UK, and the other made abroad, i.e. outside the UK. Assume that each carried broadly similar risks of being lost, either through repudiation or some other means, and also similar rewards, and it consequently appeared to the individual investor to be a matter of indifference which specific investment was actually selected. However, there were some real if concealed differences, as in cases of repudiation:

> ...the nation as a whole retains in the one case the object of the investment and the fruits of it; while in the other both are lost. If a loan to improve a South American capital is repudiated, we have nothing. If a Poplar housing loan is repudiated, we as a nation, still have the houses...With home investment, even if it be ill-advised or extravagantly carried out, at least the country has the improvement for what it is worth...A bad foreign investment is wholly engulfed.[27]

Keynes explained that 'the established system' of accepting large-scale overseas investments as natural was the result of hazardous levels of institutional inertia. In part this was the result of specific laws such as the Trustee Acts, that artificially stimulated investment in the British Empire, and the Colonial Stock Act, that falsely bolstered the risk status of colonial loans, and consequently the established system was 'capable of doing us a great deal of injury' with respects to the terms of international trade. By implication, this system must be brought to an end.

Keynes outlined that in the previous year to the issue of his article, i.e. in 1923, between one-third and a half of total UK savings, and a massive two-thirds of what passed through the UK investment markets, had been invested overseas. He concluded the article by judging that:

> ...most of this could have been usefully employed at home, and indeed must be so employed in future, if our national equipment is to grow as fast as our population and our theoretical standards of life.[28]

A clearer national–economic rationale for British investors to invest in British investments would be difficult to find. There were two possible degrees of support for such arguments. The first principle, which might be called 'weak investment nationalism', would state that, when two investments offered equal rewards and equal risks, one being in the UK and one overseas, then in such cases British investors should invariably favour British investments. The second principle, which might be called 'strong investment nationalism', would state that, even if there was a small advantage in the overseas investment compared to the British, say up to a 1 per cent higher reward, then investors should invariably favour British investments, given the 'retained fruits of investment' situation after default. Up to what precise level the remunerative advantage of the overseas investment should be ignored was arbitrary and variable, but it would seem reasonable to assume that small such advantages should be ignored in the case of applying this principle.

The question naturally arises: did Keynes employ any such principles in his own investments? There is no explicit claim by him to have done so in his writings on financial investment strategy examined previously. However, across the period 1920 to 1930, the vast majority of Keynes's security portfolio was composed of stocks and bonds denominated in sterling. Between 1920 and 1924, and then between 1928 and 1930, fully one hundred per cent of all his security portfolio investments were denominated in sterling. From 1925 to 1927, between 2 and 5 per cent of his security investments were denominated in dollars.[29] The dividends that Keynes received from these dollar securities were large, relative to the very small percentage of holdings that were so denominated, suggesting that such dollar assets had only been purchased when they promised exceptional returns.[30] Although using the currency that securities are denominated in, as a proxy of national origin, is not a perfect guide, this preliminary calculation indicates that Keynes did favour British investments vis-à-vis stocks and bonds, at least across the 1920s.

It might appear on first sight that this issue of investment nationalism was something of a sideline to the development of Keynes's more important economic theory, but in fact, it was a central concern that had been one of the main factors that had led him to begin to think outside the existing conventions of economic orthodoxy. Consequently, this nationalism is a sometimes-neglected strand in his abandonment of *laissez faire* principles that ultimately produced *The General Theory of Employment, Interest and Money* in 1936. According to orthodoxy, transferring investments from overseas to domestic sources would have no overall effect on the UK economy, as losing overseas investments would tend to have a detrimental effect on the exports out of the UK that had been generated by these investments, which would in turn counterbalance the positive effect of increased home investments. There would be no net gain to either UK trade or UK employment. Clearly, Keynes knew this orthodox theory very well, so he must have developed arguments that showed it to be erroneous, as indeed he had.

Keynes declared that it was simply wrong. A foreign investment did not automatically create a corresponding flow of exports out of the UK, as part of the overseas investment would stimulate the production of supplies exported from non-British sources.[31] Keynes developed his argument on this point in an article outlining his own recommended tests for loans to foreign governments, published in January 1925. He explained that:

> There is a great difference between foreign investments which are caused by a previous surplus of exports...and foreign investments which are the result of convention...and exercise a forcing influence on our exports in order to balance the account.[32]

If the source of the funds that were being invested overseas was an existing export surplus, as it had sometimes been in the past, then this would be fine, but according to Keynes the situation for the UK had dramatically changed. If, in order to provide for these overseas investments, the UK was trying to force its future exports above the existing level, then this could have a detrimental effect on both the prices realised for these exports, and also the state of the exchanges and the interest rate. In this latter case, investing overseas could actually exert a negative effect on the UK economy, even ignoring its subtractive effect on the total level of UK-bound investment.

It is easy to trace the wider consequences of this investment nationalism in Keynes's writings across 1924. In an article entitled 'Does Unemployment Need a Drastic Remedy?' from May 1924, he outlined his growing opposition to *laissez faire* principles in more general terms. First documenting the existing high levels of unemployment in various branches of the UK economy, he then analysed its causes and the various existing impediments to overcoming it. He explained how UK unemployment could be cured:

> Is there not a chance that we can best achieve this by recreating the mood and the conditions in which great works of construction, requiring large capital outlays, can again be set on foot? Current savings are already available on a sufficient scale – savings which from lack of an outlet at home, are now drifting abroad to destinations from which we as a society shall gain the least possible advantage.[33]

Thus, Keynes explicitly, deliberately and inextricably linked his advocacy of public works in the UK, with the idea of diverting private investments that had been targeted overseas, back into the UK. He concluded the article by declaring that he saw the ultimate cure for unemployment in two sources: firstly, monetary reform, by which he meant the establishment of a stable unit of account that was not subject to bouts of inflation and/or deflation, and secondly, 'the diversion of national savings from relatively barren foreign investment into state-encouraged constructive enterprises at home'.[34] The British government should therefore use all the financial mechanisms that were at its disposal to encourage British investment funds to invest in British stocks and securities.

Laissez faire doctrine had assumed that the use of both labour and capital was entirely fluid between nations, and hence that they both moved to where it was most rational and productive to be employed. But again, Keynes emphasised that these two assumptions were both wrong, at least in the circumstances of the 1920s: trade union organisation meant that labour was rigid, not flexible, and legal norms and institutional customs meant that capital was often invested where convention dictated. A more fundamental attack on *laissez faire* economic principles would be difficult to envisage. Although Keynes would only supply the comprehensive theoretical muscle to substantiate his criticisms of economic orthodoxy much later, in the 1930s, the origins of his radical departure from it can in part be traced back to the early 1920s, and to his articulation of the need for investment nationalism.

As further evidence of the importance of these ideas to Keynes personally, there exists a report by an economist (R.F. Harrod) who had actually attended his 1924 Liberal Summer School presentation on these themes. According to Harrod, Keynes 'spoke with vehemence and a manifest desire to persuade. The matter clearly seemed to him to be one of the utmost importance'.[35] Keynes summarised his basic position in evidence that was presented to the UK Committee on National Debt and Taxation in October 1924. In answer to a question about restrictions to investments that might be made in colonial markets if his policies were implemented, Keynes explained:

> There are some people who think it is primarily important to develop the colonies; there are others who think it primarily important to develop good conditions at home...I believe that we ought to pay more attention than we have paid lately to the conditions at home...[36]

Of course this was partly a normative judgement; that conditions in the UK only a few years after the end of an unprecedented and horrific international conflict were so precarious that it was time to modify the British concern for the whole of the Empire equally, and refocus thinking more on economic conditions at home. But the implication was that the reverse position was also a normative one, just one that worked against the UK's national interest in current circumstances.

Keynes's investment nationalism received only a mixed reception amongst economists, to say the least. According to Harrod, Keynes's Liberal Summer School audience had demonstrated some specialised interest, 'but showed no signs of sharing his sense of urgency'.[37] Indeed, wasn't this type of investment nationalism anti-Liberal in its narrow focus on the UK, and wasn't the free international movement of capital an essential part of the economist's free trade ethos? Perhaps, but it was this ethos that Keynes was beginning to question. He also received correspondence from overseas complaining about his use of the term 'colonial' in this context, suggesting that a British reluctance to invest overseas would be filled by the USA. In response to this he protested against the use of a 'blackmailing attitude' when the UK dared to consider its own interest;[38] but he could equally have declared in response to threatened US replacement of UK investments: so what? As is usual when an existing intellectual orthodoxy is questioned, there were many who did not even recognise that a crisis had developed, and that a complete change of mind-set was really necessary.

Some politicians were more sympathetic with the exhibited concern for UK economic prosperity. If the period prior to 1920 witnessed Keynes's most poisonous disagreements with Lloyd George, then the early 1920s saw the beginnings of a rapprochement. One major element of this warming in their relationship was an agreement over the necessity of government intervention in the economy of the type that Keynes called 'great works of construction'. In the spring of 1924, Lloyd George had advocated a public works programme as a Liberal cure for UK economic stagnation. Although Lloyd George's arguments were less economically grounded than those of Keynes, they were now singing from the same hymn-sheet on this important issue. But it would take some considerable period of time before the case for government intervention in the economy as a cure for unemployment would take root in mainstream economic theory.

Conclusion

Across the early 1920s, Keynes had been forced to engage with various practical policy issues vis-à-vis the British economy in detail. This in turn had led him to begin to question some of the existing shibboleths of economic theory, most notably those around the beneficial effects of *laissez faire*. But it would be wrong to give the impression that Keynes was always fully consistent on this issue in the early 1920s, or that he had articulated a fully developed theoretical apparatus within which such an approach could be understood. It would take him many years before he was in a position to declare that the existing orthodoxy had been comprehensively and convincingly dethroned.

If an underlying theme can be identified as running through much of Keynes's policy work in the early 1920s, then it was the need to focus more attention on Britain's national–economic interest. As was seen, this recommended focus brought criticism in various guises. One of these guises was the purely abstract, that Keynes's questioning of the ideology of free trade was wrong in purely theoretical terms. Another criticism was more policy-orientated, that Keynes's identification of the issue of the detrimental forces affecting the UK's standard of living as being important was wrong in empirical terms. Although usually couched in economic arguments, these issues invariably had significant political components to them, which was often why they provoked such heated controversy.

Keynes did not recoil at all from these political components, at least in intellectual terms, as his engagement with Liberal politics demonstrated. But his own Liberalism was sometimes a rather strange brew, as it included some elements of Conservatism, and also the recognition that Socialism was something of the future. Although it is probably going a little too far to state that Keynes was now a Conservative–Liberal with a Socialist tinge, there is certainly a large element of truth in the notion that he did not adhere to the conventional boundaries of political demarcation. In fact, it was one of his aims to re-fashion these boundaries as he saw fit with respects to the current issues of the period, just as it was in the economic arena.

8   The method of modern statesmen

Although the previous chapter has given the partial impression that, in the early 1920s, Keynes was principally concerned with contemporary policy and economic issues, he was simultaneously very busy with more fundamental works of philosophy and politics. This chapter will examine two of these contributions – *A Treatise on Probability* and *A Revision of the Treaty* – in more detail. These books are sometimes regarded as lesser works in the Keynes oeuvre, but they are still important for understanding how his ideas were developing at this time, and they contain much that is relevant to economic analysis.

A Treatise on Probability

Keynes's mammoth 500-page contribution entitled *A Treatise on Probability* was finally published in August 1921. By this time it had been through numerous revisions and rewritings – progress on it had been temporarily suspended by the immediate requirements of war – and it was some distance removed from its origins in a King's College Fellowship Dissertation, although large parts of it remained substantially similar. In many ways it was the most problematic of all Keynes's major works, both because of its extended gestation period and also because its subject matter appeared quite separate from his much more extensive economics writings. It was also his least influential major work in terms of its impact upon those who were working on the main subject of the investigation: there was never formed in response a 'Keynesian school' of probability theorists.

Its interest for the historian and biographer lies most obviously in attempting to elucidate connections between Keynes's theory of probability and his more influential theories in economics and in other fields such as politics and philosophy. And here its significance is rather large but perhaps especially controversial, in that commentators have proposed various different interpretations of this significance. Some of these interpretations will be considered here, together with an outline of the basic approach of the book.

In *A Treatise on Probability*, Keynes developed a version of the subjective theory of probability that might reasonably be termed a pragmatic–subjective approach. Probability concepts were concerned with that part of human knowledge obtained by argument, what Keynes called indirect knowledge, as opposed to direct knowledge, which was obtained by immediate observation. Probability concepts thus related to degrees of certainty by which the results obtained from such arguments could be declared conclusive or inconclusive. The term 'probable' described the 'degree of rational belief' about a proposition that different amounts of indirect knowledge authorised an individual to rationally hold.[1] Keynes explained that:

> All propositions are true or false, but the knowledge we have of them depends on our circumstances; and while it is often convenient to speak of propositions as certain or probable, this expresses strictly a relationship in which they stand to a *corpus* of knowledge...A proposition is capable at the same time of varying degrees of this relationship, depending upon the knowledge to which it is related...To this extent, therefore, probability may be called subjective.[2]

Although probability was partially subjective, it was not subject to human caprice or will, as once the facts that determined our knowledge on a specific topic were given, what was probable was then objectively fixed.

For Keynes, the process of inference was how the indirect knowledge garnered and evaluated by argument was obtained and processed. The theory of probability elucidated rules by which the probabilities of different arguments being correct could be compared, this being of great practical importance. Keynes continued:

The most important of these rules is the principle of indifference...
We can only discard those parts of the evidence which are
irrelevant by *seeing* that they have no logical bearing on the
conclusion. The irrelevant evidence being thus discarded, the
principle lays it down that if the evidence for either conclusion is
the same (i.e. symmetrical), then their probabilities also are the
same (i.e. equal).[3]

Ultimately, elucidating the most probable argument was of practical
importance because this argument was the hypothesis on which it
was rational for any individual to act.[4] Keynes was also concerned to
point out that the nature of the analogies being implied in the
models underlying the use of similar probability judgements must
always be kept in mind. To argue (for example) that an event had
occurred in 1,000 instances in the past, therefore it would occur
invariably in the future, was a 'feeble inductive argument', because
it took no account of the appropriateness of the analogy that was
being applied in the various instances of the event occurring.

If the reality behind the analogy changed, i.e. if the structure of
the mechanism underlying the event changed, then the associated
induction might become invalid. Hence, a series of sub-classes
should be outlined and classified according to their variety, to
ensure that the correct instances of induction were being applied to
the indirect knowledge under review. Keynes provided an example
of precisely what type of application he had in mind not in *A
Treatise on Probability*, but in a review of a book by E.L. Smith from
May 1925, which was devoted to evaluating shares versus bonds as
investment opportunities:

> It is dangerous, however, to apply to the future inductive
> arguments based on past experiences, unless one can distinguish
> the broad reasons why past experience was what it was...Mr
> Smith claims that the general causes of the relative advantages of
> general stocks [compared to bonds – VB] are discoverable, and
> they are of kind as likely to operate in the immediate future as in
> the immediate past.[5]

This type of evaluative caution meant, furthermore, that the
acquisition of additional knowledge about an event could render

the induction that was assumed to apply inapplicable in certain instances.

Keynes highlighted in conclusion to *A Treatise on Probability* that, with respects to the application of statistics to the social sciences, the various alternative outcomes of any event were not so perfectly fixed as was specified in those ideal games of chance taken from the natural sciences (such as dice throwing), as causes were always changing and evolving in the social world.[6] This meant in turn that the methodology used in applying statistical techniques to social sciences like economics could not be copied mechanically from the methodology of using statistics in the natural sciences. This latter point would be a theme that Keynes would return to again in the 1930s, when he debated the applicability of probability theory to the newly developing field of econometric modelling.

One obvious line of connection between Keynes's subjective approach to probability concepts and his work in economics and finance, related to developing an understanding of decision-making processes in these fields of human conduct. The activities of business leaders and bankers as they attempted to evaluate alternative strategies that were available to them, i.e. to invest in this business or that one, or to lend money to this person or that one, depended on them using their detailed knowledge of the industries in question, together with relevant information about the individual cases, to generate arguments that could be judged in probability terms. In choosing to invest money either in company *A* or company *B*, investors judged which company they believe was likely to have a greater chance of future success, i.e. they calculated the odds of this success as probabilities. Keynes did not explicitly outline in detail such an application in *A Treatise on Probability*, but there were passages that came close.

He explained in one instance that underwriters calculated a numerical measure of probability against specific risks, and then backed their opinion with money through offering insurance to risk-takers.[7] In another instance, he declared in relation to the suitability of gambling for different classes, 'millionaires are often fortunate fools who have thriven on unfortunate ones'.[8] He also considered the dependence of the duty of pursuing specific goods on the probable expectation of attaining them relative to an agent's existing knowledge. Specific cases of mortality statistics, the behaviour of casino croupiers and Mendelian genetics were further discussed. Thus, it is clear that Keynes's version of the subjective theory was conceived in thoroughly pragmatic terms. One of his major biographers has called it a view of probability as deductive logical insight, or as rational thought and judgement.[9]

In comparing Keynes's own pragmatic version of the subjective theory of probability with the two other main currents in understanding probability – the frequency theory (probability is the limit of observed frequency) and the logistic approach (probability is membership of a set of incompatible events) – it is immediately apparent that the pragmatic–subjective theory is the one that is most easily transferable to socio-economic realms of understanding. This does not mean that Keynes had selected his theory of probability *a priori* on this basis, but rather that his underlying manner of understanding the world provided the thread that guided him to this theory, as it guided him to an understanding of political and social affairs. This special relevance of the pragmatic–subjective theory of probability also helps to explain why it was not that influential amongst mathematicians in the 1920s. They were more concerned with strengthening the formal purity of mathematical concepts, and with providing more rigorous foundations for mathematical systems of analysis.

Other commentators have described Keynes's theory of probability as a version of an epistemological or logical interpretation, rather than as a straightforward subjective approach. This was because he believed that every individual that evaluated the shared range of knowledge available to them would come to the same (objective) conclusion as to which action was the more reasonable, after making the appropriate probability judgements.[10] However, it is clear that Keynes's emphasis within probability theory was on the level of human understanding, as revealed in the accuracy of arguments based on indirect knowledge, rather than solely on objective processes occurring in nature, and in this sense his approach can reasonably be described as a pragmatic–subjective one.

The reception of *A Treatise on Probability* was relatively favourable, at least amongst Keynes's Cambridge colleagues. Bertrand Russell praised it highly, while C.D. Broad declared in the journal *Mind* that it was 'the best treatise on the logical foundations of the subject': Broad praised 'Mr. Keynes's beautiful treatment of the Laws of Error', and concluded by congratulating him for 'finding time, amidst so many public duties, to complete this book, and the philosophical public on getting the best work on Probability that they are likely to see in this generation'.[11] F.Y. Edgeworth declared that Keynes had 'made a new contribution to an old problem', having in mind the discussion of errors of observation.[12]

The real problem, of course, was that Broad and Russell were both more philosophers than mathematicians, and that Keynes's book was soon made almost completely obsolete as a mathematical theory of probability by the publication of A.N. Kolmogorov's groundbreaking *Foundations of the Theory of Probability* in 1933, which pioneered a comprehensive set-theoretic approach to the subject. One of the most perceptive evaluations of the importance of Keynes's book was found in the *Manchester Guardian*, which declared that 'it is especially valuable on account of the extension of its subject beyond the bounds of purely mathematical probability'.[13] In fact, it would not be too far from the truth to suggest that it was *mainly* valuable for this type of extension outside of mathematics. One such pragmatic extension that Keynes was pursuing almost in parallel was his further thoughts on the economic consequences of Versailles.

A Revision of the Treaty

Keynes decided in 1921 to combine various journalistic articles on reparations that he had already published in newspapers such as the *Manchester Guardian*, with some new and further revised materials to form a book, a self-proclaimed sequel to *The Economic Consequences of the Peace* entitled *A Revision of the Treaty*, which was published in 1922. In the preface he claimed that it contained 'nothing very new' on the fundamental issues that were at stake, rather its goal was to provide an updated account of the reparations problem as it had developed in the two years or so since his first book on this topic had been published. The vast majority of the text bears out Keynes's claim, as it discussed the various ratifications, settlements, agreements, bills, commissions, debates and counter-proposals that had been forthcoming as the various governments tried to solve the outstanding issues as they had been left in 1919.

However, it is not quite true to suggest that the book contained nothing new in any respect at all. The very first chapter, entitled 'The State of Opinion', although only seven pages long, was certainly a new departure for Keynes to consider in a book, as it dealt with a topic that he had been frustratingly forced to engage with again and again since the outbreak of war in 1914: what he termed 'the method of modern statesmen', or the *modus operandi* of political leaders. He explained with decidedly mixed emotions that:

> It is the method of modern statesmen to talk as much folly as the public demand and to practise no more of it than is compatible with what they have said, trusting that such folly in action as must wait on folly in word will soon disclose itself as such, and furnish an opportunity for slipping back into wisdom...I can conceive for this terrifying statesmanship a plausible defence...A preference for truth or for sincerity *as a method* may be a prejudice based on some aesthetic or personal standard, inconsistent, in politics, with practical good. We cannot yet tell.[14]

Keynes's example here was Lloyd George, who might have admitted in private that the terms of the Peace Treaty were unwise as they were set in 1919, but who also knew the strong 'public passions' of the time had to be taken into account, at least in public pronouncements. Lloyd George consequently spent the next two years 'avoiding or moderating the dangers' of the Treaty by striving in private against the implementation of the excesses it contained, as best he could in the light of public opinion. As Keynes happily reported later in the book, it was only a slight exaggeration to say that no major parts of the Peace Treaty had actually been carried out by mid-1921, except those relating to frontier changes and disarmaments.[15] By such devious paths of statesmanship, what Keynes called 'a faithful servant of the possible' could claim to be serving mankind.

Another key element of 'the method of modern statesmen' was sensitivity to what Keynes termed outside and inside opinion, the former having two divisions. Outside opinion was the opinion of the public, as voiced by politicians and the newspapers, which was bifurcated into that formally expressed in newspapers (outer outside opinion) and that which the mass of ordinary people suspected to be true (inner outside opinion) but could not formally express. Inside opinion was the beliefs of politicians, journalists and civil servants as expressed in the private limited circles of power. According to Keynes, those who lived in these limited circles paid both too much and too little attention to outside opinion:

> ...too much, because, ready in words and promises to concede to it everything, they regard open opposition as absurdly futile; too little, because they believe that these words and promises are so certainly destined to change in due season...[16]

Successful politicians must be finely tuned to all three degrees of opinion, and have enough intellect to understand inside opinion, enough sympathy to detect inner outside opinion and enough brass to express outer outside opinion. The best politician was therefore the one who was most masterful at placing themselves at precisely the right points along these varying scales of opinion as events unfolded, circumstances changed and inside and outside opinions modified, in order to direct the overall path of policy ultimately onto the wisest course.

It is clear from Keynes's presentation of this Machiavellian method of modern statesmanship that he understood that it might have some validity in certain contexts, but it was also clear that it was profoundly uncomfortable for him to observe, and *a fortiori* to be personally embroiled in. As an academic, his natural instinct was that the greater degree of truth that was contained in a proposition, a book or a speech, the better and more useful it was to humanity, this relationship being a straightforward linear one. *A Treatise on Probability* was devoted precisely to formulating right principles of understanding in relation to the 'degree of rational belief' about a proposition that different amounts of indirect knowledge authorised an individual to believe were true, i.e. it proposed a method of finding truth amongst a range of competing evidence. Although this book was published in 1921, its extended gestation period meant that it reflected Keynes's philosophy of logic from his student days.

However, for him to then find that such an abstract devotion to finding and using the purity of truth had its definite limitations, and that public statements of political leaders were invariably 'massaged' or 'manipulated' in their truth-content by these leaders *post hoc* in line with the deeper wisdom of statesmanship, was perhaps one of the most shocking revelations that Keynes had experienced as a consequence of participating in the British war effort. Part of his strong personal aversion to Lloyd George can be interpreted as displaced aversion to 'the method of modern statesmen', of which Lloyd George was an undoubted manipulative master. Before 1914, Keynes had accumulated significant exposure to political philosophy, as represented by his study of the writings of Edmund Burke. But even political philosophers were judged by the truth-content of their statements: political leaders, by contrast, were judged by the degree to which their statements affected the world for the good, regardless of whether these statements were true in any sense at all. During and just after the war, Keynes had received a rude baptism into the world of the ordinary use of language as practised in everyday life, and he was not fully at ease with this often-devious type of language game.

Newish arguments on an existing theme

If the basic position of *A Revision of the Treaty* regarding the excessive claims being made for reparations against Germany remained the same as it was in *The Economic Consequences of the Peace*, Keynes did provide some new variations on this existing theme. One of these was that compelling Germany to pay a large indemnity would necessarily mean encouraging more direct competition with the UK and the USA. As Keynes posed the resulting conundrum: did the balancing advantages to the creditor country of receiving payments as a whole, outweigh the injury to particular industries within the creditor country of heightened international competition? His answer was that it depended partly on the time period over which the payments were made, and partly on the comparative industrial structures of the countries involved. The longer the better for the creditor country, but the closer the two nations were in industrial structure, the greater the degree of direct competition. As German exports were 'so preponderantly competitive' with those of the UK, Keynes implied that the greater German exports had to expand in order to pay reparations, the more greatly British industry would be damaged.[17]

The same argument was then applied to the USA, but with an additional twist: trends in the balance of international trade between the Old World and the New. In order to balance the existing trend of an excess of exports over imports, the US must in the future lend funds to the rest of the world, or there must be a readjustment in the balance of exports and imports. But this could not be done in association with the payment of large sums of debts, without affecting the equilibrium of international trade in a very detrimental manner. Keynes explained:

> It is useless for the United States to suppose that an equilibrium position can be reached on the basis of her exporting at least as much as at present, and at the same time restricting her imports by a tariff…If, in addition, the United States exacts payment of the Allied debts, the position will be intolerable…it is not good business for America to embitter her relations with Europe, and to disorder her export industries for two years, in pursuance of a policy which she is certain to abandon before it has profited her.[18]

Such a policy would soon be discarded partly because it would involve the complete undoing of US export industries in response to large increases in *gratis* European imports, and partly because the political consequences in Europe would quickly become intolerable in both Europe and the USA.

Another new variation on the theme was the unflattering symbolic portrait of the USA as 'a new Midas vainly asking [for] more succulent fare' after the hypothetical future shipment to them of all the bullion in the world, and the futile erection of a sky-scraping golden calf.[19] The strength of Keynes's objection to US demands for large reparations payments was then expressed in even more emotive and contentious language, as he quoted one of Shakespeare's most controversial plays prominently at the start of chapter seven:

> Shylock: I'll have my bond; I will not hear thee speak: I'll have my bond; and therefore speak no more.[20]

In the USA, and especially in the financial centre of New York, the character of Shylock could easily be taken for an anti-Semitic stereotype. The implication that the USA was acting like a small-time, revenge-fuelled moneylender was one that must have raised some eyebrows among American readers, to say the least. However, Keynes then shifted the object of his metaphorical fire to the country he believed was acting irresponsibly within Europe:

> This Settlement must be offered France on one condition only, – that she accepts it. But if, like Shylock, she claims her pound of flesh, then let the Law prevail. Let her have her bond, and let us have our bonds too. Let her get what she can from Germany and pay what she owes to the United States and England.[21]

Here Keynes meant that, if France demanded full payment of reparations from Germany, then the UK and the USA should then demand full payments of the debts that were due to them from France. As Keynes was campaigning ultimately for 'a general bonfire' of all debts, the implication was that France should not be allowed to get away with selecting for actual implementation only the most favourable components (for them) of the Allied system of financial obligations.

Conclusion

If both *A Treatise on Probability* and *A Revision of the Treaty* contained much that was relevant to Keynes's attempt to understand what could be called the impetuses to right action, then they both also expressed some deep-seated concerns about the consequences of limitations and imperfections in this regard. As the 1920s progressed, Keynes was forced more and more to deal with, and even attempt to overcome, these types of limitations in the realms of politics and economics, as what he previously termed the Carthaginian peace of Versailles began to unravel. But, as the previous chapter has clearly demonstrated, in the realms of both politics and economics, a basic additional complication was his profound concern about the precarious position of the UK within the wider European, Colonial and international contexts. What exactly did 'right action' mean in these wider geo-political contexts? As the next two chapters will demonstrate, Keynes would become even more involved in political and policy matters as the 1920s unfolded.

9 The fool's gold standard and *laissez faire*

Despite Keynes's emphatic concern to maintain the convertibility of sterling into gold throughout the period of the First World War, in March 1919 the UK formally abandoned the gold standard, an entirely understandable consequence of four years of unprecedented total war. But by this time, its central military purpose of helping to maintain the financial stability of the wartime Allied powers was no longer required, so it had served its function very well. In consequence of the uncoupling of the link to gold, in the year following, sterling declined against the dollar by around 25 per cent. However, this still left the question of the long-term nature of the UK monetary system unresolved. Should the UK at some point in the future return to a traditional form of the gold standard, or would it be better to institute a completely new form of paper currency system?

In the early 1920s, this question remained in the background of many economic debates, as the UK traversed the difficult first stages of post-war recovery. But by 1924, this question had become much more prominent, and the debates surrounding it more heated. The chapter will document Keynes's role in these currency debates, and his relations with other key figures who took part in it such as Winston Churchill. It will then consider the content and development of Keynes's wider socio-political philosophy, as it reached a stage of relative maturity in the mid-1920s.

This latter aspect spilled over in a significant way into his personal life, as his deepening relationship with Lydia Lopokova placed him in intimate first-hand contact with someone with direct experience of a country that was experimenting with non-capitalist forms of economy for the very first time. The threat of capitalist collapse also hovered over some West European states like Germany in the mid-1920s, and not entirely implausibly. Lydia conveyed to Keynes in October 1924 her feelings of guilt at having escaped from the worst of what the Bolsheviks had to offer:

> I had my Russians for tea...how much they would like to cling to any possibility to stay here or anywhere without communism... hunger and miserable salaries especially since the N.E.P. had it's end...I feel so ashamed to have all these comforts...Tea lasted 4 hours...it was very nice to gossip.[1]

She reported with irony that one of her brothers was due to stage a ballet called *Bolsheviks* that included a scene described in Orwellian doublespeak as 'the blossoming of socialism'.

In one sense, the two issues of currency reform and political philosophy that occupied Keynes in the mid-1920s were entirely separate, the former being a specific question of monetary policy, the latter a far wider topic of capitalist Britain making its way in an uncertain post-war era. But on another level they were closely connected, as the financial changes that had been necessitated by the war constituted a microcosm of the far wider structural reforms that would be required in the British economy, if it again wanted to be successful on the international stage. Keynes understood both very well, but as will be seen in this chapter and the next, not all politicians did likewise.

The return to gold

It is uncontroversial to state that the most prominent figure in British history that Keynes had significant interaction with was Winston Churchill (1874–1965), the exceptionally important and successful Prime Minister from 1940 to 1945. However, Churchill's finest hour – leading Britain through the darkest days of 1940 and beyond – was still some way in the distance at the time that the events in this chapter occurred: from 1924 to 1929 he was 'merely' the Chancellor of the Exchequer. Consequently, it was Churchill's responsibility (in association with the Conservative Prime Minister of the time, Stanley Baldwin) to decide if, when and how the UK should return to the gold standard that had been in existence for a long period prior to 1914.

It was official government policy in the early 1920s that the UK was committed to restoring the gold standard at the pre-war parity level of £1 = $4.86, but only at an unspecified future date. However, such an official commitment did not necessarily mean that it would actually come to pass, or that, if it did, the precise form that it would take was firmly established. Governments sometimes change their minds, or modify their aims in significant ways. Hence, in the early 1920s, there was still some scope for interested parties to influence the outcome of the debate.

Returning to the gold standard involved two separate but connected issues. Firstly, there was the issue of whether to restore sterling convertibility into gold at a fixed rate in itself, and by this means provide a secure basis for sterling to be traded internationally. Secondly, there was the issue of the precise rate at which convertibility should be restored. In principle, it could be set at a range of levels within a broad band. Since March 1919, sterling had floated freely against the dollar, and had been left to find its own 'natural' level on the currency exchanges. For much of 1924, the actual rate had varied between $4.30 and $4.40. Attempting to fix the rate at a higher level than it had been across 1924, at the pre-war rate of $4.86 (as was official government policy), would add an additional complication to just fixing the currently prevalent floating rate. It would mean that economic policy would have to be designed explicitly to manoeuvre the exchange rate in the required direction.

Keynes was opposed to the UK returning to the pre-war gold standard for various reasons. His opposition stemmed in part from his long-held belief that the gold standard as a system was in terminal decline across the globe, and in part from more short-term considerations of the UK's economic situation in the 1920s. He argued, firstly, that returning to gold at the pre-war rate was unrealistic, given the decline in the UK's financial position that had undoubtedly occurred following the war. Attempting to fix at the pre-war rate would have negative consequences, such as producing a falling demand for UK exports that could only be countered by price deflation, which would tend to increase UK unemployment. Secondly, he opposed the notion of the gold standard in principle, as the 'golden shackles' had previously exerted a dampening effect on economic growth. Instead, Keynes favoured a carefully managed paper currency system: his work on Indian currency and finance before the war had shown that many countries were moving towards a system in which gold played a much less active role.

The arguments were not exclusively on Keynes's side. One fundamental advantage of the gold standard was that it helped to prevent inflation, as the monetary authorities were prohibited from printing paper currency above certain fixed levels as set out in the official rules. In a purely paper currency system, the authorities had to be trusted to refrain from printing extra notes, trust that many economists warned would easily be broken when the going got tough. Another positive consequence was that it would increase trust in London as an international financial centre, and facilitate the strengthening of links between the London and New York money markets. These were major factors in its favour, but regarding the first advantage, Keynes did not believe that inflation was always the number one enemy in the economy. Sometimes the threat of deflation was the greater evil, and returning to the gold standard in the UK in the mid-1920s, especially at the pre-war rate, would be deflationary.

Regarding the second advantage, Keynes declared emphatically that it was 'most unwise to act in such a way...as to suggest that the interests of industry are being subordinated to those of international finance', as it would be the UK's industrial sector that would suffer more through deflation than the City of London.[2] Moreover, if monetary policy was set in order to manoeuvre the sterling exchange rate in the required direction – as it would have to be in order to regain pre-war parity – rather than to encourage growth, employment and price stability, then it was not being used most advantageously for the UK economy as a whole. These were many of the basic issues as the question of returning to the gold standard was debated across the early 1920s.

In the event, Keynes lost the argument of principles comprehensively, as most of the UK government, the UK Treasury, the UK banking system, the Bank of England itself, and also many economists and financiers, wanted a return to gold at the pre-war level. It duly occurred in April 1925. However, this was certainly not the end of the story, as almost immediately it was accomplished, significant problems associated with this renewed tie to gold began to appear, and Keynes's prematurely rejected arguments against the return to gold began to find more traction. His most significant work in economics of this period, *A Tract on Monetary Reform* of 1923, will be considered in detail in the next chapter; in what follows, his specific case against the return to gold will be considered in more depth.

Misleading Mr Churchill

One of Keynes's most significant interventions in this debate was the composition of *The Economic Consequences of Mr Churchill*, the title of which deliberately played on one of his previous major works *The Economic Consequences of the Peace*. Originally printed as a series of articles in the *Evening Standard* under the less personal heading 'Unemployment and Monetary Policy', *The Economic Consequences of Mr Churchill* was then published as a pamphlet in July 1925, issued by the Hogarth Press, a private company created by Keynes's Bloomsbury friends Leonard and Virginia Woolf. In sales terms the pamphlet was an immediate UK success and within months went through several new editions, suggesting that the British public were interested in these arcane financial issues.

By referring to an earlier book that had famously presented a scathing critique of its subject, the knowing reader who first saw the title of this new work would immediately expect a similar devastating attack on its subject. Although it was heavily critical of the return to gold, which had only recently taken place, its language was only a little less emotive than the former work on Versailles. Even so the first section was headed 'The Misleading of Mr Churchill', implying that Churchill as Chancellor had been hoodwinked by his economic advisers. Keynes stridently declared with respect to the negative effects of the restoration of gold on the UK's export trade that:

> The Chancellor of the Exchequer has expressed the opinion that the return to the gold standard is no more responsible for the condition of the coal industry than is the Gulf Stream. These statements are of the feather-brained order.[3]

Not many British people today would dare to call Winston Churchill 'feather-brained'. Keynes also chastised Churchill for his recent policy of increasing the sterling exchange rate by 10 per cent against the dollar (i.e. revaluing it) in order to reach pre-war parity, which had really meant attempting to reduce everyone's wages by the same amount. Increased unemployment was another compounded consequence of the restriction of credit that had accompanied the return to gold.[4]

Keynes strongly rejected the wisdom of such wage reductions partly on social justice grounds, characterising the forced reduction of wages by increased unemployment as 'a hateful and disastrous way' of regaining economic equilibrium.[5] Such wage reductions made no sense from an economic perspective either, as they exerted a deflationary influence on the UK economy. Keynes's case against attempting wage reductions was two-fold. Firstly, given recent improvements in industrial organisation, wages were sticky downwards, i.e. workers in industries such as mining would simply not accept them, and he did not blame them for this, as they were hardly living in luxury. Secondly, although it might appear from the point of view of orthodox economic theory that if miners did not like the terms and conditions of their work they could move to other sectors of the economy, in reality such changes were extremely difficult to make. This meant that the economist's resort to the hypothetical free market in labour was not a legitimate argument to present. In effect, miners were being offered a choice of submission or starvation, which was bad for them, and also bad for the British economy.

However, by mid-1925 Keynes had become partially resigned to the idea of returning to gold in itself, and had consequently focused his attention more narrowly on the question of the precise rate of the return. His main argument was now 'against having restored gold in conditions which require a substantial readjustment of all our monetary values', which was obviously 'a silly thing'.[6] It was based on the 'vague and jejune meditations' of the Treasury Committee on Currency that Churchill had asked to advise him on this issue. Keynes was so vehement in his criticisms of Churchill's monetary policy in part because the economic problems that it had caused had been entirely avoidable, simply through accepting the *de facto* level of sterling. By implication, Keynes in 1925 would have accepted the return to gold, if it had taken place at a more realistic level.

Like its earlier namesake on Versailles, *The Economic Consequences of Mr Churchill* was highly controversial, and some of its hostile reviewers 'could only fume and splutter' against its great clarity of argument.[7] Many criticisms came from the financial press. Some reviewers questioned what Keynes saw as obvious, that the return to gold had aggravated the economic problems faced by the UK in the mid-1920s, although the arguments that were adduced for this contrary position were invariably confused and baseless. Keynes replied that he should have learnt from his analysis of Versailles 'what passionate moral indignation a statement of economic truth can provoke'.[8]

Part of the difficulty that many interested parties had in accepting that sterling should not return to its pre-war level was simply the accumulated weight of convention: sterling had always been at the immediate pre-war level, so it should return there as soon as possible. Keynes in contrast realised that the sterling rate was simply a mechanism allowing flexibility on international exchanges, and market movements only reflected structural changes that had taken place in the UK/US economies since the beginning of the war. As British power on the international stage had begun to wane, so did sterling; British power could not be regained by actions on sterling alone, just as the tail cannot wag the dog.

The economic consequences of gold

It is necessary to explain more about the wider context of these controversies. Only a year or so after returning to the gold standard at the pre-war level, which had necessitated downward pressure on wages and restrictions on credit to businesses, the UK's first official General Strike had occurred in the Spring of 1926 (from 3 to 12 May). A key element of this General Strike was the actions of miners, who were being asked to accept wage cuts in order to facilitate improved profitability and increased exports of coal. Keynes was clear as to where the responsibility for this situation really rested, explaining in April 1926 that:

> ...the Government must not forget that the price problem of the coal exporters has been created largely by Mr Churchill's gold-

standard policy. The extent to which it is now essential for them to obtain higher prices by better selling methods is almost exactly equal to the lowering of sterling prices attributable to the rise in the exchange.[9]

During the strike itself, Keynes declared that his feelings (as opposed to his judgement) were with the workers: the government was at fault in allowing the situation to develop where negotiations had broken down. However, he also admitted that structural changes in the coal industry were necessary, such as a reduced workforce and a reform of the working day.[10] He recommended that the strike should be settled by further negotiations between the government and unions, rather than by the government forcibly breaking it, as the underlying structural issues would still remain unresolved, whatever the particular outcome.

Despite Keynes's clarity of analysis, in reality the return to gold was only one factor among many that had contributed to such rising levels of unrest among the British working classes, if a very important one. Keynes had pointed to one wider underlying factor in one of his own short contributions on the General Strike – the apparent halting of the 'crescendo of material progress' in the UK that had, in the past, frequently helped it out of its temporary economic difficulties.[11] This 'halting of the crescendo' was an oblique reference to his previous work on changes in the terms of trade facing the UK after 1900, and the massive structural break in international financial relations that the First World War had produced. That this issue was very much alive in Keynes's thinking at this time was apparent from a note that he published in the *Economic Journal* in June 1924. Here he warned that recent factors influencing the terms of trade in favour of some UK exports were only very temporary, and advised that some capital currently invested in the export sector should be redirected back into production destined for UK consumption.[12]

These two underlying changes – factors affecting the terms of trade and the massive consequences of war – had created the context of, first, the UK's abandonment of the gold standard, and second, the feeling of many British politicians that it was necessary to return to this standard, if the UK's previous economic position was to be regained. Ultimately, Keynes wisely recognised that this 'return to the past' was an impossible goal, that the UK could never regain its pre-eminent pre-1914 position in the world economy by restoring its old currency system, given the damaging financial consequences of the war. A Midas-like attempted return to a fool's gold standard would only exacerbate the situation rather than remedy it.

After the General Strike was officially over, in June 1926, Keynes published a more general analysis of the devastating results of the previous year of UK economic policy under the heading 'The First-Fruits of the Gold Standard'. Here he judged that the results had been what they were bound to be, given the predictable consequences of attempting a return to gold at the officially (over)-prescribed rate:

> ...we have had a million unemployed and all the penury of a slump...coal...has been reduced to the verge of ruin. Our largest group of export industries, namely textiles...are...almost in despair at their losses...The results have been what a year ago I feared they would be, but worse than I dared or cared to prophesy.[13]

Part of Churchill's defence of his gold standard policy had been that the large dollar war debt that was owed to the USA by the UK was, as a consequence of the revaluation of sterling, reduced in real terms compared to what it would have been without the revaluation. Keynes accepted that this was true, but explained that simultaneous with this nominal account book 'saving', the UK had 'lost' an equal percentage on all its exports. In addition, this policy had exerted a depressing effect on employment and on the level of exports. Given that (for example) the price of exported coal fell much more rapidly than did wages in the coal industry, the problem of re-adjustment at the required new level of equilibrium still remained, and was a significant threat to the UK's economic prosperity.[14] Thus, the return to gold had been, as Keynes had consistently predicted, an unmitigated disaster.

Despite such a major disagreement over a very important aspect of economic policy, by all reports Keynes remained on relatively friendly terms with Churchill throughout the 1920s. He tended to blame Churchill's advisers and various UK financial institutions for supporting the return to gold more than Churchill, who after all was no economics expert, and had never claimed to be. In May 1925, Lydia commented to Keynes on an astute suggestion that the post of Chancellor had not really been a suitable one for Churchill.[15] Keynes's enduring respect for Churchill was readily apparent from his review of Churchill's multi-volume history of the war. After reading it, Keynes reported feeling for its author:

> Admiration for his energies of mind and his intense absorption of intellectual interest and elemental emotion in what is for the moment the matter in hand – which is his best quality. A little envy, perhaps, for his undoubted conviction that frontiers, races, patriotisms, even wars if need be, are ultimate verities for mankind...[16]

This benign outcome of the dispute with Churchill over the gold standard was in stark contrast to Keynes's disagreements with Lloyd George over war finance, which at times had become bitter and very personal. But the second half of the 1920s would yield a rapprochement with Lloyd George with respect to some shared political aims. Aspects of these political questions will now be considered.

The Bolshevik experiment

As the 1920s progressed, one of the most significant new political developments on the international stage was the consolidation of the Soviet government in Russia. When the Bolsheviks assumed power in a *coup d'état* in October 1917, many had predicted that their rule would be short-lived. However, by the mid-1920s, it was becoming clear that the Soviet Union would remain in existence for some considerable period of time. Hence, Western politicians had to consider what their attitude to such a regime was going to be.

Keynes of course had experienced some dealings with the Russian government first-hand during the First World War, and also through his indirect participation in a failed attempt to create an alternative currency for a part of North Russia in 1918, which had yet to come under Bolshevik control. Perhaps in part because of the critical attitude of works such as *The Economic Consequences of the*

Peace to economic policy in the West, Keynes had received some positive attention in Soviet Russia. In October 1923, Lydia Lopokova wrote to her prospective husband, explaining that:

> You are very well known in Russia...you are very intelligent economist and strengthen all your sutiations with facts and figures, and when one wants to know about *victorious imperialism of Entente in Europe* (I smile like a Bolchevic writing this phrase), it becomes a nessesseity to see your work...[17]

If Lydia's spelling was sometimes questionable, then her judgement about Bolshevik interest in the economics of 'victorious imperialism' was not. And the interest was definitely mutual.

Keynes's work most explicitly concerned with the USSR – *A Short View of Russia* – was published as a pamphlet in December 1925, having previously been issued as separate articles. Although the analysis presented was indeed short, it was brimming with insight and far-reaching perspective, and even today serves as a welcome antidote to the two extremes of Stalinist adulation and ultra-Conservative vitriol that are often levied at the USSR. Keynes characterised the Leninist variant of socialism as an articulated combination of business in subordination to religion. It was religious in terms of the fanatical zeal of its advocates, and businesslike in its claim to provide a superior instrument (economic planning) to capitalism, that would generate large-scale improvements in human welfare. Keynes was rather scathing about the religious aspect:

> ...to say that Leninism is the faith of a persecuting and propagating minority of fanatics led by hypocrites is, after all, to say no more nor less than it *is* a religion...we can picture the Communists of Russia as though the early Christians...were using the equipment of the Holy Inquisition...to enforce the literal economics of the New Testament...[18]

Keynes was thoroughly sceptical as to the business aspect of Bolshevism, describing Karl Marx's *Capital* as 'an obsolete economic textbook which I know to be not only scientifically erroneous but without interest or application for the modern world'.[19] If communism did achieve any success, then Keynes predicted that it would be by means of the religious aspect of Bolshevism rather than the business aspect.

The potential danger for the West was in underestimating the strength of the former aspect of communism, given that the latter was so evidently erroneous. Using 'we' in the sense of the Western mainstream:

> We hate Communism so much…that we exaggerate its economic inefficiency; and we are so much impressed by its economic inefficiency that we underestimate it as a religion…If irreligious Capitalism is ultimately to defeat religious Communism, it is not enough that it should be economically more efficient – it must be many times as efficient.[20]

This was because the religious aspect of communism counted as an extra motivating force in tolerating any economic failings, something that was absent in capitalism. However, Keynes then expressed some definite sympathy with the quasi-Christian idea that the unmitigated love of money was 'the moral problem of our age', and declared that, if he were to face such a choice personally, then he would rather contribute his quota of labour to Soviet rather than Tsarist Russia. He concluded by suggesting that, even though the new Soviet tyrants were no less oppressive than the old monarchy, he 'should like to give Russia her chance' to make a success or failure of the new system by her own means.[21]

It might appear on first sight that Keynes's very partial and qualified sympathy for the Soviet experiment might have been conditioned by his blossoming relationship with Lydia Lopokova. In reality, Keynes's political distaste for Tsarist Russia had been a long-standing feature of his intellectual constitution. In 1917, he had even described the February revolution in Russia, which had brought the Provisional Government to power, as 'the sole result of the war so far worth having'.[22] He was less sympathetic to far-left revolutionaries such as the Bolsheviks, implying that they were 'bloodthirsty philosophers of Russia': *A Short View of Russia* demonstrated this political ambiguity very clearly[23]. Keynes believed strongly that the nineteenth-century *laissez faire* attitude was rightly coming to an end, to be replaced by a mixture of semi-socialist and semi-capitalist regulation and control. However, just as *laissez faire* had its extremist advocates, so did socialism, and the Bolsheviks were, politically at least, the most successful of such extremists.

Keynes's interest in this topic was more than just academic. He visited Soviet Russia for two weeks in September 1925, partly to see Lydia's family in Leningrad, and partly to attend bicentennial celebrations of the Russian Academy of Sciences as a Cambridge scholar. During this trip he presented two academic papers to Russian audiences, rather as a moderate Liberal in the radical lion's den. One entitled 'The Economic Transition in England' employed the notion of three economic orders through which the world had been progressing over the long run, epochs characterised by scarcity, abundance and stabilisation. He suggested the world was currently entering the latter epoch as a real alternative to Marx's Communism. However, the dangers of this epoch, which was one of collective action by various economic bodies, were Fascism on the one hand and Bolshevism on the other. Keynes explained that:

> Some of you in Russia will not agree with me in seeking help in these matters from a reformed and remodelled Liberalism, which above all things, shall not, if my idea is realised, be a class party. Leninism – so it seems to me – is at the same time a persecuting religion and an experimental technique. Capitalism too is at the same time a religion, which is much more tolerant, however, than Leninism is...[24]

The reception of Keynes's moderate political ideas amongst extremist Bolsheviks was understandably rather muted, but 1925 was the highpoint of the New Economic Policy (1921–29) in the USSR, when market relations were being officially if warily tolerated, so as to foster economic recovery after many years of conflict.

Keynes's presentation on 'The Economic Transition in England' had been based on a lecture entitled 'Am I a Liberal?' previously given to a Liberal Summer School. Regarding the historic fates of Conservatism, Socialism and Liberalism as political philosophies he explained that:

> ...I still think that there is room for a party which shall be disinterested as between classes, and which shall be free in

building the future both from the influences of Die-Hardism and from those of Catastrophism…it must emancipate itself from the dead-wood of the past.[25]

By 'Die-Hardism' and 'Catastrophism' he meant the two political extremes of ultra-Conservatism and violent revolution respectively. The party that should be 'disinterested as between classes' was of course the Liberal Party, which was under threat of being squeezed out of existence by the two outer wings of the political spectrum. For Keynes, a renewed Liberalism should focus on 'controlling and directing economic forces in the interests of social justice and social security'.[26] This meant forcibly combating the two political extremes, which in economic terms were represented by *laissez faire* and state socialism. Thus, partly as a reaction to his direct experience of the USSR, Keynes's political philosophy was beginning to develop into its mature form.

Life with Lydia

Although Keynes and Lydia Lopokova had, on the face of it, very different intellectual interests, they corresponded in intimate terms about their respective professional and social activities when they were temporarily separated by the geography of London, Cambridge and elsewhere. Lydia maintained a constant and enthusiastic interest in Keynes's economic work, writing to him in February 1925 that: 'I have read again 'the return to gold'…and again was impressed with its truthful mastery'.[27] Much earlier, she had admitted that 'When I read what you write somehow I fell bigger than I am'.[28] In one instance she even wrote in exasperated mood of the 'high falluting nonsense' of politicians, declaring in response that 'Even I, a non economic person, see that deflation in the extreme just as bad as inflation in the extreme'.[29]

In turn, when they were separated Keynes provided frequent updates for Lydia on the daily triumphs and frustrations of his academic and policy work, and also his more relaxing Bloomsbury escapades. For example, in March 1925 he reported to her that:

I have wasted two more whole mornings over that same mathematical rubbish which I was doing on Thursday. Now at last this morning…I have satisfied myself that there is nothing whatever in it and have cheerfully torn it up.[30]

In April 1925, he described to Lydia a vitalising visit to Keswick in which he went hill walking and 'puffed and blew, and lost my breath and my heart beat hard'. After tea on the same day:

I explained and discussed and argued my new views about Theory of Money (Yes! – P = M/wT + C) with Dennis [Robertson] and the other economists for about two and a half hours. And after dinner we have read out loud Shakespeare's *Coriolanus* taking the parts in turn.[31]

Keynes referred to Lydia in his letters affectionately and variously as 'darling pupsik', 'dearest pupsikochka', and 'darling Lydochka', while in turn Lydia often referred to Keynes as 'Maynardochka'. She sometimes ended her letters with suggestive flirts such as 'I kiss your face and other Holy places' and 'I taste your buttons', and she occasionally signed off more brazenly as 'Your gobbling dog'.

Partly in order to cement his new marriage with Lydia, in 1925 Keynes began negotiations to obtain the lease for Tilton, a detached country farmhouse situated within several acres of its own land in the South Downs region of Sussex. Although the house was in need of some renovations, the location was picturesque and the life it promised was idyllic, and after the lease was finally acquired following extensive negotiations in 1926, Keynes and Lydia would spend the holiday periods of the rest of their married life there. Tilton was certainly not at the very large or opulent end of the country house spectrum, but it did require a small number of staff to manage it, mostly living nearby on the grounds. However, it was reported by other members of the Bloomsbury group that Lydia and Maynard were not especially extravagant hosts when it came to supplying their guests with food and drink, despite Keynes's own taste for fine art.

Some Bloomsbury friends took the irresistible opportunity of Tilton to jibe the country house-owning Keynes as 'the Squire', something that in reality he was most definitely not. Lydia even chastised him on occasion for wearing old trousers with holes worn in them. These were certainly friendly taunts, from which even the

Lord Jesus Christ was not immune when in the illustrious company of Bloomsbury. Keynes reported to Lydia in May 1925 on a party in Cambridge at which one of Lytton Strachey's cantankerous sisters:

> ...spent all the time...proving to a very serious Christian undergraduate that Christ never happened. I read out the book of Jonah to show what a funny old fellow God was, and we all laughed a good deal.[32]

In the same month Lydia described to Keynes attending first a dinner party of her own and then afterwards a ballet, complaining semi-humorously about 'those Greeks, I wish they would wear tights instead of bare legs. I suppose what looks nice on the vases somehow losses the beauty in...movements'.[33] At such social events, the apparently anomalous pairing itself sometimes came under scrutiny, Lydia reporting an overheard conversation that was only initially flattering:

> 'How charming what a radiant person was Mme Lopokova, but she could not say the same about her friend M. Keynes.'... Maynarochka, is it not a wicked combination between you and me, at other parties it will be the opposite; how interesting and charming M. Keynes is and how unsignificant is his friend Loppy.[34]

Such temporary doubts about the suitability of the combination were very quickly dispelled when the couple were again together.

Tilton became very much a place for spending the holidays (summer, Christmas and Easter) and a contemplative retreat, and consequently Keynes still retained a house in Gordon Square in London, at which he resided in the middle of the week, with Cambridge reserved for most weekends. After 1925, Lydia continued with her artistic and dancing interests – 'we all labour like dogs, no difficult steps and yet it is difficult' – appearing for example at the Coliseum in London in various Serge Diaghilev productions, which continued with success in the summer of 1926.[35] Also during 1926, the opportunity for Keynes to become the Provost of King's College arose, but in the event he vacillated over the decision, and then arranged for another candidate to take his place. He had been fatally torn between his College duties and the freer life outside Cambridge: more time for the former would inevitably mean less for the latter and for his increasingly important socio-economic writings.

The End of Laissez-Faire

The intellectual point of culmination of all Keynes's political and economic philosophising in the first half of the 1920s was expressed very clearly in his 1926 pamphlet entitled *The End of Laissez-Faire*. And by 1926, this was no longer a question being posed by a questioning mind, but an emphatic declaration of an undeniable truth that had recently come to pass. The end that was under review can be understood in two distinct senses. It was the end of the epoch of *laissez faire*, i.e. an era of increasing free trade and individual liberty among an increasing number of nations that had unfolded across the nineteenth century; but it was also the end of the doctrine of *laissez faire*, i.e. an ideology in which individual self-interest was asserted always to operate in the public interest, as had been articulated by classical economists such as Adam Smith. And the end of the former sense had squarely provoked the end of the latter.

Keynes began *The End of Laissez-Faire* with the controversial lesson that the doctrine of self-interest was '*not* a correct deduction from the Principles of Economics'.[36] Many previous economists had asserted that it was, and Smith's 'hidden hand' of the market was a metaphor for this principle of social good coming from individual self-interest. But according to Keynes, this was simply wrong, as individuals acting separately were often too weak or ignorant to attain even their own narrow aims. The problem, consequently, was to decide precisely what the state should take upon itself to direct in the wider public interest, and what was truly best left to individual action. Note that Keynes's approach was supremely non-ideological. Whether the state or the market should govern an area of human activity should be resolved on an individual case-by-case basis, looking solely at the facts at hand, without any preconception as to whether the state or the market was superior.

The title of Keynes's pamphlet was thus somewhat misleading. It could more accurately be formulated as *The End of Universal*

Laissez-Faire. He was not arguing that the market was always an inappropriate mechanism for governing human life, only that sometimes it was. In these instances, the state must assume control. The opposite was also the case; he was not arguing that the state was always an appropriate means of governing human life. The real goal should be to find the happy medium between the two, a combination of what he called semi-socialism and semi-capitalism. In contrast, the doctrinaire state socialism of the Bolsheviks was merely a 'dusty survival of a plan to meet the problems of fifty years ago', and itself sprang out of the ideology of free competition, the two being 'different reactions to the same intellectual atmosphere' of the mid-nineteenth century.[37] These ideas were a direct continuation of the principles that had been presented in earlier works, such as 'Am I a Liberal?' and *A Short View of Russia*, but they were now brought together in a more forceful and coherent statement.

A more novel idea was that real progress 'lies in the growth…of semi-autonomous bodies within the State' whose criterion of action was the public good, and who were subject to the sovereignty of democracy expressed through Parliament.[38] Examples provided by Keynes included the Universities, regional authorities and perhaps even railway companies as 'semi-autonomous corporations'. Another more controversial idea was that the scale of savings of the whole community and the degree they were invested overseas, and also the size of the national population, should not be left entirely to private judgements, but should be gauged according to the national interest by a 'co-ordinated act of intelligent judgement'.[39]

Keynes's most substantial and detailed biographer, Robert Skidelsky, was not especially impressed by *The End of Laissez-Faire*, declaring that its author 'fails to develop any sustained critique' of the *laissez faire* doctrine, that his articulation of the state/private functional division 'is a misleading way of stating the task', and agreeing with the existing criticism that the superb style of this pamphlet concealed some hasty arguments.[40] Although Skidelsky is a superb historian of Keynes's life and times, his judgement here was to a considerable extent mistaken. *The End of Laissez-Faire* was deceptively simple, yet hid within its surface ease, great wisdom and complexity. It had the theoretical potential to operate as a manifesto of socio-political moderation nearly on a par with other epoch-making declarations such as *The Communist Manifesto*.

One of its apparent failings was really part of its strength: it lacked the fanatic's flair for fire and brimstone. But by definition, moderates forcefully shun fanciful extremism and the blusteringly plain poles of black and white that its advocates portray in order to whip up support. *The End of Laissez-Faire* could thus be seen as an anti-manifesto manifesto, or a pragmatist's programme for the moderating mixture of the multitude of political colours. As correctly evaluated by another of his biographers, Keynes was one of the most important ideologues of the new Liberalism that was being articulated in the 1920s.[41] In was a 'new' Liberalism in the sense that it was much more interventionist in the economic arena than Liberals had been in the past, but it still held to the old Liberal ideals of supporting individual freedom with a parallel concern for social welfare.

It was true that not all its arguments were exhaustively developed. But here Keynes was, like other pioneer political philosophers, sketching the pillars and arches of a new approach, the detailed economic components of which had to wait until later to be fully articulated. But many were present in embryo in *The End of Laissez-Faire*, as can be seen from the following astute declaration:

...I think that Capitalism, wisely managed, can probably be made more efficient for attaining economic ends than any alternative system yet in sight, but that in itself it is in many ways extremely objectionable. Our problem is to work out a social organisation which shall be as efficient as possible without offending our notions of a satisfactory way of life.[42]

The objectionable features were basing society, to the extent that it currently was, on 'the money-motives of individuals', and the concomitant rejection of all ascetic notions, plus the fact that fortunate individuals were able to take advantage of a prevalent state of ignorance. The trick was to utilise the money-motive where it was best suited, but in a controlled and directed fashion, in combination with what might reasonably be termed 'the social motive' where it was best suited, in order to achieve the optimal type of society desired. Another feature of the moderate's programme must be that the collection and dissemination of all data relating to business activity should be undertaken by a directive intelligence of society.

Of course, Keynes did not explain exactly how all these great improvements were to be accomplished in full detail in 1926. He would spend the rest of his life exploring how economic policies, mechanisms and ideas could help to bring about the sort of happy medium that had been sketched in bare outline in *The End of Laissez-Faire*. But this is why it was such an important text for elucidating the mature Keynes's political philosophy. In effect, he had produced one of the first anti-communist manifestos of the twentieth century; and it was simultaneously, if only partially, anti-capitalist. How successful he ultimately was in this social terra-forming goal is another matter, as was the actual political impact of *The End of Laissez-Faire*, but the nature of the goal itself was very clear. It was to combine the best of capitalism and the best of socialism to form a superior hybrid of the two: what might be called social-capitalism, or perhaps state-managed capitalism, or in more modern and familiar terminology, the third way.

Conclusion

It is apparent that by the mid-1920s, Keynes 'mature' concern with the nature of capitalism as an economic system, especially as it was constituted in the UK, was beginning to be clearly articulated. This concern brought together various important intellectual and personal threads in his life up until this point in a cogent and coherent manner. There was the concern with the role of the financial and monetary system within the economic system as a whole. There was the concern with the impact of large-scale socio-political events, such as the First World War and the Bolshevik revolution, on how the capitalist economic system was evolving and then its long-term fate. There was the concern for how the parliamentary political system operated in relation to finding solutions to ongoing economic problems. There was the concern with long-run trends in international economic relations and how they were affecting the UK. And then there was the concern to articulate a political philosophy that could provide a framework for solving many of these political, social and economic problems in a rational and coherent way.

In outlining Keynes's interrelated set of concerns in this way, it becomes apparent that he was much more than just an academic economist, at least as the term has come to mean today. He was more akin to the economic philosopher as previously exemplified by Adam Smith and Karl Marx. Indeed, Smith, Marx and Keynes are sometimes identified as 'the big three' in economics. But the real truth of this characterisation is not always brought out. If Smith was the philosopher of free market capitalism, and Marx the philosopher of state-controlled socialism, then Keynes was the founding philosopher of the median between the two, or of socially managed capitalism. Of course for philosophical extremists like Smith and Marx, the idea of combining the best of both economic worlds was anathema and was actually impossible, akin to being a little bit pregnant. But in fact, all fertile women are a little bit pregnant; they just need the final male component to bring their potential children to fruition.

Keynes's underlying goal from this time onwards was thus to help to bring into realisation the prospective system of state-managed capitalism that was already in partial existence, but needed further development and refinement to reach its full potential. And this goal was not a luxury, the success of which was just an interesting option for those who favoured it; it was an immediate and pressing necessity, as the two alternatives, free market anarchy and socialist barbarism, were both knocking on the historical door with forceful abandon.

10 The fluctuating value of monetary reform

The previous chapter deliberately avoided discussing Keynes's most significant work in economic theory from the first half of the 1920s – *A Tract on Monetary Reform* of 1923. This was his first book-length analysis of purely economics topics since *Indian Currency and Finance* of 1913, and since the latter was 'merely' a study of the financial institutions of one single country, *A Tract on Monetary Reform* represented Keynes's first major work in economics more widely conceived. From a purely historical perspective it had only moderate impact on the economics of its day, and had its author not subsequently published much more significant theoretical works, it would probably be regarded as not especially original or influential. However, this does not mean either that it was uninteresting in itself, or that it was not important from the point of view of the intellectual development of its author. According to R.F. Harrod, it had 'an important place in economic history', due to its analysis of the post-war monetary histories of various European countries.[1]

Before analysing the book itself, it is necessary to consider its rather unusual title. Before 1914, academic economists had rarely named their books as 'tracts'. The term 'tract' meant a polemical discourse aimed at arguing a specific point of view, rather than a considered analysis for purely theoretical ends. In fact Keynes's 1923 book was both, in that he was arguing passionately for a specific type of monetary system, but did so by employing a more considered analysis of monetary theory. The brilliance of the book was in how these two elements were brought together. Keynes had developed much of the material in it previously, either as articles or lectures, but it was his first post-war attempt to bring together many contemporary monetary concerns into a major statement of economic analysis.

The sociology of monetary changes

Perhaps a little surprisingly for a work of monetary theory, the book began with a sociological analysis of the impact of fluctuations in the value of money on various different classes of society. True to the traction generated from the book's title, this concern with structural issues was not tangential to Keynes's approach, but formed part of the underlying basis from which the rest of the work was generated. As has been demonstrated previously, Keynes's essential political goal in this period was to provide a philosophical foundation for what was characterised as state-managed capitalism or the third way. *A Tract on Monetary Reform* can be seen as its author fleshing out some aspects of this philosophy in the financial arena.

Keynes began with a tripartite sociological classification of society into an investing class, a business class and an earning class, each having its own specific economic interests. The investing class benefited from stability in the value of money over time, as it wanted the value paid out on its investments in the future to remain steady in real terms, or even to appreciate. As the business class were in general debtors, they benefited from a reduction in the value of money over time, as the nominal value of their repayments would remain constant, while their real value declined. The earning class in the past suffered losses if the value of money declined over time, as the value of their wages fell, but improved labour organisation had tended to negate this effect in some instances. Keynes concluded here that:

> …Inflation redistributes wealth in a manner very injurious to the investor, very beneficial to the business man, and probably in modern industrial conditions, beneficial on the whole to the earner. Its most striking consequence is its *injustice* to those who in good faith have committed their savings to titles to money rather than to things.[2]

After sketching the structural positions of these three classes in relation to long-run changes in the value of money, Keynes then embarked upon his real goal: to analyse how more recent changes had affected these classes, and the consequences of these changes for the nature of the economic system as a whole.

Due to the massive call upon existing funds that it necessitated, the war had consumed a large portion of the funds of the investing class, and brought about a far-reaching change in the relative positions of the different classes. Given these facts, new savings would have to be attracted in the future in order to encourage productive investments to be made by the business class. However, and here was the key point, new savings could only be attracted if the people making them were sure as to the stability of the monetary unit over the long term. In order to obtain the new investments required in order to promote British economic growth, the standard of value had to be kept stable, and significant levels of inflation (or deflation) had to be avoided. In addition to affecting the investing class, very high levels of inflation also affected the earning class, as it watched powerlessly as profiteering eroded the value of wages. Hence, for Keynes in the first half of the 1920s, the most important monetary issue was to maintain stability in the value of money, and thus to help to promote business investment.

The contextual reasons for Keynes's underlying concern with monetary stability were obvious. During the First World War, the Russian government had been overthrown partly in consequence of the inflationary issue of vast amounts of paper currency, a technique that Keynes had been closely involved with advocating and implementing, and which he later came partially to regret. After the war, monetary chaos in Germany had also threatened political disaster. In 1922, Keynes had been directly invited by the German government to advise on currency reform as part of a larger group of experts.[3] But as Keynes explained, the 'collapse of the currency in Germany...was the chief contributory cause of the fall of Dr. Cuno's Government in August 1923'.[4] As *A Tract on Monetary Reform* was being written in the summer of 1923, and then published at the end of the year, these dangerous political events were uppermost in its author's mind. Keynes even warned a certain Benito Mussolini against attempting to raise the value of the lira to its former level, before acknowledging that, fortunately, 'the lira does not listen even to a dictator'.[5] Thus, although *A Tract on Monetary Reform* appeared in much of its contents as merely a technical analysis of

Plate 1 Keynes in the early 1920s. (Photo by Keystone-France/Gamma-Keystone via Getty Images)

Plate 2 Keynes in 1925 with his wife the Russian ballet dancer Lydia Lopokova. (Photo by Keystone-France/Gamma-Keystone via Getty Images)

Plate 3   Keynes formulates a plan to finance the war and to avoid its most disastrous
economic consequences: from *Picture Post* in 1940. (Photo by Tim Gidal/
Picture Post/Getty Images)

Plate 4 Keynes in his study with his extraordinary collection of rare and valuable antiquarian books. (Photo by Tim Gidal/Getty Images)

monetary theory, in fact its aims were supremely practical and political.

The preferred system

One major reason why these issues were so important for the UK was that the question of restoring the gold standard for sterling had become a very live policy issue in the early 1920s. As Keynes had opposed this return in principle, he needed to outline an alternative system. *A Tract on Monetary Reform* provided this theoretical alternative by declaring that, through adapting the existing system as it had developed after 1918, a broadly correct system would be achieved:

> ...we have already gone a long way towards the ideal of directing bank rate and credit policy by reference to the internal price level and other symptoms of under- or over-expansion of internal credit, rather than by reference to the pre-war criteria of the amount of cash in circulation (or of gold reserves in the banks)...[6]

The internal price level was the key variable, which had to be kept relatively stable in order to provide the monetary context for businesses to grow successfully. In this ideal system, the amount of credit in the banking system should be regulated in order to maintain price stability. Banks usually adjusted their credit creation up to a limit that was set by formal criteria, such as what were deemed by convention as 'safe' proportions between bank deposits and credit. Bank deposits or cash were, in turn, determined by public demand for money in combination with Treasury and Bank of England currency issue. Since the latter was under the control of these institutions themselves, Keynes believed that the price level 'depends in the last resort on the policy of the Bank of England and of the Treasury'.[7] These institutions must consequently regulate their policy in order to achieve the required price stability. This, in basic form, was Keynes's preferred system of currency control, which required no fixed link between sterling and gold at all.

The standard objection to this type of state-managed paper currency system was that governments could not, in the long run, be trusted to maintain the stability of the price level, as printing additional currency was too great a temptation when governments found themselves short of revenue. Keynes's own reply was, firstly, that he believed Western governments were now mature enough to be trusted with the operation of a paper currency system, and secondly, that even the use of a gold standard did not negate all the dangers of fluctuations in the value of money. This was because the value of gold itself was not fixed, but fluctuated on the international markets in response to variations in demand and supply, and hence even gold could not prevent any changes in the value of money at all.

In a paper currency system, the monetary authorities still retained a significant level of gold reserves as one means of affecting the price level, it was just that the relation between this reserve and currency notes was not fixed. Keynes's system did contain one preventative measure against the risk of profligate governments printing money: the existence of two separate management authorities. As he recommended his system for use in the UK and the USA, the Bank of England would have to collaborate with the US Federal Reserve in order to regulate the exchange rate between the two currencies, one being forced to serve as a check on the other.[8] Keynes concluded about gold:

> As an ultimate safeguard...no superior medium is yet available. But I urge that it is possible to get the benefit of the advantages of gold, without irrevocably binding our legal-tender money to follow all the vagaries of gold and future unforeseeable fluctuations in the real purchasing power.[9]

Thus, he believed that a properly managed paper currency system could be superior to a gold standard system in maintaining purchasing power stability, as currency value would be entirely under rational governmental control.

Currency systems and the quantity theory

There were various complicating issues of course, such as the demand for money, which was variable and depended on other factors, such as the amount of purchasing power that it suited the public to hold and the amount required by businesses. In order to facilitate a more formal analysis, Keynes assumed that the public held an amount of money having a purchasing power over k consumption units, k thus being cash held by the public:

> Let there be n currency notes...and let p be the price of each consumption unit...then it follows from the above that $n = pk$. This is the famous Quantity Theory of Money. So long as k remains unchanged, n and p rise and fall together; that is to say, the greater or the fewer currency notes, the higher or the lower is the price level in the same proportion.[10]

The variable n was thus total notes in circulation and p the index number of prices. In reality, what was declared as k (consumption units in cash), and what was termed as money available at banks against cheques (k'), was not fixed but varied in line with convention. Moreover, the quantity theory of money was only fully true 'in the long run'; in the short-term, changes in currency in circulation could affect the amount of money held by the public, rather than the price level. These complicating factors led Keynes to present perhaps his most famous short statement of all, a one-liner of immense seduction: in the long run we are all dead.[11] What he meant of course was that short-term consequences, while fleeting, could have a major impact on the situation at hand.

Even given these various complicating factors, Keynes still maintained that 'the price level is not mysterious, but is governed by a few, definite, analysable influences'.[12] Both the total number of currency notes issued (n), and the proportion of bank liabilities to the public that were kept as cash (r), were under the control of the banking authorities. As the public demand for cash was not directly controllable:

> The business of stabilising the price level...consists partly in exercising a stabilising influence over k and k', and...deliberately varying n and r so as to counterbalance the movement of k and k'. The usual method of exercising a stabilising influence over k and k'...is that of bank rate.[13]

By 'bank rate' Keynes meant the interest rate set by the authorities. By increasing the interest rate, the authorities could make borrowing more expensive, and thus reduce the volume of loans and the demand for cash. Hence, although Keynes readily admitted that exerting a stabilising influence on the price level was more complicated than just regulating the amount of currency in circulation, he still believed that by the various means outlined, stability in the price level could be maintained by government policies, without the need for a formal link to gold.

Keynes's adherence to the quantity theory of money in the early 1920s has led Monetarist economists like Milton Friedman to declare that *A Tract on Monetary Reform* was Keynes's most significant work. But Friedman was missing the essential nature of the book; he was neglecting the (policy aim) wood for the (purely theoretical) trees. The quantity theory of money was only a technical tool that Keynes was using to substantiate the underlying policy aim. As often with Keynes, the economic analysis was subordinate to the more general practical goal.

Reception and influence

As the UK did return to the gold standard in 1925, in one important sense *A Tract on Monetary Reform* was a total failure. It did not, on first publication, convince the relevant authorities that a managed paper currency system would be superior. Neither did it convince many UK economists, who remained sceptical as to whether governments could be trusted with a paper currency system. Keynes was also accused of downplaying the virtues of the gold standard. However, its longer-term impact was arguably much greater. According to R.F. Harrod, the book caused a lively controversy that was remembered for many years, at which politicians and bankers were forced to take note, and thus the 'seeds of doubt' regarding the gold standard were sown.[14]

As highlighted in the previous chapter, in fact there were two separate issues at stake in the case of the UK: the gold standard as a system in itself, and the precise rate of any return to it. In deciding to launch a blistering book-length attack on the entire system of gold backing for currencies, Keynes had chosen the more radical path of criticism. But in simultaneously neglecting the seemingly less important question of the rate of any return, he had missed the opportunity of having an influence on this second, and perhaps more open-ended, issue. If *A Tract on Monetary Reform* had either solely or mainly focused on arguing for a more sensible rate of sterling's return to gold, it might have been more immediately successful.

Some commentators have been critical of the book purely as economics, characterising it as 'not a fully integrated performance', and declaring even more disapprovingly that 'Keynes had not begun to analyse the major issues in his field of specialisation'.[15] This latter remark belied a partial misunderstanding of what Keynes was trying to achieve in *A Tract on Monetary Reform*. It was certainly not a book of pure economic theory, and through its tactile title, this could not have been made any clearer. Keynes in the early 1920s had spent a great deal of time and effort on 'his field of specialisation' – it was just that the previously quoted remark contained a partly incorrect characterisation of what this field really was. It was the application of economic (and other) ideas to improve the socio-economic system. It was not the development of abstract economic theory in itself.

In the wider international context, Keynes's call for price stability to be the central aim of monetary policy was not unique. In the USA, the economist Irving Fisher had in 1920 published a book entitled *Stabilizing the Dollar*, which carried the subtitle 'A Plan to Stabilize the General Price Level without Fixing Individual Prices'. The details of Fisher's plan were different to Keynes's, as Fisher desired to 'fix the purchasing power of the dollar', but the underlying issues that were tackled were very similar.[16] Fisher also opposed the traditional form of the gold standard, wanting to create instead 'an ideal composite or "goods-dollar", consisting of a representative assortment of commodities'.[17] Again as with Keynes's own plan, the relevant US authorities ignored Fisher's call for monetary reform. Keynes had met Fisher before the war, corresponded with him thereafter, and reviewed Fisher's classic book-length statement of the quantity theory *The Purchasing Power of Money* of 1911.

A major difference between Keynes and Fisher was that the former employed what was called the Cambridge version of the quantity theory of money in the analysis, as outlined above, whereas the latter was the progenitor of the more conventional basic form of the quantity theory of money, $MV = PT$. In the Cambridge version,

$n = p (k + rk')$, greater emphasis was given to a consideration of the demand for money. Keynes brought out this difference in a comment published in the *Economic Journal* in March 1924. Here he called the policy of looking only to the volume of legal money in circulation as the regulator of value 'old-fashioned', pointing out that k (consumption units in cash) and money available at banks against cheques (k') were capable of violent fluctuations. This meant that:

> ...the policy of fixing the value of n by law is unsound, because the right value of n is not always the same but is constantly fluctuating...those responsible for monetary policy must keep their weather eye on almost everything except the volume of the note issue...For the note issue tells much more about how they have been acting in the past than about what they should do in the future; and a big movement in it proves...that the navigation is already at fault and that they are on the rocks.[18]

Thus, it should be assumed that current note issue had been correctly regulated, but to rely on this element alone in a mechanical manner would be equally as dangerous as the abandonment of all note issue regulation. The quantity theory of money used in too simplistic a form could be misleading.

Undoubtedly, the greatest and most important immediate impact of *A Tract on Monetary Reform* was on Keynes himself. Soon after it was first published, he began outlining a plan for a sequel, a new book on monetary theory that would 'throw much new light on my fundamental arguments in favour of the dogmas to which I have rashly given utterance without sufficiently substantiating them'.[19] The implication of this statement was clear. After publication, he had quickly seen through the 'dogmas' of *A Tract on Monetary Reform*, thereby realising the need for a new, deeper level of understanding of the issues in question. But only through the process of composing the book had this been possible. This is not to suggest that Keynes then reversed his opposition to the gold standard, as his underlying policy goals remained as they were before. What would change was the theoretical apparatus of economics that he employed to substantiate them. In the next two chapters, the processes that resulted in the publication of his next major work *A Treatise on Money* of 1930 will be considered in full detail.

Conclusion

What was the precise link between the specific proposals for monetary reform outlined in *A Tract on Monetary Reform*, and Keynes's wider socio-political concern with outlining the third way? One component of this link was the desire to bring financial policy under rational human control, rather than it being left to the vagaries of a so-called free market for gold. As Keynes had previously pointed out, if the 'right' amount of new gold was mined that was required to generate the 'right' amount of monetary expansion in order to accompany the actual level of the economic growth of nations in any given period, then it would be merely coincidental. An important part of a system of state-managed capitalism would be to bring monetary policy fully under the control of government. Supporters of the gold standard saw only greater risks in this change, but Keynes saw it as part of a wider trend not towards state socialism in itself, which he strongly opposed, but towards an optimal combination within the ideal mixed economy. In the short run the UK authorities rejected Keynes's ideal monetary system, but in the long run it absolutely came to pass.

11 Organising prosperity

In the UK and across Europe in the second half of the 1920s, various important political and economic developments were progressing at a fast pace. In 1925, an Unemployed Insurance Act was passed in the UK, giving workers some increased measure of assistance if they lost their jobs and extending the 1911 Act formulated by David Lloyd George. From 1926 onwards, problems with a decline in the exchange rate of the French franc risked widespread political disruption, and in Germany in 1927, a looming financial crisis threatened to scupper the whole European war repayments scheme. Keynes continued to write insightful commentary on the reparations problem, which had become firmly enmeshed with various other ongoing economic issues such as the international role of the gold standard and the rising importance of the USA in the world economy.

Indeed, the second half of the 1920s witnessed in the USA what Keynes described in 1930 as 'one of the greatest "bull" Stock Exchange movements in history', and there was an atmosphere of easy optimism that permeated many areas of American life.[1] The assorted European problems that have just been sketched meant that such financial bullishness was not observed in anything like the same degree in most of Europe. In the UK in 1929, Labour won the General Election but without an overall majority, and with the Liberal Party (as supported by Keynes) in a very poor third in terms of seats, even though they had gained extra votes. One of the central economic issues facing the UK in the 1920s was the decline of many of its traditional manufacturing industries as they started to face increased competition from overseas, a developing trend that had been temporarily disguised by the war. As an economist very concerned with Britain's industrial decline, Keynes became personally involved with this issue on a number of occasions.

Personal Life

Keynes's wife Lydia continued her dancing career in the second half of the 1920s, although much more sporadically than she had previously. In 1927 she performed only once, but in 1930 she gave a number of performances in *A Masque of Poetry and Music*. One temporarily alarmed houseguest of the Keyneses recollected that:

> I well remember staying at Tilton in those days. There were great thuds and the house shook. What could be happening? It was too continuous for an earthquake, too violent for the pumping of water or other domestic machinery. I came out of my bedroom in alarm. It was Lydia doing her exercises at the top of the stairs.[2]

Lydia also began to experiment with acting on the amateur stage, and Keynes was keen for her to explore the artistic potential that she demonstrated, although her heavy Russian accent proved something of a hindrance, especially when she acted in a Shakespearean piece. Even so she did receive some positive reviews for her straight acting. There is some evidence to suggest that they made some attempts to conceive a child in 1927, and then a rather distressing indication that either they were unsuccessful, or worse, that the child did not manage to survive to its birth, although the remaining documentation is not completely clear about its possible unhappy fate.[3]

Famous visitors in this period included the philosopher Ludwig Wittgenstein, who had recently ended his teaching term in Austria. In January 1929, Keynes reported semi-humorously from Cambridge that 'God has arrived', but then complained to Lydia about Wittgenstein's 'tremendous self-centredness', forlornly suggesting that they should quickly try to exchange guests for an easier life.[4] As a fellow European outsider in Cambridge, Wittgenstein soon became friends with Piero Sraffa, an Italian-born economist who became a Fellow of Trinity College in 1927, and the two émigrés sometimes boated in concert on the River Cam. Keynes and Sraffa often frequented antiquarian bookshops together, after the latter's position at Cambridge was secured by Keynes's active intervention. Sraffa had previously translated Keynes's *A Tract on Monetary Reform* into Italian, and he went on to edit the standard edition of the works of David Ricardo, which is a little ironic given Keynes's long-standing preference for Malthus over Ricardo.

A less benign connection was that Anthony Blunt, the noted art historian and (as later revealed) notorious Soviet spy, was inaugurated into the Cambridge Apostles in 1928, although by this time Keynes had moved substantially beyond his youthful university associations. He was never tempted by the pseudo-scientific ideology of Marxism, and found it very difficult to comprehend how others could fall for its erroneous class-hate stereotypes. But at the very end of the 1920s, a momentous series of events would occur that could be seen as the closest that capitalism had yet come to fulfilling the Marxist prediction of its complete collapse and annihilation.

The Lancashire cotton industry

As was outlined in chapter nine, in the early 1920s Keynes was very concerned with the detrimental effects of recent economic changes on the British coal industry. Although significant portions of his intellectual efforts across the 1920s were directed towards international financial issues, his 'real economy' considerations were being increasingly focused on the UK. And his evaluation of the calibre of British businessmen was not always very flattering, calling some of them 'third-generation men' who had been handed control of their empires only through the hereditary principle, thereby producing a 'weak and stupid' leadership.[5] This general evaluation was confirmed in a very specific case.

Towards the end of 1926, Keynes turned his substantive attention to the position of the British cotton industry, which was mainly located in Lancashire. As he explained in his first article on this topic published in November 1926, more than one third of the world's total cotton spindles were located in Lancashire.[6] However, similar to the coal industry, the British cotton industry in the

1920s had been experiencing major problems in re-orientating itself to the new realities of the post-war world, problems that had been compounded by government policies such as the return to gold.

Compared to the volume of pre-war exports, Lancashire had (on average) lost around one third of its trade in the first half of the 1920s. Various temporary external factors, such as the high price of raw cotton and a falling off of world trade, had been blamed, but Keynes suggested that more troubling factors might also be at work. He provided data that showed that while some countries like Germany and Russia had also seen a decline in cotton consumption compared to pre-war levels, others like France, Italy, Japan and the USA were producing more for themselves in the mid-1920s than they had been in 1913.[7] He concluded that Lancashire had suffered a definite loss of trade since the war, at least with respect to those spindles that employed coarser grades of cotton. What Keynes called 'the greatest of British exports' had lost around half of its former trade in the post-war period (for coarser cotton). The key questions in response of course were: what was the underlying cause of this decline, and how could it be reversed?

Keynes listed various causes for the decline – tariffs, high labour costs, increased overhead costs caused by short-time working and the effects of the gold standard. Many of these were outside the control of the Lancashire cotton industry, but this did not mean that no response could be attempted. Keynes's proposed solution was the reduction of overhead costs by rationalisation, by which he meant the re-grouping of mills by amalgamation, and the ending of the practice of short-time working. However, the strength of his feelings on this matter becomes clear in the final paragraph of the article, where he bemoaned:

The mishandling of currency and credit by the Bank of England since the war...[and] the apparently suicidal behaviour of the leaders of Lancashire raises a question of the suitability and adaptability of our business men to the modern age of mingled progress and retrogression. What has happened to them...Are they too old or too obstinate? Or what? Is it that too many of them have risen not on their own legs, but on the shoulders of their fathers and grandfathers?[8]

Such heavy criticism provoked newspaper responses from the cotton industry's leaders, and Keynes was subsequently invited to Manchester to discuss his article by the Committee of the Federation of Master Cotton Spinners. He then published a second article on this topic where he developed and refined his arguments in response to the new information that had been provided in the various replies.

The additional contribution that Keynes provided in this second article was to clarify what he meant by the 're-grouping' of mills, which was *a fortiori* still his offered solution to the problem of high overhead costs:

> ...this problem of excess productive capacity is not a new one in the world at large, and there are recognised ways of tackling it. All these are variations on the cartel, the holding company, and the amalgamation...by these means only, can the surplus capacity be withdrawn from competition and held in reserve against future requirements, so that the rest of the industry can earn normal profits meanwhile.[9]

The scale of the problem was made clear when it was explained that, in one section of the cotton trade specialising in spinning coarser yarn, there were around 350 separate firms each in competition with each other.[10] Thus, Keynes's solution to the problems of the cotton industry was its re-organisation into an industrial cartel, which (he admitted) might grate against the 'intensely individual temperament' of Lancashire traditions, but which was necessary if its business prospects were to improve.

Just after his second article was published, Keynes received a promising letter from a member of a nascent Cotton Yarn Association. In response he declared that 'this Association probably represents by far the most hopeful move in the direction'.[11] He composed a substantial article discussing its merits, where he outlined three objectives for the cotton trade: firstly, the elimination of weak sellers and the replenishment of working capital; secondly, the adjustment of capacity to demand; and thirdly, the securing of organised economies and then the recovery of markets.[12] The first aim came from the prevalence of what Keynes called 'excessive competition' resulting from surplus capacity, which led to hand-to-mouth buying and weak selling. The existing lack of bargaining resistance came from the fact that producers were so poor that they could not carry unsold stocks even for a few days, and were forced to sell at excessively low prices.

Keynes believed that the second and third objectives, supply adjustment and the recovery of markets, would follow once the first had been achieved. In order to accomplish the first objective, a minimum selling price for cotton yarn must be set, preferably a protective minimum that allowed some degree of competitive play. Separate output quotas for each district should then be fixed to avoid senseless overproduction, which could be transferable with a view to the concentration of production.[13] In order to achieve these types of controls, an umbrella organisation for the industry as a whole was required, which could be a cartel, or an Association like the one that was being proposed.

Thus, in his analysis of the Lancashire cotton industry, Keynes was advocating the conscious planning of prices and production levels. Here was one part of the detail of what he had previously called socially managed capitalism. Another term for it could be 'planned competition', to distinguish it from the 'free competition' of *laissez faire*. As Keynes had shown in the case of cotton, so-called free competition had sometimes led to disastrous results, as foreign competitors had begun to take away market share from UK producers. His response was that British industry should be re-organised in order to regain these markets. This involved partly a traditional market response – the competitive restructuring of industry – and a partly socialised response – the planning of industrial structure and the social control of business behaviour. In fact the two went hand in hand.

In January 1927, Keynes was again in Manchester, addressing another meeting organised by the Committee of the Federation of Master Cotton Spinners. In this speech he characterised the banks that were involved in financing the cotton industry as 'professional deaf-mutes...some distinguished representatives of which I see here in person', as they were continuing to prop up unprofitable firms. He warned that there were 'plenty of people in Lancashire who would like to keep the spinners in a weak competitive position'; the notion of trying to 'win back markets by selling at a loss is cant'; and the real problem underlying everything was 'surplus capacity...there is no solution for anyone except in united action'.[14] A report of this speech was then published in a local newspaper, which is worth quoting for its insight into his personality as well as his policies:

> Mr. Keynes has an interesting presence...dark, with a high forehead and deep-set eyes, when he stood up to address the meeting he immediately obtained close attention. His hands thrust into the pockets of his open jacket, he was not so much an aggressive figure as of rock-like steadiness. He had calmness and poise...He spoke rapidly, but in a clear and cultured voice...In precise and direct tones he began swiftly to annihilate the various opposing schools of thought...It required courage thus to beard the lions in their den; courage to say that the banks were professional paralytics, and that the ignorance with which Lancashire carried on its trade was horrible...[15]

Throughout 1927, the Lancashire Cotton Yarn Association attempted valiantly to carry through a Keynes-type amalgamation plan, but with one essential flaw: not all producers became members, as membership had not been made compulsory. Only around 200 of the 350 firms spinning the coarser yarns joined. This meant that the minimum price and the quotas could still be undercut/exceeded by those beyond the Association's control. As Keynes explained in August 1927, outside firms could just underbid the Association's minimum price, without making any contribution towards the Association's regulation of output. He recommended in response that the British Board of Trade should extend Association rules to the whole industry.[16]

This flaw eventually proved fatal, however, and the Association was forced to abandon its central goals. In November 1927, the obligation to observe minimum selling prices was dropped. As Keynes duly explained, a cartel covering not more than 70 per cent of the industry was not strong enough for effective operation in conditions where demand declined to 50 per cent of total capacity. He was desperately disappointed that the Association's price control and quota idea had proved unsuccessful, and he gave vent to his barely-concealed anger in a passage of near-Shakespearean intensity. In part he blamed:

...the temper of the minority spinners, sturdy, independent, greedy, short-sighted, as full of Guelphs and Ghibellines of local jealousies and passions and ruthlessness to neighbours across the way, born of ancient feuds and ancestral struggles to survive. The Capulets of Royton will not lie down with the Montagus.[17]

He also blamed those in Manchester's larger industries, such as the export houses and the finishing trades, who exhibited 'a certain contempt for the small men, the spinners', an unhelpful attitude in impartial quarters of 'half-malicious hostility', and the underlying 'sterile unhelpfulness of the Manchester atmosphere' of business.[18]

On a more theoretical level, it might be asked what an economist of the stature of Keynes was thinking about with his advocacy of industrial cartels, which are currently illegal in the UK for their anti-competitive consequences. The answer was that he distinguished between two types of cartel: the first aimed at monopoly advantages either through tariffs or monopoly controls, while the second existed only to mitigate the evils of excess capacity through enabling rationalisation. Keynes only supported this second type in certain specific industrial circumstances, and remained opposed to the first type in principle.

All was not yet lost in Lancashire, however, as in January 1929, the Bank of England belatedly helped to organise a Lancashire Cotton Corporation, which as Keynes explained was a 'vast combine which will absorb at the start approaching one third of the whole industry – and perhaps much more before long'.[19] He supported this move wholeheartedly, and explained that such a vast combine was a significant step further than an Association or even a cartel, since:

...economies will come from several sources...To dispense with five hundred directors and reduce the host of independent managers, salesmen and secretaries will be something to begin with. The bulk buying...may be worth a good deal...A further integration with other branches of the cotton industry...may be the beginning of a movement which will transform the whole structure of Lancashire's traditional organisation.[20]

The Lancashire Cotton Corporation did continue to exist for some time, and had some success in halting the long-term decline, but its year of initial creation (1929) was not a fortuitous one from the point of view of the general economic weather. If such a radical solution had been attempted in the mid-1920s, rather than on the eve of the Great Depression, then the longer-term results might have been noticeably better.

Liberalism evolving

For Keynes, the effect of the sobering experience with what was called Lancashire progression to industrial perdition was to provide further support for his belief that the free competition assumed within *laissez faire* was not only an unrealistic model, but could be utterly disastrous in cases of its implementation. In January 1927, he delivered a speech entitled 'Liberalism and Industry' to the National Liberal Club, in which he analysed the new industrial reality in more theoretical terms. He declared that the old notion of numerous small capitalists staking their own fortune on their own firms was increasingly out of date. With a direct reference to his recent Lancashire experiences, he explained that:

> Businesses are increasingly owned by the public, who know nothing about the details of the true financial position of the concern, and they are run in their daily management by salaried persons who, perhaps, are risking little or nothing of their own fortunes...small investors who own these businesses have no power whatsoever of controlling them...[21]

This was a direct formulation of the increased separation of business ownership from control that had been developing within capitalism in the first few decades of the twentieth century. For Keynes, the solution was neither the 'anti-communist rubbish' of a return to competitive chaos, nor the 'anti-capitalist rubbish' of complete nationalisation, but rather 'the maximum degree of decentralisation which is compatible with large units and regulated competition'.[22]

He listed various policies that would assist in this regard: governmental responsibility for collecting economic data; governmental powers to provide preventative policies for industrial mishaps; concern that private investors could invest their savings with security; experimentation with new forms of partnership between the state and private enterprise; the conscious regulation of wages towards the betterment of workers' welfare; assistance in enabling the mobility of labour; and restoring a greater link between financial interests and the daily management of firms.[23] Such a 'vast programme' of economic reforms Keynes labelled as '*the* task lying to the hand of the new Liberalism', and he named his old adversary David Lloyd George as being a key supporter of such a plan within the Liberal Party.[24] This rapprochement with Lloyd George had been brewing for some time, as Keynes declared in June 1926 regarding splits in the Liberal Party that 'I support the line which Mr Lloyd George has taken lately and find myself thoroughly agreeing with him on policy for the first time for years'.[25]

As a measure of how important these issues were in the wider context of the UK's economic future, in July 1926 Lloyd George initiated an official investigation into many of them under the general title of a Liberal Industrial Inquiry. The membership included Keynes, Lloyd George, fellow economists such as D.H. Robertson, Hubert Henderson and Walter Layton, other Liberal politicians such as Herbert Samuel, and businessmen such as B.S. Rowntree and L.J. Cadbury. This Inquiry lasted through the second half of 1926 and until the end of 1927, and published a detailed report entitled *Britain's Industrial Future* in February 1928. Keynes's contribution to it was extensive, as he drafted various chapters on his own, as well as contributing to the composition of others. Although he supported the vast majority of what the report contained, after it was completed he commented jadedly that he hoped 'never again to be embroiled in cooperative authorship on this scale'.[26] One of his main criticisms was that the report was long-winded and would have been better and more useful at half the length.

The achievement of *Britain's Industrial Future* in terms of Keynes's goals was to flesh out in more detail the ideas about creating a mixed economy of socially controlled capitalism that were proposed only in outline in shorter works such as *The End of Laissez-Faire*. Some of these more specific ideas were: the creation of a National Investment Board to direct the accumulated investments of the public sector; the issue of National Investment Bonds; the creation of Public Boards for the management and control of state and semi-socialised enterprises; the making of a General Staff for economic understanding in order to co-ordinate governmental policy-making; the reform of private company accounts to overcome abuses such as insider information; the reform of National Budget accounts to provide a clearer indication of government actions; and greater restrictions on industrial monopolies through increased inspection.

Britain's Industrial Future was 'only' a Liberal Party proposal, albeit a detailed and substantial one; the British government had not officially commissioned it. Little of its content was directly and fully implemented, at least on its first issue. However, over the medium- and longer-term, some elements did find their way into official policy. For example, Keynes noted in May 1928 that 'Churchill has moved slightly in the direction recommended by the Liberal Industrial Inquiry in his proposed changes in the form of the Budget'.[27] In 1930, a special Economic Advisory Council was created by the Labour Government of the day, which resembled a General Staff of economists. After 1945, when state control of parts of British industry increased substantially, some public companies did find themselves under the control of Public Boards. It would be wrong to give the impression that this brand of ideas came solely from Keynes, as other economists and politicians proposed elements of them also, but he was certainly a major intellectual force behind developing them.

The Cambridge Circus

As Keynes's applied analysis was developing in response to ongoing world events, the economists that he interacted with in a University context were also evolving. In the second half of the 1920s, the group of people who would later become very important as members of a younger cohort of 'Keynesian' economists began to coalesce around Keynes in Cambridge. The term 'Keynesian' has here been placed in quotation marks, as it is an essentially contested concept: what it 'really' meant has been the subject of continuous debate, with different currents in economics having different understandings of its meaning. These later currents will not be considered here, but what was indisputable were the people that Keynes interacted with as he was writing his major works in economics from this period onwards.

In 1928, Austin Robinson came to Cambridge as a lecturer in economics after having graduated from Christ's College in 1921. In 1931 he published *The Structure of Competitive Industry*, and in 1934 he became assistant editor of the *Economic Journal* (alongside Keynes). He was married to Joan Robinson, also an economist who had graduated from Girton College in 1925. She was appointed as an assistant lecturer in 1931, and in 1933 published an important book entitled *The Economics of Imperfect Competition*. She also published some key later works that interpreted Keynes's contributions to economic theory in various specific ways. Already long established at Cambridge was A.C. Pigou, who had succeeded Alfred Marshall as Professor of Political Economy in 1907. In 1927 Pigou published a book entitled *Industrial Fluctuations*, which provided a summary and a typology of existing theories of the trade cycle, but did not provide that much that was really new.

Perhaps the single most important figure at Cambridge who had a direct, ongoing and personal influence on Keynes's economic theory across the 1920s was D.H. Robertson. Robertson was a lecturer in economics from 1924 onwards and also a Fellow of Trinity College. His 1915 work *A Study of Industrial Fluctuation* had exerted some early influence on Keynes's understanding of trade cycles, and also *vice versa*. Robertson's major contribution from the 1920s was *Banking Policy and the Price Level* of 1926, which again had been closely read and commented upon by Keynes in draft form. The favour was reciprocated, as Robertson provided detailed commentary on the substantial work in economic theory that Keynes was working on at the end of the 1920s. For example, towards the end of 1928 Keynes commented in an early draft of his new book that Robertson exerted 'a most salutary influence on contemporary thought'.[28] In turn, Robertson readily accepted that his own textbook on *Money* was partly Keynes's own work.

Another significant (if rather younger) associate was R.F. Kahn, who became Keynes's student in 1927 and then a Fellow of King's College in 1930. Kahn was a special favourite of Keynes, and it was Kahn who was instrumental in first developing the concept of the multiplier – the idea that a positive change in demand could have a cumulative effect on economic activity through compounded re-spending, and thus that the effect of an initial investment could be multiplied. Another important member of what would retrospectively be called 'the Cambridge Circus', appearing on the scene a little later, was James Meade. Meade was Oxford-educated but spent the period 1930–31 in Cambridge.

There has been much debate about who in these groupings influenced Keynes the most, in what manner was this done, in what particular stages of his development, and in respect to what elements of his theories. These questions will not be considered here, except to say that all these individuals had ongoing interactions with Keynes (and with each other) over a number of years, and that some degree of exchange and collective refinement of ideas must have occurred. What was unquestionable was that all of them (except perhaps Pigou and Robertson, who were not really members of the Circus) regarded Keynes as very much the leading figure at Cambridge, both in terms of his natural talent as a theorist, and also vis-à-vis his wider influence outside academia. This does not mean, however, that members of the Circus were afraid of disagreeing with Keynes if they believed he was wrong.

The Cambridge Circus was not really a formal 'school' of economics in the conventional sense, it was more like a convivial association of sometimes like-minded individuals who, for creative stimulation, interacted with each other profoundly over a significant period of time. This was partly the case because the theoretical foundations of the 'Keynesian' approach to economics had not yet been fully articulated, so the demarcation lines of a Cambridge 'school' of economists had yet to be invented. As later explained by Austin Robinson, the various younger economists at Cambridge at the end of the 1920s:

> ...formed a "circus" which met weekly for the discussion of the *Treatise*, and R.F. Kahn retailed to Keynes the results of our deliberations. We managed quickly to seize on the formal importance of some of the implied assumptions regarding employment and output levels and within a few weeks Keynes had not only seen the force of our criticisms...but was dashing ahead of us in re-deploying his ideas in terms of a variable level of employment.[29]

Later, across the 1930s, members of the Circus went their different intellectual ways; in particular, Robertson came to disagree with

Keynes's work to a considerable degree, but at the end of the 1920s, the fault lines that generated these later divergences were not yet fully apparent.

The storm clouds gather

In the period leading up to 1929, it is fair to say that few accurately predicted the scale and consequences of the economic downturn that would follow, and Keynes was no exception. Of course, the booms and slumps of the business cycle (the American terminology) or the upturns and downturns of the trade cycle (the British terminology) were well-accepted features of capitalism that many had analysed in detail before 1929. So were specific financial crises such as banking panics, asset bubbles or stock market crashes, although the outbreaks of these specific crises were not always linked to the more general progress of economic conjuncture in any consistent way. And individual financial crises could sometimes occur without causing a wider economic depression.

Up until this time, Keynes used the term 'credit cycle' to designate his own conception of 'standard' economic fluctuations, which to the non-economist might have given cycles the connotation of being tame technical features of the monetary system that had few wider consequences. What would follow after 1929 would banish forever the notion that periodic variations in industrial activity had little greater significance for the social and political world. What came later to be known as 'the Great Depression' was especially damaging for the world economy and important for economic theory, as many separate individual problems – a stock market crash, a banking crisis, a wider industrial downturn, mass unemployment, ongoing liquidity shortages and a prolonged period of depression – were combined together to form a toxic sequence of major economic disasters that had never before occurred to the degree and proximity that they did after 1929. And they never did again – until nearly eighty years later in 2008.

However, although no-one accurately forecast the exact timing and nature of the various elements that constituted the Great Depression, it would not be true to say that no-one had expressed concerns about how the economies of the West were developing in the period leading up to 1929. As already explained, Keynes was very concerned with problems in certain sectors of British industry after 1925, and he also expressed worries about the UK economy as a whole. For example, in July 1928 he published an analysis of wider issues under the provocative heading 'How to Organise a Wave of Prosperity'. The title itself implied that, if such prosperity were not consciously organised, then it would not occur, i.e. economic prosperity did not necessarily come about 'naturally' through the workings of the market system. In this article, Keynes brought together and refined various ideas that he had expressed up until this time in more isolated form.

The basic economic problem that Keynes identified as facing British industry as a whole was one he had been articulating for a number of years: a deflation of prices, in part due to the return to gold, but also due to credit controls and increased foreign competition, had been occurring, but a necessary deflation of costs had been absent, which had produced the disastrous combination of low profits and high unemployment. There were only three ways to deflate costs and thus to improve profits and employment levels in the future: by assaulting wages, which had proved impossible for political reasons; by rationalising and concentrating production, which many employers had been postponing in a forlorn hope of rising profits in the future; and by working existing plant and resources at full capacity, and thus improving unit costs. Keynes suggested that British industry might afford higher wages if it could work at 100 per cent effort, which it was not, and 'the increased purchasing power of a working population in full employment would react quickly and cumulatively on the prosperity of numberless industries'.[30] Here was found an early formulation of the concept of the economic multiplier.

Keynes was rightly cautious about whether an attempt to consciously organise prosperity in such a situation would be successful, but declared unambiguously that 'it ought to be tried'. As it was outside the power of individual businesses to take the initiative, the task of beginning the process fell to the Chancellor of the Exchequer and the Bank of England. The practical steps that Keynes recommended were: the Bank of England should increase the reserve resources of the joint-stock banks and thus facilitate the availability of more credit to businesses; the Bank of England must refrain from encouraging a deflationary atmosphere by relaxing its insistence that the gold reserve requirements of state banks should forever be fixed; and the Chancellor of the Exchequer should reverse his pressure against increased public spending.

Keynes then made a clear link between two elements of his favoured policies for organising prosperity that are not always highlighted by commentators:

> When we have unemployed men and unemployed plant and more savings than we are using at home, it is utterly imbecile to say that we cannot *afford* these things. *For it is with the unemployed men and the unemployed plant, and with nothing else, that these things are done.* To have labour and cement and steel and machinery and transport lying by, and to say that you cannot *afford* to embark on harbour works or whatever it may be is the delirium of mental confusion.[31]

The standard 'sound money' reply against schemes of public works was that the financial resources to command the unemployed men and plant were lacking, and should not be created out of nothing by printing additional money, which would be inflationary. But note Keynes's very clear solution in this passage: it was not by printing money that such resources should be put into action, but (in part) by retracting existing British savings that were currently invested overseas, and then by re-investing them back into the UK. There are a number of cautionary responses to this aspect of Keynes's solution: that such a supply of foreign investments did not exist (he clearly believed that it did); that it might be difficult to re-direct them in the manner suggested (this could be done by giving favourable tax rates to British investments as against foreign); or that the effect on foreign countries might be negative (Keynes gave priority to the British economy in this situation).

Some commentators have ignored this important aspect of Keynes's solution to the problem of organising prosperity in Britain – instead they have allowed the tacit misrepresentation to be propagated that he was (in 1928–29 at least) arguing solely for monetary expansion. Monetary expansion was part of the solution, but so equally was retracting foreign investments. This latter element was a theme that Keynes had been pursuing for a number of years, from as far back as 1924, and hence it was not an added extra that was tacked onto the analysis at the last minute.[32] It was an essential element on equal footing with the other measures for organising prosperity that he had outlined. As has been correctly identified, Keynes's policy advice for the UK in this period arose directly from his concern that a rise in foreign lending would automatically issue from a reduction in the interest rate, which was the standard monetary method of stimulating economic expansion.[33] As it was a rise in domestic lending that Keynes desired for the UK, not increased foreign lending, such a policy response would produce inadequate results.

The effects of overseas investment

Acutely aware of international developments, as early as October 1926 Keynes had questioned the wisdom of UK investors 'gaily lending almost as usual to smarten up the emporiums of our trade rivals – Tokyo, Hamburg, or wherever' at a time when the UK economy was facing a coal strike.[34] The UK would jeopardise its economic revival after the strike was over, if the flow of future savings was allowed to drain away into foreign loans. The solution that Keynes recommended in 1926 was an official governmental embargo on foreign investment from the UK, as:

> ...it is broadly efficient on the whole in attaining the desired end of checking new foreign investment by the great body of ordinary investors. We ought to devise a permanent centralised control for the regulation of foreign investment. [35]

The idea prevalent among many economists that a *laissez faire* attitude to overseas lending would automatically correct itself, if problems with the flow of savings to the UK arose, was 'obsolete and dangerous', as this area of the economy was not one that should be left to the 'irresponsible actions of individuals'. Although problems with the effective policing of such embargoes were sometimes raised, Keynes believed that overall they were worth considering; in fact, they were actually used by the Bank of England in this period, but only in a semi-official manner and sporadically, and not as part of a coherent set of policies directed to the common goal here outlined.[36]

He did not at all give up on this theme as time progressed; rather he added new layers of argument to it. Consider the following passage from an article by Keynes entitled 'The British Balance of Trade, 1925–27' that was published in December 1927:

> ...foreign investment since 1924, both by Great Britain and the United States...has not translated itself...into a demand either for goods or for gold, but has been hoarded in liquid form in the foreign centre where the borrowing has occurred...We and the United States have been continually creating purchasing power for foreigners on a very generous scale in relation to our true surpluses, but they have not been using it.[37]

As Keynes explained in another article from March 1929, 'the volume of foreign investment has tended, I think, to adjust itself – at least to a certain extent – to the balance of trade, rather than the other way round'.[38] What was meant here was that any additional foreign investment, if it exceeded an amount that corresponded to the balance of trade generated by the economic structures of the two countries involved, might well remain idle. Keynes evidently believed that the UK had been investing overseas to a degree that exceeded the natural structure of the balance of trade between the UK and the foreign countries in question, which was why such overseas investment was being wastefully hoarded. Hence, this excess foreign investment could be returned to the UK for use in bolstering home investment, and this would have little detrimental effect on the countries from which it was being withdrawn.

Keynes explained more about this aspect of his solution in an article entitled 'A Cure for Unemployment' published in April 1929. Here he clearly identified the 'orthodox Treasury dogma' – the idea that no additional permanent employment could be created by increased state expenditure – as fallacious. As savings did not automatically materialise in investments, it was possible that some definite amount might remain idle. By extrapolation, savings also did not automatically materialise in home investments, as they might go overseas instead. Hence, one available source of funds for increased capital investment in Britain:

> ...will be found by a reduction of foreign lending. But this will not operate...by a reduction of our exports...partly it will take

the form of an increase in our imports; for the new schemes will require a certain amount of imported raw materials...[39]

As Keynes had indicated in 'The British Balance of Trade, 1925–27', at least a portion of British overseas investment had been hoarded, and hence curtailing this investment would not necessarily result in the reduction of exports out of the UK, as such exports had not been increased by the overseas investment in the first place. Retracting foreign investments would not, therefore, necessarily have a significant dampening effect on the UK's export industries.

Keynes was so convinced of the importance of this policy that he included it as one of three strategic methods of funding increased state investment in his political broadside programme of expansion written together with Hubert Henderson, and published as a Liberal pamphlet in May 1929 under the 'edge-of-your-seat' title *Can Lloyd George Do It?* Austin Robinson characterised this pamphlet as 'of much more than ephemeral interest', as it first analysed 'the cost to the community of putting men to work' by government-supported means.[40] Keynes and Henderson admitted that:

> The embargo was a crude instrument, suitable only for temporary use...But the need which that embargo was designed to supply still remains...we are investing abroad dangerously much... partly because there are insufficient outlets for our savings at home. It follows, therefore, that a policy of capital expenditure... would serve mainly to divert to home development savings which now find their way abroad...[41]

Diminishing the volume of foreign issues 'would be welcomed by the Bank of England' as the UK exchange position was precarious, this being the Bank's own reason for maintaining a semi-official embargo a year or two earlier. But for Keynes and Henderson, this reason had been only a partial one, as there was a far more important justification for restricting foreign issues: its effect on UK investment.

Keynes presented a clinching argument on this issue in an article entitled 'The Bank Rate' published in October 1929. Here he identified a rather astonishing fact: the UK had in the recent past been lending overseas on its capital account at a rate that exceeded the level of the surplus on its trading account. The UK's trade surplus with overseas countries, i.e. the excess of exports out of the UK over imports into it, was less than the amount it was lending to foreign countries as investment. This had necessitated an increase in the UK interest rate from 5½ per cent to 6½ per cent in September 1929. This was required in turn in order to discourage the outflow of gold from the Bank of England to overseas countries, which had been needed to cover the excess of British lending overseas compared with the UK's trade surplus. Thus, the UK had been 'shooting itself in the investment foot' by such an excess of foreign transfers.

This was because a higher interest rate would have a detrimental effect on the level of home investment in the UK, as higher payments would be due on any money borrowed to fund increased investments at home. Keynes hoped in response that:

> ...the discouragement to loans to foreign countries will be as great as possible, and that investors will be reluctant, for the present, to subscribe to new loans to overseas. For the prime purpose of raising the Bank Rate is, on this occasion, to diminish our foreign lending...[42]

Thus, according to Keynes, the UK authorities were in the autumn of 1929 trying themselves to effect a reduction of UK investment that was directed overseas.

Some commentators have not fully understood this crucial aspect to Keynes's thinking at the end of the 1920s. For example, it has been declared rightly that Keynes advocated mobilising savings that had been going abroad, but then wrongly asserted that he 'had not explained why this would increase employment' in the UK.[43] The answer was clear: it would increase UK employment by enabling greater investment in UK domestic industry, and it would not simultaneously detract a similar amount from the UK's export industries, as these had not been bolstered to a large degree by the overseas investment anyway. Other commentators have accepted this element to Keynes's thinking, but have provided various criticisms: that it was only a remedy for one country alone (correct, but Keynes was concerned with the UK at this time), and that it would be necessary to offer higher interest rates compared to foreign borrowers in order to attract increased home investment (not necessarily, as either physical or tax restrictions could be placed on foreign investments).[44] Keynes did sometimes suggest higher interest rates for home investments, but as the previous commentator actually admitted, 'a tax or an embargo on foreign loans' could constitute other plausible methods of achieving reduced foreign investment.[45]

Of course, this latter policy would be anti-free trade: but Keynes at this time was precisely articulating an economic philosophy based on the idea that the dogmas of free trade were damaging and unrealistic. Why would he baulk at the idea that state controls should influence the balance of domestic and overseas investment? His own previous idea for a National Investment Board demonstrated that he had been articulating a mechanism for such controls for some time. And in *A Treatise on Money* of 1930, Keynes's most substantial work on economic theory up until this date, the author explicitly recommended 'differential terms for home investment relatively to foreign investment' in certain instances.[46] In 1930 he also considered treating foreign government bonds and foreign company shares differently, i.e. allowing overseas investments in the latter, as they represented enterprises that offered the possibility of 'a real bonanza', but not in the former, as the returns from bonds were fixed and generally somewhat lower.[47]

Other arguments against Keynes's position are more complex. Would a reduction in overseas investment really have had little impact on British exports in the period under review? But for such a policy to make sense, it would not have to be true that such a reduction should have no effect on UK exports, only that the downward effect on exports would be less than the gains made within UK industry through increased home investment. In a letter to *The Economist* in March 1929, Keynes did accept that foreign lending could sometimes stimulate British exports, but the killer point was the damaging mechanism by which this was achieved. Foreign investment would increase exports 'because it will make the maintenance of full employment impossible at the present level of wages, so that unemployment will continue until British wages are reduced'.[48] Thus, foreign investments by UK funds were, according to Keynes, actually generating unemployment and reduced wages for workers back home in the UK.

In truth, finally resolving this issue was an empirical question that would have required a calculation of the various factors involved in order to come to a definite answer. Such techniques and complete information were not readily available to those debating this question at the end of the 1920s, so it is not fair to criticise Keynes for not providing an elaborate calculation: neither did his opponents. However, he did in March 1929 indicate as a rough guide that he thought 'not more than 20% of the money lent [overseas] created additional exports'.[49] This meant in turn that he thought a significant portion of the money lent abroad could be returned without curtailing UK exports, as long as the appropriate foreign investments were selected.

One contemporaneous estimate of the overall magnitude of the figures involved was that in 1928 alone, total overseas capital issues on the London market amounted to £143 million.[50] In May 1929, Keynes presented a similar figure of £125 million for the UK's annual 'investment abroad'.[51] As a comparison, the Liberal Party state investment programme articulated by Keynes proposed that the UK government should spend £100 million a year extra for three years, in order to increase UK employment significantly.[52] Of course the first and the last figures were not directly comparable: 'overseas capital issues' were not the same as investment in foreign countries, and Keynes was certainly not suggesting that overseas investment should be forced down to zero, only that it should be substantially reduced. But without question, the scale of foreign investments that were made by UK sources at this time was large.

This raises indirectly one further potential criticism of Keynes's idea of withdrawing overseas investment: its possible impact on London as an international financial centre. If direct physical controls on capital flows, or even indirect financial controls through differential taxation, were placed on foreign investments made by the London investment market, it seems reasonable to assume that this policy could have exerted a negative effect on London as an institution. As Keynes was a pre-eminent expert on the UK's financial markets, it can only be assumed that he thought either that such an effect would be minimal, or that this was a price worth paying, if UK employment and business prospects could be substantially improved.

Keynes received some definite support for such policies from his Cambridge colleague D.H. Robertson. In his evidence given to the Macmillan Committee on Finance and Industry in May 1930, Robertson argued that if private individuals in the UK tried to invest abroad on a bigger scale than had recently been occurring, then they should 'be stopped by some discouragement of foreign investment, by differential taxation or any other way'.[53] Robertson also added a new element to Keynes's argument: an attempt to force UK exports above the existing level should not be made, instead any free investment resources should be used 'in other directions', i.e. to produce goods that would be consumed at home. Robertson explicitly called this policy 'increased national self-sufficiency', a theme that Keynes would soon be echoing.[54]

Even R.G. Hawtrey, a well-known supporter of the 'Treasury view' of public-works ineffectiveness, submitted a separate memorandum to the Macmillan Committee, in which he acknowledged that the diversion of investment funds from external to internal use was a possible means of increasing UK investment, without having to elevate government expenditure. He did raise some potential problems about how a differential tax (for example) would affect the investment market overall, but he did not completely reject the idea in principle.[55] Thus Keynes was not alone in identifying reduced foreign investment as a possible source of increased UK business activity at the end of the 1920s.

Unemployed savings equals unemployed people

It would be inaccurate to give the impression that withdrawing overseas funds was the only source of increased home investment that Keynes identified in this period, although it is today the most commonly neglected. The other more often acknowledged sources were: harnessing UK savings that were being kept idle through the lack of availability of credit, savings made through reduced welfare payments to the unemployed following increased employment, and a cumulative impulse to prosperity once the increased investment had begun to operate. Perhaps the most controversial of these was the first: was there really a pot of unused savings lying idle somewhere in British financial institutions, that could be put to work with some simple encouragement? Here was a crucial point of intersection between Keynes the theoretical economist and Keynes the practical policy adviser.

According to those who opposed the idea that the UK government should fund increased capital investments as a cure for unemployment, 'all the savings of the country, or approximately all, find their outlet in employment'.[56] That they did so naturally was what Keynes in 1929 called 'the Treasury dogma'. But he disagreed with this idea fundamentally. Instead he argued that:

> ...savings...do not necessarily materialise in investments. The amount of investment in capital improvements depends, on the one hand, on the amount of credit created by the Bank of England; and, on the other hand, on the eagerness of entrepreneurs to invest...So far from the total of investment, as determined by these factors, being necessarily equal to the total of savings, disequilibrium between the two is at the root of many of our troubles.[57]

Thus, the actual level of investment was determined by the supply of credit and entrepreneurial impulses, while the actual level of saving was determined by the returns that were available from interest and the thrift-habits of individuals. There was no necessary reason why these two elements would always be equal. There could be circumstances envisaged in which, due to the low availability of credit and fears about the economic situation, savings exceeded investment by a significant amount. According to Keynes, this type of disequilibrium had caused the UK unemployment situation at the end of the 1920s. The solution was to encourage the unused savings back into active investments through government policies. He was so sure of the notion that, if the total investment of a country was less than its current savings, then it was 'absolutely certain that business losses and unemployment *must* ensue', that he fearlessly promised to the Governor of the Bank of England in May 1930 that 'I am ready to have my head chopped off if it is false!'.[58]

The notion that there was a pot of unused savings that could be put to work to cure unemployment was very convenient, and also very controversial. It was easy and eye-catching to make such a bold claim, but more difficult to substantiate it with detailed facts and financial data. That Keynes found it difficult to supply all the required data for 'idle savings' was evident from a letter that he published in *The Times* in August 1929. In this letter he highlighted six sources where the hypothesised £100 million per year for the Liberal Party investment scheme could be found. They were: 1) savings made through employed spending rather than unemployed spending; 2) additional home production of consumption goods generated by the increased capital investment; 3) higher Treasury tax receipts from the proposed increased production; 4) reduction of foreign lending; 5) an increase in credit due to more wages and business receipts in circulation; 6) an increase in credit in itself.[59] 'Idle savings' were not now mentioned specifically, although they might conceivably be found within items five or six.

Keynes supplied some numerical estimates of what could be obtained by these six sources. One, two, three and five together would generate £75 million, and four and six together the remaining £25 million. Note that the majority of the scheme was self-funding, as sources one, two, three and five were generated by the very act of the state increasing its own investment. Only items four and six involved sources outside the processes being advocated. Source six was what 'the Treasury dogma' so opposed (forced credit expansion), and source four was the retraction of overseas investment that has already been considered in detail. Consequently, opponents of such a scheme found an easy target in response: the notion of the majority of it being funded by its own results was declared as wishful thinking and tautological.

There was another more intangible element of a Keynes-type government investment stimulus programme that has yet to be considered. The authors of *Can Lloyd George Do It?* wrote of the expectation of state-funded schemes being implemented as providing an 'immediate fillip' to trade, i.e. they proposed the operation of a positive psychological effect on business sentiment. Much mainstream economic theory had traditionally been rather sceptical about the relevance of psychology to economics, instead favouring the search for objective laws akin to those of the natural sciences. Perhaps in part because Keynes had become sceptical of the *laissez faire* ideology of free trade, he was more open to considering the effects of psychology and sentiment on investment behaviour.

Conclusion

By 1930, Keynes had gone a long way towards producing a more sophisticated explanation of business cycles that looked, at least to some significant extent, beyond traditional mechanical notions of equilibrium being automatically maintained within an economy. From this explanation emanated various concrete policies for improving the specific employment and business difficulties that were being encountered in the UK at the end of the 1920s. However, although the basic outlines of this new approach were present in much of his policy writings from this period, its more substantial theoretical expression would only occur in the book that Keynes had been composing across the second half of the 1920s, but which did not finally appear until 1930. The next chapter will consequently examine this work, and its link to more immediate policy issues, in more detail.

12 It all comes out in the wash

The publication of *A Treatise on Money* in October 1930 was the culmination of Keynes's ongoing work on monetary theory and trade cycles across the whole period since 1918. It was certainly his longest book, issued in two thick volumes and a total of nearly 800 pages. It is also not that easy to follow straight through from beginning to end, containing numerous subtle definitions of economic quantities that are then linked by means of various interconnected equations. Thankfully, the meaning of these equations is explained clearly in words, but these explanations are themselves complex and demanding, and hence the reader frequently has to pause in order to 'come up for air': I doubt whether many people have read the entire *Treatise* from beginning to end in one continuous sitting. And compared to Keynes's previous books, such as *The Economic Consequences of the Peace* and *A Tract on Monetary Reform*, there was less discussion of the wider socio-political context of the economic ideas being considered, although there were a few chapters devoted to a consideration of historical examples in the second volume.

In the following chapter, some of the basic features of the book will be explained and its wider significance discussed, but it is as well to admit that every element of such a long and complex work cannot be fully considered in a relatively short chapter; hence this chapter cannot claim to provide a comprehensive guide to every feature, nuance and debate in the book.

The basic elements

Keynes ended the two volumes of *A Treatise on Money* with the apparently self-deprecating statement that 'Monetary Theory, when all is said and done, is little more than a vast elaboration of the truth that "it all comes out in the wash"'.[1] What was meant was the quantity theory-style supposition that, in the long run, many monetary (and other) factors were 'flushed through' the economic system leaving little long-term impact. But, and this was a very important but, in the short- and medium-run, they could have very significant impact, i.e. the precise nature of 'the wash' was what monetary economics should be concerned with.

Remember Keynes's famous quip that 'In the long run, we are all dead': consequently, the situation after 'the wash' was completed, was irrelevant to the immediate concerns of most people. The real question was: what happened to specific variables like savings, investment, the price level, the demand for money and so on as they went through the process of 'the wash'? This was part of the task that Keynes set himself in the book, to explain how equilibrium and disequilibrium were established and then lost, as an economy went through the sometimes-painful experience of 'flushing' various changing quantities through itself.

At the heart of the explanation of economic fluctuations, in Keynes's 1930 view, were two key variables: savings and investment. The purchasing power of money, or in other words the general price level (in relation to the goods and services required for consumption in a community):

> ...oscillates below or above the equilibrium level according as the cost of current investment is running ahead of, or falling behind, savings. A principal object of this Treatise is to show that we have here the clue to the way in which fluctuations of the price-level actually come to pass...[2]

This statement was the crux of Keynes's explanation of the changes in the price level (and other quantities) that were known as trade cycles. It was not simply monetary factors that were causing the oscillations of trade, but the overall relation between savings and investment. A key realisation that he had come to by 1930 was that there was no natural mechanism that automatically brought actual investment in line with actual savings, i.e. the two quantities could diverge, at least for a definite period of time. Thus, there were three possible scenarios for any given period. Savings could equal investment, savings could exceed investment, or savings could be less than investment. The consequences for the economic system of departing from and regaining this equilibrium between savings and investment was the essential driving force behind the changes that were called variously the trade cycle, business fluctuations, or the economic weather.

As was sketched in the previous chapter, what actually determined the level of investment and the level of savings in any given period were two entirely different things. The scale and the terms on which the banking system granted loans and other monetary facilities to businesses set the rate of investment. The decision of the community as a whole as to how much they spent and how much they saved set the rate of savings:

> ...therefore, as the banking system is allowing the rate of investment to exceed or fall behind the rate of saving, the price-level...will rise or fall...But this disparity between investment and saving sets up a disequilibrium in the rate of profit...[3]

If savings equalled investment, then the price level would be stable, which corresponded to the average rate of remuneration on factors of production. If credit was available to businesses at terms lower than the equilibrium level, prices would increase as demand rose, and more profits would be made, until such time as the terms of credit were brought back to their equilibrium level. If credit was available to businesses at terms higher than the equilibrium level, prices would decline as demand fell, and less profits would be made, until such time as the terms of credit were brought back to their equilibrium level. Thus, booms and slumps were simply the result of the oscillation in the terms of credit around their equilibrium level, these terms being determined partly by the policies of the banking sector, and partly by the decisions of the community about how much to save.[4]

This approach to explaining trade cycles diverged significantly from what could (for simplicity) be called the classical theory of economic equilibrium. In the classical theory, it was the function of the interest rate to bring continuous equilibrium to the supply and demand for credit, which would also bring savings and investment into balance. Keynes accepted that such a rate existed in theory, and he called it the natural-rate of interest. However, those who set the actual interest rate considered not only whether it would bring balance to the supply and demand for credit or to savings and investment, but also many other factors such as the wider state of business, the supply and demand for money, confidence in the currency, the state of the bond market and so on. This meant that the actual rate of interest, what Keynes called the market-rate, often diverged from the natural-rate, i.e. the rate that brought equilibrium to the credit market:

> Thus the natural-rate of interest is the rate at which saving and the value of investment are exactly balanced…Every departure of the market-rate from the natural-rate tends, on the other hand, to set up a disturbance of the price-level…[5]

Moreover, the interest rate also affected the degree of investment and the degree of savings. The higher the interest rate, the more businesses had to pay to borrow money in order to increase their investment, and the less they would invest; similarly, the higher the interest rate, the more savers would be encouraged to increase their level of savings. Overall, an increase in the interest rate would tend to force the rate of investment to fall relative to the rate of savings. But there was no necessary reason why the market-rate would automatically create a position of equilibrium between the two, i.e. would exactly balance savings with investment. Keynes was beginning to think in terms outside of the confines of the neoclassical approach that had so disastrously failed to prevent the onset of the Great Depression.

Enough of the analysis has now been provided to demonstrate that, above all, Keynes was in 1930 concerned to show how various types of disequilibrium were generated, and how these disequilibria would work their way through the economic system. In this sense the phrase 'it all comes out in the wash' applied not only to monetary changes, but also to changes in investment, savings, consumption and production. All the disequilibria created by the various influences affecting these economic quantities were, however, not permanent, as they created new situations out of which a tendency towards the re-establishment of equilibrium would follow. In this sense Keynes still partially adhered to the classical doctrine of automatic harmony. But where he diverged was in insisting that the economy rarely remained in a position of stable equilibrium for very long, implying that disequilibrium was a more common reality for much of the time. And if this was the case, then economists should make more of an effort to understand these periods of temporary but frequent disequilibrium, rather than assuming that a state of full equilibrium was the natural one. Keynes had reached nearly half way towards the 'new economics' that he would invent a few years later in *The General Theory*.

One final innovative element of the 'pure' part of *A Treatise on Money* requires consideration. The actual rate of interest, what Keynes called the market-rate, was in reality divided into long-term market rates (for example those on government bonds), short-term market rates (for example those on three-month bills of exchange) and then the official Bank rate set by the monetary authorities. Long-term rates were 'sticky' in relation to mimicking changes in the natural-rate, while the Bank rate affected short-term rates more than long-term. Part of Keynes's originality was to direct greater attention to 'the complex of interest rates effective in the market at any time', suggesting that actual rates which prevailed in private markets were not necessarily a simple reflection of the official rate set by the Central Bank.[6] Understanding what was later called 'the term structure of interest rates' was thus important to explaining how equilibrium and disequilibrium were generated.

The international dimension

The above analysis applied to economies of individual nation-states, but *A Treatise on Money* also contained a substantial consideration of international factors. As was explained previously, one source of increased funds for UK investment that Keynes had identified in his policy writings across the second half of the 1920s was the withdrawal of funds from overseas sources. It might consequently be expected that in *A Treatise on Money*, Keynes would explain this element in more detail. And in a sub-section of a chapter presenting the fundamental equations of money entitled 'Foreign Lending and the Foreign Balance' this was indeed the case.

He defined two basic quantities as follows. The foreign balance (B) was the excess of home-owned output placed at the disposal of foreigners (exports), over foreign-owned output in UK hands (imports). Foreign lending (L) was the excess of the amount of UK money put at the disposal of foreigners (investments abroad), compared to the amount expended by foreigners on investments in the UK. An equation related these two elements as follows:

$$L = B + G$$

G was the amount of gold exported out of the UK. Hence, if the foreign balance (B) were less than foreign lending (L), the difference would have to be made up through the export of gold.[7] Keynes identified the existence of a 'traditional doctrine' here, which was that foreign lending automatically stimulated the foreign balance, i.e. that increased exports automatically resulted from increased foreign investment, and hence additional exports of gold would not be necessary to balance the two. He then questioned whether this was always the case, as an outflow of gold might instead be the result, if some other conditions were also met.[8]

In Keynes's model, the basic condition of external equilibrium for a country was that L = B (foreign lending equalled the foreign balance). However, since the foreign balance depended on relative prices at home and abroad, but foreign lending depended on relative interest rates at home and abroad, there was no automatic link between the two, and therefore disequilibrium was a possibility.[9] However, there was a radical difference between a disequilibrium created by price level divergences, and a disequilibrium created by interest rate divergences. In the former case, the cure was simply a change in price or income levels without any change in interest rates, but in the latter case a change in price levels and also in interest rates would be necessary. Changes in interest rates affected the capacity for future investment, and had a greater knock-on effect in the economy than only price changes.

At the end of volume one of *A Treatise on Money*, Keynes explained the importance of this emphasis on international investment for the UK. An increase in the demand for investment overseas was capable, in certain circumstances, of producing a fall in money-earnings at home, as it could cause an outflow of gold that might only stop when money-earnings at home had fallen sufficiently compared to money-earnings abroad.[10] In effect, investing abroad could function as a way to reduce the comparative standard of living of the investing country compared to that of the recipient country. Keynes left it to the reader to work out in frightening detail:

> ...what a pickle a country might get into if a higher rate of interest abroad...leads to most of its savings being lent abroad, whilst at the same time there are tariffs abroad against most of its exports and a tendency to raise these tariffs from time to time to balance the gradually rising level of costs in the protected country...[11]

In this particular instance, the suckered investing country would be blindly digging its own economic grave by means of its foreign investments.

In order to analyse more accurately the effects of foreign investment on a lending country in any given instance, Keynes created an equation that could calculate the net national gain (NNG) or loss across any two specific periods of time:

$$NNG = s.L' - E_2 (p_1 - p_2) + F_2 (q_1 - q_2).$$

where the subscripts referred to two time periods (the old position and the new position), E was the volume of exports, F the volume of imports, s the proportionate rise in the interest rate, L' the amount of foreign lending in the new position, and p and q the prices of exports and imports respectively. Through this equation any loss through the fall in prices of exports relative to prices of imports was subtracted from any gain in the advantage of foreign lending through a rise in the interest rate $(s.L')$, to see whether there was an overall loss or gain. Keynes admitted that this equation neglected certain other elements involved, but concluded agnostically about net national gain that 'I see no presumption in favour of this quantity being positive rather than negative', i.e. there could well be an overall loss from foreign investment in some instances.[12] It is evident that Keynes considered this issue to be very important, as he had dealt with it both in his policy writings and theoretically, in *A Treatise on Money*. Here he also raised additional issues on the best form of an international monetary system that deserve some consideration.

The problem of national autonomy

In the second volume of *A Treatise on Money*, devoted to the applied theory, Keynes provided a more concrete analysis of what so worried him about excessive international investments by the UK. In the nineteenth century, the UK was the 'conductor of the international orchestra' of foreign investment, as London was the only major global trading market, and this enabled a successful *laissez faire* attitude to prosper. However, British economists had erroneously 'attributed the actual success of her *laissez-faire* policy, not to the transitory peculiarities of her position, but to the sovereign virtues of *laissez-faire* as such'.[13] After 1914, New York had become a rival to London as a funnel of international investments, in part because the financial strength of the UK had been seriously affected by the war. As a result, the relative importance of the London market had been substantially reduced, and the consequences of large levels of foreign investment flowing out of the UK would be greater.

This led Keynes to consider a wider question: the problem of national autonomy with respect to the international standard of value and fixed exchange rates, which was another reason to question the wisdom of the UK using the gold standard. In an ideal international gold standard system, differences in national interest rates inevitably produced gold flows towards those countries with higher rates, until uniformity of rates was re-established. However, for Keynes this would mean that the degree of an individual country's power of independent action over interest rates 'would have no relation to its local needs'.[14] Thus, the dilemma of an international monetary system was to maintain the advantages of local currency stability, and 'to preserve at the same time an adequate local autonomy for each member over its domestic rate of interest and its volume of foreign lending'.[15] For Keynes, the diminution of national autonomy that the use of the international gold standard system entailed was another reason why the UK should not have been using it after 1925.

Keynes finally outlined the concrete measures that he believed should be applied in order to reduce foreign lending out of the UK. Firstly, foreign bonds should not be traded on any UK stock exchange except with the prior approval of the Bank of England. Secondly, British holders of securities that had not received the *imprimatur* of the Bank of England should pay higher taxes on the income received. Thirdly, London's international short-term deposit business should be clearly segregated from its domestic business, so that any new regulations that applied to the former did not automatically apply to the latter. At another point in the book, he raised the possibility of providing subsidies to home investments, in order to neutralise any advantages of returns on foreign investments, 'so as to bridge the difference between the market-rate of interest…and the natural-rate of interest at which a profitable outlet could be found at home'.[16] By these various means, the level of foreign investment could be controlled to a degree that was in the long-term interest of the UK, a policy that Keynes in 1930 believed was crucial to maintaining the UK's future economic prosperity.

Explaining the slump

How did all these planks of analysis come together to explain the profound economic difficulties of the early 1930s? At the very end of *A Treatise on Money*, Keynes discussed what he called 'the world-wide slump of 1930' and its basic causes. Using the theoretical framework outlined in the first section of this chapter as his foundation, he blamed 'an unusually wide gap between the ideas of borrowers and those of lenders, that is, between the natural-rate of interest and the market-rate', which had persisted in many countries across the post-war period. By this he meant that actual interest rates had been far higher than they should have been vis-à-vis long-run economic trends, this being for various contingent reasons such as post-war reconstruction, reparations payments, a long line of 'distress borrowers' ready to pay higher rates and the inappropriate return to gold. This meant that, eventually, borrowers for genuine purposes of making new investments had been squeezed out of the credit market, which in turn had produced a decline in demand for investment goods, a falling price level and then the onset of a self-propagating 'slump' psychology. The stock market collapse in 1929 was only a secondary cause of the economic decline, but once it had occurred, it aggravated the situation by further discouraging investment and lowering the natural-rate of interest.

A lasting economic recovery would not occur until the market-rate of interest fell internationally to near its pre-war level, but this would not happen naturally. The remedy was a deliberate policy of controlling the rate of investment so as to assist in the reduction of the market-rate of interest towards its long-term natural-rate. Keynes consequently recommended that banks should offer private depositors the very low figure of 0.5 per cent as interest, that the government should lend to local authorities and public boards at the low rate of 3 per cent when the proposed investment schemes were new and immediate, and that the government should place a large amount at the disposal of a newly-formed Bankers' Industrial Development Company at 3 per cent in order to re-equip the private industries of the UK.[17] This latter policy would be a subsidy to private investment in the home market so as to divert funds away from foreign investment. Thus by 1930, Keynes had fully accepted the need for conscious intervention in the economy both in specific policy terms and also in more general theoretical terms, but still conceived of this intervention as a means of getting the 'natural' movement towards equilibrium back on track.

As *A Treatise on Money* was designed mainly for professional economists, it gave only short intimations of Keynes's wider socio-political analysis of the slump. In October 1930, he published an article entitled 'Economic Possibilities for our Grandchildren' that gave such a wider analysis in non-technical terms. He believed that to see the slump and associated pessimism as an indication that a long epoch of continuous economic progress was over was mistaken; rather it represented only the 'growing-pains of over-rapid changes', a painful readjustment caused by one period of development transmuting into another.[18] He expressed a firm belief that wealth creation would in the long run continue unabated, and that when in the future wealth had accumulated beyond a certain point 'there will be great changes in the code of morals'.

This reference to morals brought Keynes partially back to his youthful concern with the philosophy of ethics. In perhaps one of the most unexpected passages ever to be penned by a mainstream

Western economist, Keynes then characterised the love of money purely as a possession as 'detestable' and as a 'disgusting morbidity, one of those semi-criminal, semi-pathological propensities which one hands over with a shudder to the specialists in mental disease'.[19] For someone who had just published a two-volume work called *A Treatise on Money* this was a rather surprising admission. But it demonstrated clearly his existential anger with those (mainly in the business and financial worlds) who had acted at the end of the 1920s without any concern for the wider consequences of their actions.

Conclusion

A number of more general observations about *A Treatise on Money* are worth making. Firstly, although many commentators have pointed out that it still employed the 'traditional' framework of fluctuations around an equilibrium level to provide its underlying theoretical explanation of cycles, it is noticeable how often, when providing examples of what was meant in concrete instances, Keynes turned instead to institutional and behavioural explanations such as investor psychology, traditional customs of financial behaviour and context-specific economic policies. For example, when discussing the factors that influenced the movement of security prices, he declared that the market price of a stock was not determined by the value of 'the whole block of the outstanding interest' of a going concern:

> ...but by the small fringe which is the subject of actual dealing...
> Now this fringe is largely dealt in by professional financiers...It
> is natural, therefore, that they should be influenced...by their
> expectations on the basis of past experience of the trend of mob
> psychology.[20]

Even worse, the vast majority of those who were concerned with buying and selling securities 'know almost nothing whatever about what they are doing', as they did not possess 'even the rudiments of what is required for a valid judgement' about long-run future economic trends and conditions, instead falling prey to 'transient events' and easily aroused fears.[21] Such a stark characterisation of capitalist investors was not often found in neoclassical economics, although both A.C. Pigou and Alfred Marshall had emphasised that forecasting errors had a role in determining investment decisions.[22]

Furthermore, in relation to the desired hypothetical equilibrium between savings and investments, according to Keynes there was always a 'fringe of unsatisfied borrowers' that remained after banks had made their investment loan choices, as banks lent money not only in response to changes in the interest rate obtainable from customers, but also in respect of 'the borrower's purpose and his standing with the bank'.[23] This 'borrower rationing', today officially called credit rationing, meant that bank lending could produce investment effects out of all proportion to those which corresponded to the changes that were occurring to the interest rate. Such institutional factors meant that equilibrium between savings and investment could be more difficult to create, as even if the market-rate of interest coincided with the natural-rate, banks operated additional factors of control over their loans.

Secondly, as Keynes readily admitted, *A Treatise on Money* was the result of a mind in continuous creative flux, or as he declared in the preface to the book, 'my ideas have been developing and changing, with the result that its parts are not all entirely harmonious with one another'.[24] One example of this potential disharmony was the tension between his apparent equilibrium-style claim that 'it all comes out in the wash', and the more specific analyses of particular instances of financial behaviour that he provided, where few tendencies towards automatic harmony could be detected. Some hostile reviewers picked up upon this disharmony in a major way.

For example, the Austrian economist F.A. Hayek provided one of the most substantial early criticisms in a two-part article for the journal *Economica*. Hayek admitted that the book was stimulating, but argued that Keynes's analysis of the concept of investment was obscure and inadequate, as it failed to consider changes in the value of existing capital across the business cycle, and how its replacement affected the investment process. This meant in turn that Keynes's explanation of cycles was incorrect, as he had not considered changes to the structure of capitalist production (the lengthening or shortening of the average period of manufacture as capital was renewed), which he had erroneously relegated to only a long-run phenomenon. Thus, what had been provided was only a variant on the existing purchasing-power fluctuation explanation of cycles.

Keynes was rather stung by Hayek's criticism, suggesting rather mutedly in reply that Hayek had 'misapprehended the character of my conclusions', but privately he recognised that the book was significantly less than perfect. Another related criticism to emerge was that some of Keynes's conclusions required the illicit assumption that output was fixed and not variable, a partial consequence of the long-standing dichotomy between the theory of money and the theory of employment that he had (only partially successfully) attempted to overcome.[25] And as he acknowledged in the book, the key notion of a distinction between the natural-rate and the market-rate of interest was not entirely original, as the Swedish economist Knut Wicksell had suggested something similar in a work entitled *Interest and Prices* first published in 1898.

Thirdly, although the composition and publication of *A Treatise on Money* were very important events within the Cambridge Circus, it cannot really be considered as a greatly influential book in the wider world at the time of its first issue, or at least no more so than numerous other works by economists on trade cycles from this period. Although a substantial part of Keynes's analysis presented in evidence to the Macmillan Committee on Finance and Industry starting in February 1930 was based on the theory outlined in *A Treatise on Money*, he was only one (albeit a significant one) of a number of people who provided such verbal evidence, and the book itself did not create an immediate revolution in the subject. As he himself readily admitted, it was almost immediately overtaken by the unfolding events of the Great Depression and his own ongoing reactions to them.

And although Keynes was indeed a major force behind the final report of the Macmillan Committee, *A Treatise on Money* was only one part of the background of the analysis that was presented there. As he admitted in the preface to the book itself, 'the practical suggestions contained in Volume II represent my opinions as they stood before the work of the Committee commenced rather than what they may be when the time comes for the Committee to report'.[26] The momentous events of 1929 and 1930 had made economists acutely aware that the rate of change of actions, ideas and their interaction had accelerated, and threatened to throw into doubt any economic analyses that were presented as fixed for eternity. In Keynes's case, this acceleration of new understanding produced his most famous and influential work, *The General Theory of Employment, Interest and Money*, which is a main subject of the next two chapters.

13 Multiplying (un)employment by expectations

The Great Depression of the 1930s, initiated by the Wall Street crash of October 1929 that then produced its concomitant business decline across 1930, was only initially an American phenomenon. The falls of commodity, stock and asset prices that were triggered by the New York crash quickly spread internationally, and Keynes was soon forced to deal with the consequences of the collapse of the 'greatest speculative boom in history' (so-called, or at least until 2008).

The most important financial development for the UK occurring in 1931 was that, on 21 September, the convertibility of sterling into gold at a fixed rate was officially suspended, and thus the UK finally abandoned the gold standard that Keynes had campaigned against for so long. The immediate cause of this was a sterling crisis starting in the summer of 1931, provoked by data showing that the debtor position of the London markets had worsened and that the UK government was facing a large budget deficit, partly as a consequence of the developing depression. Some initial attempts to save the gold standard had been made, including the creation in August 1931 of a national government expressly to do so, but eventually the Bank of England was forced to admit that it could no longer support the official sterling exchange rate.

Keynes was on the one hand relieved that the burden of maintaining a fixed level for sterling was over. But on the other hand, he was painfully aware that the financial position of the UK was still precarious, and that suspending the gold standard was not a 'magical fix' that would cure all of the UK's economic ills, especially as much of the damage from re-introducing the gold standard had already been done: by 1931, it had been in renewed operation for six years. Recriminations about the UK's exit from the gold standard then followed internationally, with some in the USA blaming Keynes for its demise. He had, they argued, by his arguments against deflation across the second half of the 1920s and his support for maintaining workers' pay rather than bearing down on wage levels, prevented the 'classical' remedy of automatic readjustments from taking effect.

Firstly, this characterisation gives Keynes too much influence, and secondly, a stronger operation of the proposed 'classical' remedy might have given just enough political ammunition to have enabled the UK General Strike in 1926 to turn into something much worse. Throughout the 1920s, Keynes had been very conscious of the 'new model economy' that was being created in the USSR. The onset of the Great Depression in 1929 only exacerbated the economic problems that were facing the UK, but for Keynes, this perilously evolving context would produce the work and the policies that would forever be associated with his name.

Life in the 1930s

Perhaps in (only poetic) coincidence with the wider deteriorating economic situation, Keynes's health began to suffer during 1931: in the autumn he was confined to his bed with chest pains for some time, experiencing what he referred to as 'rheumatic twinges'. Following this episode he then developed bronchitis, and this period of intermittent poor health lasted (off and on) until the spring of 1932. After the initial period of bed-rest was over, he was able to resume many of his work duties, but this health scare would turn out to be a harbinger of worse to come much later in the decade.

Despite the maelstrom of the developing depression, the first half of the 1930s was a time when Keynes continued his lecturing duties at Cambridge. A captivated attendee has lucidly outlined that at this time:

...Keynes continued his practice of giving eight lectures annually, usually in the Michaelmas Term...these lectures became something wholly unlike anything else that I have ever known in Cambridge lectures. Apart from the third-year undergraduates...there were to be found the whole body of research students, at least half the members of the Faculty, a visiting Professor or two from America, Australia or where you will, and on occasion a few spies...from London, Oxford or elsewhere. Gradually year by year the essential features of the *General Theory* emerged.[1]

In using the term 'spies' this attendee meant the inquisitive eyes of economists from different currents of thought, for example the Austrian school (such as F.A. Hayek at the LSE), not Communist spies loyal to the USSR (although this was not inconceivable, given the reputation of Cambridge in this regard). Another of Keynes's undergraduate students described attending intimidating supervisory sessions in this period as follows: 'His overwhelming brilliance made interruption undesirable...It was amazingly exciting and inspiring...after many months, it became almost too much': in large quantities, pearls of wisdom sometimes became indigestible.[2]

Keynes also spent time at Tilton in the early 1930s whenever he could, writing what eventually would become *The General Theory of Employment, Interest and Money*, and even expanded his landholdings in the surrounding area. He became more interested in the practical aspects of agriculture; for example, he starting rearing pigs on the estate (with some necessary external help) and learnt more about animal husbandry.[3] For some time he had, as a speculator, been investing in agricultural products such as cotton, rubber, wheat and sugar to make a profit; now he turned his hand to actually making some agricultural goods.

While at Tilton and now feeling entirely at home, a brazen Lydia would occasionally sunbathe 'stark naked' on the veranda that overlooked the slopes of the South Downs, even though a public footpath 'crossed in front of it only a few yards away'.[4] Less audaciously, she continued to pursue her performing interests through the creation in 1930 of the Camargo Society, an organisation designed to fund and arrange ballet performances in England, which lasted until 1933. It was responsible for various notable productions such as William Walton's *Façade* in 1931, with Lydia in a dancing role, although in some other productions she merely assisted and advised. A particularly innovative collaborative effort was a version of *Job* written and designed by Geoffrey Keynes, a leading scholar of William Blake and Keynes's own brother, which used Blake's visionary drawings as background settings and had music composed by Ralph Vaughan Williams.[5]

The Camargo Society eventually led (in a fashion) to the creation of the Royal Ballet, as many of its closing production assets were transferred there.[6] Keynes played a background role in the Camargo Society as a patron and then its treasurer, as he did with various other artistic and cultural institutions in this period. For example, he had helped to create the London Artists' Association in 1925, a co-operative organisation for the exhibition and selling of its members' art (which included Bloomsbury associates such as Vanessa Bell, Roger Fry and Duncan Grant). This Association lasted, with Keynes's full involvement in the acquisition and selling of pictures, until 1933. After 1930 he argued passionately for the inclusion of younger artists, but eventually its most famous members (Grant and Bell) left the Association to follow an offer of better financial rewards elsewhere.

In addition, between 1933 and 1935, Keynes was a major player in the funding and construction of the Cambridge Arts Theatre. With his substantial help (both financial and organisational) and the approval of the King's College Estates Committee, which controlled some suitable land, this new Theatre opened successfully in February 1936. Of the £20,000 of capital initially required to fund construction, Keynes had provided £17,500, although the actual cost eventually escalated to £36,000.[7] Lydia was soon performing on its stage as a lead in two Henrik Ibsen plays, for which her noticeable Russian accent was not inappropriate. Regarding the selection of plays to perform, Keynes was always:

> ...interested in the programmes and spent many long hours discussing these matters...He was deeply interested also in the character of the audiences and in the kind of people who were attracted by the various productions...Favourable terms were given for organised parties from factories in the neighbourhood.[8]

By such favourable means, those he had previously characterised as the 'boorish proletariat' might be educated to appreciate the true 'quality in life'.[9]

It has reasonably been argued that for Keynes, art was the highest form of human activity, and hence that his developing critique of *laissez faire* capitalism was inspired to a major degree by what he saw as the detrimental effects of allowing art to be governed solely by money-making motives.[10] It was certainly true that Keynes deeply loved the arts (and their usual creators the intelligentsia), and devoted a significant amount of his time across the 1930s to promoting them, but the case against *laissez faire* capitalism did not need the special case of the arts to be convincing in the early 1930s, as the business world had been doing fine in making the case against *laissez faire* by itself.

Given that, even with some not insignificant investment losses suffered in 1929–30 (see below), Keynes still remained a relatively wealthy individual living a privileged life across the 1930s, it is remarkable how many of his policy efforts in this period were devoted to attempting to assist those who were much less fortunate than himself. Finding a cure for economic depression and mass unemployment could be seen purely as a conceptual problem to be solved by the disinterested theorist, like an abstract intellectual puzzle, but for Keynes there was an additional component as well. In *The General Theory* he would comment positively on the 'significant progress towards the removal of very great disparities of wealth' that had been made since 1900, and thus his genuine concern for the personal consequences of unemployment was also a humanist one (but certainly not a socialist one: remember the 'boorish proletariat'). His early interest in the philosophy of ethics never left him, and this ethical concern invariably sat alongside a passion for the arts and a sincere interest in more conventional business matters. The real trick for Keynes was to find the perfect balance between these three, sometimes divergent, forces.

The slump turns to depression

When the economic crisis first broke in 1929, there had been no way for anyone to know that it would not follow the 'normal' lines of such economic downturns, and automatically generate the beginnings of a new upturn (say) in 1931 or 1932, rather than continue 'with varying severity, for ten years'.[11] In 1930, Keynes had been commonly referring to the problem as a 'slump' and then a 'worldwide slump', but by the beginning of 1932, he was describing it as 'an acute slump' with significant added financial complications. In January 1932, he gave a lecture entitled 'The Economic Prospects 1932' to a German audience, where he presented his heightened negative evaluation of the ongoing slump, before presenting a revised version entitled 'The World's Economic Crisis and the Way of Escape' in the UK in February.

Keynes opened both versions of the lecture with the same sentiment: the problem in 1932 was 'essentially different' from what it had been a year ago. Previously the issue was 'merely' of recovering from a significant (if conventional) slump, but in 1932 there was a new 'primary problem': avoiding a far-reaching financial crisis on an international scale, which threatened to topple the entire economic system. He did not downplay the seriousness of this crisis at all:

> Can we prevent an almost complete collapse of the financial structure of modern capitalism? With no financial leadership left in the world and profound intellectual error as to causes and cures prevailing in the responsible seats of power, one begins to wonder and doubt...The immediate causes of the financial panic...are to be found in a catastrophic fall in the money values not only of commodities but of practically every kind of asset...a collapse of this kind feeds on itself.[12]

This type of 'catastrophic fall' in the value of all assets is now known as a structural depression. Moreover, the worsening situation had by 1932 generated a 'competitive panic' for liquidity, a desperate game of musical chairs for cash, which had exerted a further downward effect on asset values. This panic had even extended to governments, who were restricting imports and forcibly stimulating exports, in order to improve their international balance sheets.

Keynes was concerned both with the UK's own immediate economic prospects, and those of the international financial system as a whole. He was, however, in early 1932 cheered by some positive developments, namely the UK's abandonment of the gold standard, which had produced an abatement of the deflationary pressure that had threatened new signs of recovery in the UK. He believed that various other countries (in central Europe and elsewhere) would soon follow the UK and abandon their fixed links to gold, thus further entrenching the division of the world into two country blocs: those on and those off the gold standard. This turn against gold promised a possible way out of the deepening crisis, as the deflationary pressure that had been exerted internationally by the gold standard would be mitigated, and the restoration of equilibrium by means of breaking the creditor positions of the two leading gold countries (the USA and France) could begin.[13] Exchange depreciation would, therefore, succeed in reinvigorating economies where deflation had not.

Perhaps the most uncompromising part of Keynes's 1932 analysis was a section about war debts. Recent events had, he claimed, utterly vindicated his own position as presented a decade previously in *The Economic Consequences of the Peace*. As neither reparations nor war debts were really being paid, the choice was that which Keynes had posed long ago: a much reduced final settlement or a general default. His own position was still in favour of total cancellation:

> We now know that the whole system of ideas and policy for which these obligations stand was a disastrous error – one of the greatest errors of international statesmanship ever committed... an agreed settlement could be made today for an annual payment by Germany of less than a third even of the amount which I proposed...in my *Economic Consequences of the Peace*.[14]

In 1933, he even cited the war debts as having played an important part in creating the international economic tension of the early 1930s.[15] Not everyone agreed with Keynes's analysis on this issue. Some argued that allowing Germany off too lightly after 1918 had prevented a decisive crushing of German pan-European aims, but he was at least consistent in supporting the same position across the decades.[16]

It was clear from the earlier part of the 1932 lectures that Keynes believed 'beggar-thy-neighbour' policies, or what he called 'competitive panic', were inevitable in conditions of a prolonged and acute slump. The UK's exit from the gold standard, in so far as it had involved a devaluation of sterling, was one such competitive policy. However, he was certain this was a positive move not only for the UK, but also for the global economy, rather than it representing 'the uselessness of one country gaining at the expense of another'. The explanation was that:

> ...it is a necessary preliminary to world recovery that this country should regain its liberty of action and its power of international initiative...we and we alone can be trusted to use that power of initiative...to the general advantage...I therefore welcome... that there should be a material strengthening of the creditor position of Great Britain.[17]

By 'creditor position' Keynes meant improving the trade balance, which in turn would help the UK to finance new international investments, a process the leadership of which had recently passed into the hands of the USA and France. The implication was that the UK was more skilled and experienced at financing global industry, and also better connected, than either the USA or France.

This latter element might be seen as signalling a change of heart on allowing foreign investment, as Keynes in 1932 wanted the UK to restart home economic activity by increasing the volume and affordability of credit, and also to 'lend abroad to the utmost of our powers'.[18] However, this last statement was conditional, as 'the utmost of our powers' depended on the UK's economic strength, which had been seriously affected by the slump and the ensuing financial difficulties. In an article from September 1932, he recommended re-opening the new issue market in London, which had been closed to new borrowers by the UK Treasury, but then warned that: 'At the same time I hope that we shall not return to complete *laissez-faire* in overseas lending'.[19] In another article from the same month, he recommended more clearly that the task should be 'a division of the aggregate of new lending between foreign and domestic borrowers which is appropriate to the foreign exchange level best suited to the stability of domestic prices', i.e. the amount of foreign lending should be determined by the needs of UK currency stability.[20]

Keynes expanded on this idea in a pamphlet entitled *The Means to Prosperity* issued in March 1933, a publication that his most substantial biographer judged as marking 'the emergence of Keynes as a world statesman' in terms of its balanced analytical maturity.[21]

It also marked the temporal mid-point between *A Treatise of Money* of 1930 and the new book on economic theory that he was concurrently composing, *The General Theory of Employment, Interest and Money*. In intellectual terms, *The Means to Prosperity* was closer in spirit to the latter book than the former. *The General Theory* was eventually issued in 1936: its theoretical content will be considered in more detail in the next chapter.

In *The Means to Prosperity* Keynes admitted that protective measures designed to improve the UK's foreign balance helped no one if they were applied simultaneously in all countries, but even so: 'A moment came when we were compelled to use them, and they have served us well'.[22] Their use in the UK had not only been for selfish reasons, as world output could be increased by the UK *at the appropriate time* using such national measures, as they served to 'increase loan-expenditure by strengthening confidence in a financial centre such as Great Britain and so making it a more ready lender both at home and abroad'.[23] The sequence of measures adopted to overcome the slump had been important, as the UK had to be 'saved' earlier rather than later because of its key role in facilitating global investment: thus, economic nationalism (at the right moment) had facilitated internationalism.

Also in *The Means to Prosperity*, Keynes more clearly than ever before blamed the worsening slump squarely on psychological causes: it came from 'some failure in the immaterial devices of the mind' and from problems with the 'working of the motives which should lead to the decisions and acts of will' necessary to bring into action the physical and technical means that were in existence, but were lying idle.[24] This greater emphasis on psychology would form a key part of the conceptual apparatus of *The General Theory*. The solution to the slump proposed in 1933 was a 'blend of economic theory with the art of statesmanship' plus some clear thinking. Such thinking from Keynes yielded the result of encouraging increased loan-expenditure throughout the world, i.e. a co-ordinated programme of government investments on a large scale from many individual countries, and he provided a formal scheme for precisely such a programme (see below). In the UK, the total figure declared necessary would be around £100 million per annum.

Robert Skidelsky evaluated *The Means to Prosperity* as 'a key document in the history of the Keynesian revolution', as it provided a more sophisticated theoretical foundation for public works.[25] This pamphlet, and the associated articles in *The Times*, had some immediate effect, as the UK Chancellor of the Exchequer (Neville Chamberlain) requested that Keynes should visit him in mid-March 1933 and discuss the issues outlined.[26] If any hopes had been raised at this meeting that Chamberlain would adopt Keynes's approach, then they were soon dashed when Chamberlain unveiled his new Budget at the end of April. Keynes's analysis of this budget was scathing; it mocked Chamberlain as a 'faithful accountant', complained that he had 'done nothing' to make the economic situation better, and decried that he was 'starved' of any larger conception of what was really necessary to increase national income: such a Budget represented a 'deliberate decision to mark time' only.[27] By implication, it had been a wasted opportunity. Although the Keynesian 'theoretical tools' for policies designed to multiply prosperity were beginning to be forged, many of those in government were not yet taking them at all seriously.

Terrific tariffs

Another element of the 'competitive panic' that Keynes had identified in his articles from 1932, both in the UK and internationally, was the levying of protective tariffs, a topic that he had been discussing for some time prior to 1932. Of all the policies that so infuriated doctrinaire supporters of *laissez faire*, it was restrictive import tariffs that were usually the most denigrated and reviled. Would Keynes dare to go as far as supporting even these monstrosities of custom, which, for supporters of free trade, were the most extreme expressions of economic ignorance ever encountered?

Keynes began to consider tariff protection for the UK positively at the very end of the 1920s. For example, in his questioning of witnesses for the Committee on Finance and Industry in May 1930, he hypothesised a case in which the general wage level of a country was 10 per cent too high, this then being remedied by a 10 per cent import duty and a 10 per cent bounty on exports.[28] The theory behind this was that wages were not as flexible as the free trade doctrine had assumed, and hence other means might be required in order to restore equilibrium. Keynes was also one of a group who participated in a Committee of Economists of the Economic Advisory Council, which gave advice to the UK government on various issues. In September 1930, he composed a detailed Memorandum for this Committee in which he developed his ideas on UK economic policy to some significant degree. Here he advocated the setting of tariffs on certain imported industrial goods for various inter-related reasons.

The first was that tariffs would help to improve the UK's balance of trade by restricting imports; the second was that they would encourage home production vis-à-vis the imported goods that were targeted; the third was that they would help to reduce real wages by raising prices (rather than by the more politically incendiary method of wage cuts); the fourth was that they 'raised the spirits of business men' in the UK; and the fifth was that they were less likely than other remedies to turn the terms of trade against the UK.[29]

Another more overtly political reason was that there were 'certain fundamental industries' which Keynes wished to preserve in the UK for non-economic reasons, for example agriculture, and all European countries were taking this view. The implication was that agriculture was so important strategically that to lose it significantly might be disastrous in any future conflict situation. From 1926 onwards, Keynes had been advocating the idea that the government should accumulate stocks of primary commodities in order to protect national producers from excessive price instability. Tariffs were just a logical extension of this concern, the aim being to protect staple industries, not to exploit a monopoly advantage.[30]

In the 1930 Memorandum, tariffs were only one of a number of economic policies that were discussed, but in November 1932, Keynes published an article in *The Listener* under the more focused heading 'Pros and Cons of Tariffs'. This provided a substantial theoretical basis for protection, and hence was even more likely to provoke dissent from orthodox economists. He began by stressing that he had some sympathies with both sides of the argument, but more from a practical point of view than a theoretical one. The purely theoretical arguments on both sides were 'invalid or misapplied', whereas both sides had 'got hold of an important practical maxim'. On the free trade side, the idea that everyone would be richer if they concentrated on activities for which they were best suited, was an 'obvious conclusion of common sense'.[31] Consequently, more often than not the free trader was speaking words of wisdom. However, free traders had 'greatly overvalued the social advantage of mere market cheapness', and had undervalued the 'virtues of variety and universality, the opportunity for the use of every gift and every aptitude', and they also ignored the value of tradition.[32] In effect, Keynes was suggesting that there should be an optimal combination of specialisation and variety, of free trade and protection, designed to get the best of both worlds for the UK. In addition, he conceded that temporary tariffs could be used to combat unemployment in certain situations.

He considered three specific examples. Firstly, as it would be a 'shocking thing if we were to be without a prosperous' motor industry, this being a sector in which the UK's natural national aptitudes were excellent, then protection here was 'wise and beneficial'. Secondly, tariffs could be one part of the solution for the UK's decaying iron and steel industry, although Keynes admitted that tariffs alone would not regenerate this sector. Thirdly, the active pursuit of agriculture was part of a 'complete national life', and hence protecting it was essential, as a country that could not afford 'art or agriculture, invention or tradition, is a country in which one cannot afford to live'.[33]

It is apparent that Keynes's arguments for protection were not purely economic in nature, but were conceived on the wider plane of national–cultural preservation. He accepted the economic argument for free trade as a maxim that could be applied in certain instances, but was concerned that it must be tempered by other considerations of a cultural and national nature. Blindly following the pure arguments for either free trade or protection in all circumstances would lead to negative results. The wise choice was to know when it was best to follow the one and when it was best to follow the other, in a type of conditional 'protectionist free trade' (this was not Keynes's own term), in the sense that protection would only be employed to achieve positive national goals. As he was arguing, the context was everything in relation to selecting correct trade policies: an unprecedented context might require unprecedented policies. Supporters of free trade who always stuck rigidly to their doctrinal certainties would doom the UK to ongoing decline.

Someone who fully understood the significance of Keynes's rejection of the free trade doctrine to his wider approach was his Cambridge colleague Joan Robinson. She later explained that:

> The great outcry against Keynes' treachery to the Free-Trade cause, which made strong men weep, shows how long an ideology can survive its usefulness; the doctrines that...it was desirable to preach when England was the greatest exporting nation, made precious little sense at any level in the nineteen-thirties. The Free-Trade doctrine is the clearest case of how the moral problem was abolished by the neo-classicals and how the Keynesian revolution brought it back.[34]

The 'moral problem' here was the idea that virtue and self-interest were indivisible. According to Robinson, Keynes 'spoilt this happy concatenation' by destroying the delusion that protection was never successful: in fact, the uncomfortable reality was that the level of international unemployment was indeed a zero-sum-game between competing nations, at least in periods of high involuntary unemployment. By implication, beggar-thy-neighbour policies were sometimes the only reality.

An example of someone who remained diametrically opposed to protection throughout this period was Lionel Robbins, a professor of economics at the London School of Economics, a noted departmental rival to Cambridge. In his own book explaining the causes of *The Great Depression* in 1934, Robbins called those who had been turned by the context into supporting tariffs 'feeble-minded and the paid agents of vested interests'.[35] The implication being made was clear: for Robbins, Keynes was either feeble-minded or a paid agent, or perhaps even both. As the British government must also have been: a tariff on imports was introduced soon after the general election in October 1931. The effects of economic policy on performance are always contested, but one respected economist judged that the abandonment of the gold standard and the adoption of import duties in the early 1930s 'ushered in the fastest period of economic growth in British history', from 1933 to 1937, at least in the manufacturing sector.[36]

There was another area of emerging economic policy in which Robbins disagreed with Keynes profoundly. Robbins dismissed planning entirely as the 'chaos of bilateral bargains between State monopolies', judging that it offered no hope for future political stability or economic progress.[37] Keynes on the other hand was again moved by the context to seriously consider the benefits of positive planning.

Positive planning

The early 1930s were, up until this date, economically the starkest and politically one of the most divisive periods experienced by developed Western capitalism. Consequently, it is to some degree understandable how those on the left and right came to believe in cataclysmic theories of the most extreme nature (Soviet Communism and German National Socialism), which mirrored each other in terms of the dangerous messianic messages that were conveyed.

Even Keynes caught the bug in a very mild and innocuous way, declaring in a broadcast from March 1932 that there was a new conception of the function of government in the air – state planning. However, he very wisely understood that:

> We can accept the desirability and even the necessity of *planning* without being a Communist, a Socialist or a Fascist…To bring in the collective deliberation, is not to disparage the achievements of the individual mind or the initiative of the private person. Indeed it is the achievements of this initiative which have set the problem. It is the failure of the collective intelligence…not to fall too disastrously behind – the achievements of the individual intelligence, which we have to remedy.[38]

Thus, for Keynes the need for (innovative) collective enterprise fitted alongside the (continued) need for individual private enterprise – the former most certainly could not replace the latter. It was this 'collectivist individualism' that he started to advocate in his political writings of the early 1930s, alongside the previously articulated support for 'protectionist free trade' and the soon-to-be-made case for 'internationalist nationalism' (see below).

According to Keynes, there were two general areas of the economy where state planning would be most suitable – consciously controlling the rate of interest and the rate of investment, as well as in various specific areas such as town planning, rural conservation, industrial location and tax distribution. Elsewhere in 1932, he wrote that the planning task was 'to maintain the level of investment at a high enough rate to ensure the optimum level of employment'.[39] He ended the broadcast analysis by making a direct, but conditional and limited, parallel between the developing five-year plans in Russia, the emerging corporative state in Italy and the desired 'state planning by Public Corporations responsible to a democracy in Great Britain'.[40]

However, for Keynes a key political difference between the latter case and the previous two was that state planning in the UK would be woven together with the existing democratic institutions of the country, rather than being designed to destroy and then replace them. Another difference was that UK planning would only be directed towards the general organisation of society's resources, and would leave the particular issues of production and distribution to the province of businesses and technicians. Thus, microeconomic decisions would remain within the realm of the individual. With this conditional promotion of protectionism and planning, Keynes had completed an intellectual evolution a long distance from the liberal *laissez faire* ideas of his early years, indicating that he had reached a more profound understanding of the complex historical varieties of the capitalist system. He had not yet provided the completed economic theory to go alongside this deeper understanding, but by 1932, he was actively working on it.

Personal investments

The depression also affected Keynes in more personal terms. At the very end of the 1920s his private investments had suffered terribly, alongside those of most others. However, by 1936, he had recovered his personal wealth and even made some noticeable gains. For example, his income from dividends denominated in sterling declined in 1929 and 1930, but then increased dramatically in the period 1934–37, whilst his negligible receipts from dividends denominated in dollars across the 1920s suddenly increased massively in the period 1934–37.[41] His total income declined between 1927 and 1930, but any losses had been recovered by 1932 and his total income increased significantly in the period 1936–

38.[42] Alongside this changing personal fortune, Keynes's own investment philosophy changed appreciably from the market-barometer style 'credit cycling' that he had favoured in the 1920s, to a much more considered approach.

For example in November 1933, he wrote that 'The more I have to do with investment, the more I believe in a certain continuity of policy', by which he meant that he now favoured a more medium-or long-term approach of holding investments until they matured, rather than a short-term strategy of profiting by predicting immediate market swings.[43] As he explained in August 1934:

> As time goes on I get more and more convinced that the right method in investment is to put fairly large sums into enterprises which one thinks one knows something about and in the management of which one thoroughly believes.[44]

Then the task for the investor was simply 'to hold the shares obstinately for a period of years for a really large appreciation'. Examples of the type of shares that Keynes selected to hold in this fashion after 1929 were UK car manufacturers, US utility companies and gold stocks. Part of this shift from a short-term to a long-term strategy can be explained by the latter method being (for Keynes in the 1930s) the more profitable approach, but it was also partly linked to a wider shift in his attitude to the moneymaking motive within capitalism.

He now believed that it was the job of the responsible investor principally to take a long view, as it better served the social function of facilitating continuity in investment, and helped to enable stable economic growth in the long-term. Thus he changed from favouring short-run speculation to long-run asset accumulation, a distinction that he would soon label as speculation versus enterprise.[45] In *The General Theory*, he would describe speculation very negatively as a 'bubble on a whirlwind' and liken it to the precarious activities of a casino. As he was acutely aware, precisely this type of short-term speculation had been a major factor in generating the Wall Street crash of 1929.

Despite Keynes's undoubted (if partial and sporadic) success as an investor in stocks and commodities, some of his greatest financial successes were (arguably) in a much more arcane area of investment:

that of antiquarian books. Across the 1920s and the 1930s he was an avid collector of books in various esoteric fields such as the history of ideas, the history of science and classical literature, in a period when the first two of these fields were not at all fashionable amongst bibliophiles. He bought mainly through dealers and auctions, and although his purchases were not primarily made as financial investments, they have shown his judgement of selection to be overwhelmingly accurate. Some of his 'greatest' purchases were as follows.

He acquired a second folio edition of the collected plays of William Shakespeare in November 1924 for the grand sum of £78.[46] At a UK auction in 2008, a copy of the same second folio made £75,000. Annoyingly, he had to pay £180 for a Shakespeare fourth folio a few years later (in June 1927). He acquired a first edition of Isaac Newton's *Principia Mathematica* in January 1928 for £60: today it would be worth around £100,000.[47] This was not his first Newtonian success, as he had in 1905 obtained a copy of the third edition of the same book for only four shillings. He eventually ended up in total with two copies of the first edition of Newton's *Principia*, two of the second edition and one of the third.

Perhaps his canniest ever book purchase in the field of science was a first edition of Nicolaus Copernicus's *De Revolutionibus Orbium Coelestium*, bought in 1934 for the princely sum of £150: today an auction estimate would be in the eye-watering range of £300,000–£500,000.[48] It was no accident that Keynes purchased this particular book in 1934, when he believed himself to be working on a revolutionary book in economics, since, if one single book is taken to have begun the scientific revolution in the mid-sixteenth century, then it was that on the revolutions of the heavenly spheres by Copernicus. To show that this purchase was not an isolated fluke, Keynes bought a copy of the superlative Aldine *editio princeps* of Aristotle's works in 1934 for £160. At Sotheby's in January 2001, a copy of this same book fetched precisely £583,250 (including the buyer's premium).

But without doubt his greatest contribution to bibliographical preservation was his purchase of a significant number of the lots at Sotheby's sale of an important collection of the personal manuscripts of Isaac Newton in July 1936. As they were sold at what today appear like bargain-basement prices, partly due to the context of the ongoing economic depression, Keynes managed to 'save' a large number of the items and keep them together by buying them for the purpose of donating them (as he eventually did with the rest of his book collection) to King's College. He initially bought only 38 of the 329 lots at the sale, but subsequently managed to re-assemble 92 of the other lots from dealers and other sources, complaining that:

> The greater part of the rest were snatched out of my reach by a syndicate which hoped to sell them at high prices, probably in America, on the occasion of the recent tercentenary.[49]

That a number of the manuscripts of England's greatest ever scientist had to be rescued for posterity from private dispersion by the individual efforts of England's greatest ever economist, purely on his own fancy and at his own expense (around £3,000 in total), accurately indicated the neglectful attitude of the British academic authorities towards the appreciation of their own heritage of scientific endeavour.

(Inter-)national self-sufficiency

The ultimate culmination of Keynes's long-standing concern with articulating the UK's national interest by means of financial and investment policy, tariff protection and industrial strategy in an increasingly volatile world, was a long and bold article entitled 'National Self-Sufficiency' published both in the UK (by the *New Statesman* in July 1933) and in the USA (by *The Yale Review*). Politically this was one of Keynes's most controversial sketches of contemporary affairs. Although at the time of its publication it did not make nearly as much of a storm as *The Economic Consequences of the Peace*, today it is often treated in rather arms-length fashion by commentators. Some are oblivious to it, declaring erroneously that Keynes 'abhorred the nationalist spirit'.[50] Others acknowledge the article as existing, but then immediately distance it from the contemporary reader by painting it as a short-lived 'anomaly' or 'phase' through which Keynes was (unfortunately) progressing.

A characteristic account is that by Roy Harrod, who dismissed the article very briefly as 'rambling' and as lacking Keynes's 'usual precision of thought': in fact it was extremely precise and clear.[51] Skidelsky, although giving due attention to this article, then described it as exhibiting 'Keynes the patriot rather than the balancer of economic advantages', whereas in fact it showed precisely the opposite: Keynes the patriot *resulting from* the balancing of economic advantages.[52] It showed how he had seen through the *laissez faire* argument that free trade was always the best way to bolster economic advantage, finally realising that in order to guarantee the UK's lasting economic prosperity, some degree of protectionism and national self-assertion would be required in certain circumstances. In this sense it was not an anomaly in Keynes's thinking that was soon discarded, but the culmination of a long process of liberating himself from the ill-fitting dogmas of nineteenth-century political economy.

Another of his biographers, Donald Moggridge, while discussing 'National Self-Sufficiency' together with 'Pros and Cons of Tariffs' of 1932, bizarrely concluded from them that Keynes 'accepted the basic logic of the free-trade position', whereas in fact, he rejected both free trade and protectionism as pure and absolute principles.[53] As he declared unambiguously in answer to questions from the British Prime Minister in 1930, 'I am no longer a free trader', although neither had he become an out-and-out protectionist.[54]

Keynes began the 1933 article on 'National Self-Sufficiency' by explaining that his dramatic change of heart regarding free trade was due to the preoccupations of the current situation being very different from those of the nineteenth century. Perhaps having in mind the protracted disruptions caused by the First World War, he warned that 'the penetration of a country's economic structure by the resources and the influence of foreign capitalists' and the 'close dependence of our own economic life on the fluctuating economic policies of foreign countries' were certainly not safeguards of international peace.[55] Moreover, the divorce between ownership and control of businesses that was proceeding at a fast pace, when applied internationally, would be 'in times of stress, intolerable'. Consequently, Keynes now sympathised with 'those who would minimise...economic entanglement between nations'.[56] This was because national self-sufficiency 'may tend to serve the cause of peace', as economic internationalism had proved itself unsuccessful in avoiding war. In this later admission he was referring to the 'economic imperialism' explanation of the First World War, where imperialist expansion of capitalist states had contributed to the outbreak of war on an international scale.

The other major component of what Keynes called 'the reorientation of our minds' that had been occurring, was that in the nineteenth century, 'self-destructive financial calculation' had been carried to unwise lengths, yielding a 'parody of an accountant's nightmare' and a generation that was 'beclouded by bogus calculations'.[57] It is important to stress that his argument was not that a maximising computation was always necessarily wrong, but that, taken to its extreme in accounting purely for financial gain, it missed significant areas of human life. The example given was of 'the beauty of the countryside' being destroyed, because the splendours of nature had no formal economic value. Here Keynes was alluding to what are called public goods, i.e. essential goods that are shared by all (e.g. national parks) but not traded privately as commodities. Given that some of these public goods had no market price, ignoring them was a real danger in financial calculations. The solution was either to give a rightful value to such benefits in any calculations made, or to protect them through legislation.

Despite Keynes's apparent turn to nationalism (what Skidelsky called 'Keynes the patriot'), he then stressed that 'I must not be supposed to be endorsing all those things which are being done in the political world today in the name of economic nationalism'.[58] This was a fine distinction, but a very important one. What he meant was that he was not a narrow-minded nationalist who only supported British goods because they were British, regardless of the economic reality of the situation; as he declared in this very article, 'a certain degree of international specialisation is necessary'.[59] He was only supporting a greater emphasis on self-sufficiency because he believed that it was in the economic interests of the UK and her international neighbours at this point in time.

With an increasing divergence of economic systems, as was illustrated by post-war developments in Russia and in other states like Germany, the UK required greater self-sufficiency in order to control its own system more directly. International free trade might be fine as an ideal in a trouble-free environment and when all countries adopted this model, but if they did not, for the UK blindly to adhere to it on its own, then this would be disastrous for its future prosperity. Keynes concluded the article by stating contrary-wise that, if the idea of self-sufficiency was also treated too dogmatically, then he would 'soon be back again in my old nineteenth-century ideals'.

Overall, Keynes could be characterised as advocating national self-sufficiency on supremely internationalist grounds. Given the realities of the situation in the mid-1930s, all states would be better off if they stepped back from forcing a pseudo-internationalist agenda and considered the interests of their own people to a greater degree. But, just as free trade should not be supported blindly, neither should self-sufficiency be taken to its extreme: as always with Keynes, the point was to find the happy medium between nationalism and internationalism that was most appropriate for the circumstances.

That Keynes did not quickly abandon what could reasonably be called his 'internationalist nationalism', was evident from by far his most important work of pure economics, *The General Theory*. Here he declared that:

>...under the system of domestic *laissez faire* and an international gold standard...there was no means open to a government whereby to mitigate economic distress at home except through the competitive struggle for markets...if nations can learn to provide themselves with full employment by their domestic policy...there need be no important economic forces calculated to set the interest of one country against that of its neighbours.[60]

It was the 'simultaneous pursuit' of an interest rate autonomous from gold, and a 'national investment programme directed to an optimum level of domestic employment' by all countries together, which was 'twice blessed' as helping a given country and its neighbours at the same time.[61] A clearer statement advocating a mature form of (inter-)national economic self-sufficiency could not be envisaged. Thus for Keynes, the best expression of internationalism (in certain contexts) was conditional nationalism, just as (no doubt) in other contexts, the best expression of nationalism would be conditional internationalism.

New dealings in America

As the 'acute slump' was an international phenomenon, it was unsurprising that Keynes paid attention to its progress in partner countries like France and the USA. In June and the first half of July 1931, he went on a visit to the USA, spending time in Chicago, New York, Washington and Boston, meeting key officials at the Federal Reserve, lecturing and giving seminars, and meeting US economists such as F.W. Taussig. In his lectures to the Harris Memorial Foundation in Chicago entitled 'An Economic Analysis of Unemployment', he argued that the case for a significant level of government-funded public works in the USA was 'much weaker' than it was in the UK. This was because the US economy was much more of a closed system than the UK. In the latter's open system, attempts to reduce the interest rate produced too much lending and a loss of gold internationally, but these consequences did not apply to the same degree in the USA, so reducing the US rate of interest would be a more effective means of encouraging recovery.[62] This type of analysis suggests that in 1931, Keynes was still employing the theoretical framework of *A Treatise on Money*.

Nearly two years later, in March 1933, F.D. Roosevelt had become the new US President, and in December 1933, Keynes published an open letter to Roosevelt in which he attempted to encourage the economic policies that he hoped Roosevelt would implement. Keynes strongly advocated 'the increase of national purchasing power' by means of government expenditure, which should be 'financed by loans and is not merely a transfer through taxation, from existing incomes'.[63] This should be directed to a large programme of public works: he had abandoned his belief that interest rate policy would be sufficient for regeneration in the US context. He was hopeful that a bold approach to public works would be adopted, as to him, Roosevelt was:

...the ruler whose general outlook and attitude to the tasks of government are the most sympathetic in the world. You are the only one who sees the necessity of a profound change of methods and is attempting it without intolerance, tyranny or destruction.[64]

Regarding the public works schemes that Keynes favoured, he declared a preference for those that could 'be made to mature quickly on a large scale' such as the rehabilitation of the railroads. The interest rate should also be reduced so as to aid the flow of cheap credit, for example by reducing the rates given on long-term US government bonds, but this measure would not be sufficient on its own.

Keynes returned to this same theme again in January 1934, when he reported positively that for the first time 'theoretical advice is being taken by one of the rulers of the world as the basis of large-scale action'.[65] He explained that:

> The President's recent sensational budget statement...means vast expenditure under these heads in the near future...Public works, railway renewals, unemployment relief, subsidies to local authorities, further aid to farmers...if the President succeeds in carrying out a substantial part of his programme, for my part I expect a great improvement in American industry and employment within six months.[66]

Keynes subsequently undertook a visit to the USA across most of May 1934, in part resulting from the offer of an honorary degree from Columbia University, during which he met with various high-ranking governmental luminaries, and then on 28 May, he finally met the US President. Roosevelt later reported of their hour-long meeting that he had undertaken a 'grand talk with Keynes and liked him immensely', but no complete record of their meeting was made. Keynes's most substantial written comment focused on a physical description of the President, particularly Roosevelt's hands, which were 'Firm and fairly strong, but not clever or with finesse'.[67] Keynes reported that meeting the President had been 'fascinating' but he was not impressed by Roosevelt's economic illiteracy.[68] One US economist suggested by extrapolation that 'the session was no great success; each...seems to have developed some doubts about the general good sense of the other'.[69]

Many have argued that this meeting was not especially important for Roosevelt, who had already decided to pursue an employment creation programme for his own political reasons, not because Keynes provided novel economic arguments for why it was necessary in theoretical terms.[70] Even so, letters emanating from the participants of some of Keynes's US meetings suggest his visit did have wider effect. With respect to securing new housing legislation, one reported that 'Your conversations with the Senators had a most salutary effect', while another from a government statistician declared that 'The whole Division felt greatly stimulated by your visit'.[71] An intellectual highlight for the US side was that early draft chapters of what was to become *The General Theory* were presented as lectures to the American Political Economy Club, which included amongst its membership leading economists of the day such as Wesley Mitchell and Joseph Schumpeter.

There was to be no easy victory for the US government's stimulus approach to exiting from depression. By the spring of 1934, Roosevelt's recovery programme was facing some significant problems of implementation, with opposition to increased expenditure coming from various quarters, and hence the predicted 'great improvement within six months', as Keynes had forecast in January 1934, was still some way off. Consequently, Keynes found reason to expand the timescale of the effect of public works. If in January he had predicted an improvement in the US economy within six months, then by June 1934, he had elongated the temporal delay to a full year before positive results would be seen. He also modified his favoured targets, as in December 1933 he had directed that the rehabilitation of the railroads should be the first port of call for US government expenditure, but by December 1934, it was the building of houses that was 'the best measure of all' for the USA to spend itself back into prosperity.[72]

Although a charge of some inconsistency might therefore be made, it should be recognised that Keynes was a pioneering advocate of ideas that were only just beginning to be developed and taken seriously by governments. He readily admitted that the appearance of new data would modify the details of his analysis. Despite such teething problems, he remained resolute in support of a large-scale public works programme, arguing at the end of his trip that the US government loan programme should be further increased rather than reduced. He recommended that a higher figure of $400 million a month should be spent, rather than a decline to $200 million that was beginning to occur.[73]

The question remains of Keynes's ultimate influence on US

economic policy in this period. Most commentators have detected only a nebulous general impact on the mood of the time, rather than any direct impact on individual policies or government decisions. Moreover, there were indigenous advocates of increased government expenditure in the USA (such as Lauchlin Currie, an economist and Roosevelt adviser), and Keynes's own theoretical apparatus for supporting such expenditure was (in 1933–34) only half completed in his own mind, which meant it had to an even lesser extent been publicly aired. Hence, Roosevelt's New Deal cannot be directly linked to Keynes's emerging policy solutions, and any indirect effect that operated on the wider context was not decisive. Even so, the fact that Currie for example took *The General Theory* as confirmation of the course he was already urging, indicated that such an 'argument from authority' was not without its American effect.[74]

International affairs

The international consequences of the depression continued to develop across the first half of the 1930s. In July 1932, the remaining reparations payments that had emanated from the First World War were cancelled, but not the war debts themselves. Keynes was pleased about the former, although from his point of view this should have happened many years previously. In June 1933, a World Economic Conference of sixty-six nations assembled in London with the partial aim of attempting to co-ordinate an international response to the slump. A few months earlier, *The Means to Prosperity* had contained a section entitled 'A Proposal for the World Economic Conference' in which Keynes sketched a bold globally co-ordinated plan to supply the treasuries and central banks of the world with 'more adequate reserves of international money' based on gold, so as to enable the increase of international loan-expenditure that he believed was required to overcome the depression.

In order to do this, it was proposed that an international authority for the issue of gold-notes should be created, with such notes being able to be issued up to a maximum of $5,000 million in total, and being obtainable by participating countries against an equal value of new government gold-bonds up to a given nation's gold-note quota. Each country's quota would be set in relation to its own existing gold reserve level, and the gold-notes would be accepted as the equivalent of gold for contractual purposes and held by the monetary authorities against domestic note issues.[75] They would gradually be withdrawn when an index of the main articles of international trade had recovered to an agreed level, i.e. when their function of returning the world to economic prosperity had been accomplished. The point of this new system was to enable national governments to more easily fund their own public works schemes, and for central banks to overcome any fears they harboured about losing or expending their gold reserves in the process.

In a previous article from December 1932, Keynes had called the proposed new international monetary authority the Bank for International Settlements. Actually, he had not been the very first to outline such a scheme, as Hubert Henderson, a fellow Cambridge economist and co-author (with Keynes) of *Can Lloyd George Do It?* of 1929, had initially proposed a similar idea in May 1932. Henderson's version was different in some major details (it used export levels instead of gold reserves to set the country quotas) and overall Keynes's scheme was much bolder ($5,000 million to be allowed in total instead of $1,000 million). Hence the idea is sometimes referred to as the Keynes–Henderson plan.

Unfortunately for Keynes (and Henderson), the outcome of the World Economic Conference in 1933 was hugely disappointing, as the draft proposal for a new Bank for International Settlements was rejected. In an article from July 1933 marking the end of the Conference, Keynes lamented that 'there was no cat in the bag, no rabbits in the hat – no brains in the head'.[76] He labelled the Conference itself a 'fiasco' and blamed its ultimate failure on too many cooks (sixty-six attendant countries) and a mentality that only universal agreement amongst everybody was acceptable. However, the plan was not a complete loss for, as has been noted, it bears a 'remarkable resemblance to the International Monetary Fund with its quotas' and elsewhere it 'looked forward to the International Monetary Fund and the Bretton Woods system'.[77] The design and development of these institutions would occupy Keynes a great deal more after the outbreak of the Second World War in 1939.

Conclusion

It would be accurate to say that by the mid-1930s, although various methods had (rather haphazardly) been applied in an attempt to overcome the depression in different countries, there was no universally accepted consensus as to the best way to encourage prosperity. This was partly a failure of economic policy itself, partly a failure of policy implementation and partly a failure of the theoretical underpinnings of the policy. In January 1935, Keynes wrote to George Bernard Shaw expressing the extremely bold and, on first sight, even a little self-important view that:

> ...I believe myself to be writing a book on economic theory which will largely revolutionise – not, I suppose, at once but in the course of the next ten years – the way the world thinks about economic problems...in particular, the Ricardian foundations of Marxism will be knocked away.[78]

The book in question was of course *The General Theory of Employment, Interest and Money*. Keynes had begun to realise the urgent need for a radically new theory to explain the ongoing 'acute slump' towards the end of 1931, and for the next four years (off and on), he devoted a significant amount of his time to resolving exactly this problem. He did this analysis and writing sporadically, in intermittent contact with various other economists, and alongside the policy-related work he was pursuing. As this chapter has demonstrated, much of this policy work was either directly or indirectly relevant to this attempt to forge a bold new theory to explain the depression.

For example, during the summer of 1932 he reported that he had composed nearly a third of a new book on monetary theory then to be called 'The Monetary Theory of Production'. In Cambridge lectures prepared during 1933, further parts of the analysis were developed. By the autumn of 1934, a more familiar version of the title was being considered for the much more advanced version of the chapters – 'The General Theory of Employment'. This title was partially framed in response to the publication of A.C. Pigou's 1933 book *The Theory of Unemployment*, which Keynes would controversially take as representative of the orthodox approach to the subject that had (he claimed) failed to account for the reality of persistent unemployment.[79]

Draft chapters of 'The General Theory of Employment' were subsequently read and commented upon variously by colleagues such as Richard Kahn, Dennis Robertson, Piero Sraffa, Ralph Hawtrey, Roy Harrod and Joan Robinson, although some of these commentators (Kahn and Robinson) were much more favourable to what they were reading than others (Hawtrey and Robertson). The general consensus amongst commentators is that Kahn was most intimately involved in the book's composition – Keynes rated him a 'marvellous critic and suggester and improver' – although on exactly which parts each of the aforementioned individuals exerted their greatest influence is more contentious.[80] By the autumn of 1935, Keynes was correcting the proofs of his revolutionary new book, a process that was completed by the end of the year. Thus, all told, *The General Theory* was nearly half a decade in gestation, if the author's almost immediate dissatisfaction with *A Treatise on Money* of 1930 is considered as the very earliest spark for the instigation of its sequel.

However, Keynes turned out to be entirely mistaken about the extensive decade-long timing of his thought revolution: 'not, I suppose, at once but in the course of the next ten years' – in fact, it took not ten years but closer to ten weeks for the revolution to (at least) begin. And although the first part of the previous quotation predicting 'the Keynesian revolution' is well known and frequently discussed by commentators, the later sentence in the quote in which the author implied part of his motivation is less frequently highlighted: to 'knock away' the Ricardian foundations of Marxism. In an article from November 1934, he explained that the nineteenth-century economic orthodoxy that he was aiming to demolish in the book included Marxism 'equally with *laissez-faire*', these two extremes being nineteenth-century twins.[81] Thus, both ideologies were as dangerous as each other: what was actually needed instead was that the 'English principles of compromise' should lead statesmen to temper the errors of the erroneous extremist economic teachings in which they had been brought up. And he was about to provide the original theoretical tools with which this extremism could more effectively be countered.

14 Liquidising the classical theory

Macmillan published *The General Theory of Employment, Interest and Money* in February 1936 at a price of five shillings per copy, bound unceremoniously in blue cloth and with an ordinary light beige dust-jacket. On the front of the jacket was emblazoned a box of advertising text that declared that the book constituted 'a general assault on the adequacy of the existing orthodox economic theory'. Although this text was unlikely to have been written by the book's author, it was not a completely inaccurate characterisation of the author's aim. Today a good copy of the first edition without the dust-jacket is worth around £600, and a copy including the scarce jacket a great deal more.

As a collector of great discernment, Keynes would have appreciated the irony that even though *The General Theory* was a far more important contribution to economics than his very first book *Indian Currency and Finance*, a first edition of the latter is worth much more as a commodity than a first edition of his 1936 masterpiece, only because it is much more uncommon. As Keynes wrote in chapter 21 of *The General Theory*, economists had rightly been 'accustomed to teach that prices are governed by the conditions of supply and demand'.[1] Part of what was original in the book was that its author wanted to apply this type of reasoning more extensively than it had been previously to the theory of money.

Although, at approximately 400 pages, *The General Theory* was only half the length of *A Treatise on Money*, it was still a complex and demanding work, only the main elements of which can be considered in a short chapter of a few thousand words. Rather than presenting an exhaustive summary of the book in the sequence in which it was designed, the method adopted here will be first, to consider each of the central theoretical innovations that it contained separately, and then second, to connect them together to demonstrate the main elements of the original understanding of the economy that Keynes had proposed. In describing the individual elements as 'original components', it is not being implied that no economist had ever previously considered them in any respect at all, only that the precise way Keynes understood and used them together in the context of the economic theory of the period was original.

And by stating that Keynes had proposed various 'original components', it is simultaneously being implied that there were some things called 'existing components' prevalent in the literature that he was bringing into question. Keynes labelled these 'the postulates of the classical school', by which he meant those principles developed by the founders of Ricardian economics (Adam Smith and David Ricardo) and also their more contemporary neoclassical heirs (Alfred Marshall and A.C. Pigou). In a note from the drafts, he more clearly specified his target as the 'orthodox equilibrium theory of economics'.[2] The two main existing postulates of the classical school that he outlined were that wages were equal to the marginal product of labour, and that the utility of the wage at a given amount of employment was equal to the marginal disutility at that amount of employment. In a note from the drafts, he again more clearly articulated his underlying target: the idea that there were 'natural forces' constantly tending to bring the volume of economic output to an optimum level.

Keynes went on to argue not that such postulates of the classical theory never pertained at all, only that they were special instances of a wider reality where many other positions of equilibrium/disequilibrium were possible. Thus, he was allowing a much more flexible (or liquid) approach with respect to potential levels of employment and business activity. And it was, he suggested, these more flexible cases that better described 'the economic society in which we actually live' for much of the time.[3]

The original components

The first original notion that Keynes deployed was effective demand, which was 'the aggregate income (or proceeds) which the entrepreneurs expect to receive...from the amount of current employment which they decide to give', or the expected volume of sales.[4] In other words, it was the level of real demand backed by money (from the actual given level of employment) that businesses expected to encounter as they sold their products on the market in any given time. This concept was outlined in explicit opposition to the idea that underlay 'all orthodox economic theory', that supply created its own demand (Say's Law), which (if true) meant that the aggregate demand price always accommodated itself to the aggregate supply price.[5] According to Keynes this was not necessarily so, as an increase in supply did not necessarily lead to a corresponding increase in demand, due to the operation of psychological factors that will be explained further on.

The second original notion that Keynes deployed was expectations, for example that it was current expectations of what consumers would be prepared to pay for goods in the future that determined the behaviour of entrepreneurs in deciding how to make their investment decisions. Thus, the level of employment (the result of entrepreneurial investment) at any given time depended on both existing expectations of future demand, and the states of such expectations that had existed over a certain past period. Expectations were, at least to some degree, a psychological phenomenon, based partly on existing facts and partly on estimated forecasts of future events which were uncertain, and thus they could turn out to be either true or false, depending on the outcome of all current and future activities.[6] Keynes distinguished between short-term and long-term expectations, the former being concerned with sales predicted to occur from existing production processes, the latter with sales that might occur with additional production capacity.

The third original notion that Keynes deployed was propensities, for example, the propensity to consume, which was the degree to which consumers decided to spend their income on consumption, as against the degree to which they saved this income for future use. He famously asserted that it was a 'fundamental psychological law...that men...increase their consumption as their income increases, but not by as much as the increase', i.e. they saved more in percentage terms as their income rose.[7] Such propensities were again, at least in part, psychological in origin, and depended on the existing habits of culture and circumstance, such habits only adjusting imperfectly and over long periods to changes in income.[8] This propensity was the reason that Say's Law did not always apply, as if saving increased alongside income then spending necessarily decreased, leading to demand falling below supply.

The fourth original notion that Keynes deployed was the multiplier, for example the investment multiplier. This applied when there was an increase in aggregate investment, which would then increase income by an amount (k) times the increase in investment. He wrote that there was a 'law that increased employment for investment must necessarily stimulate the industries producing for consumption and thus lead to a total increase of employment which is a multiple of the primary employment'.[9] Such a multiplier effect could (in theory) be measured empirically, and it explained how relatively small fluctuations in investment could generate fluctuations in employment (either upwards or downwards) of much greater magnitude. As was readily admitted, it was R.F. Kahn who had first introduced the multiplier as an explicit concept in its own right, but Keynes had in *The General Theory* transformed Kahn's employment multiplier into his own investment multiplier.

The fifth original notion that Keynes deployed was the marginal efficiency of capital, which was a percentage rate by which the summed yearly returns from a capital asset purchased by an entrepreneur (for example a piece of machinery) were equated to its supply price or replacement cost. Accordingly, the actual rate of investment in capital assets by an entrepreneur would be taken to the point at which the marginal efficiency of capital was equal to the actual interest rate.[10] The marginal efficiency of capital thus depended on the relation between the supply price of an asset and its prospective (or expected) yield, the latter of course being only an estimate that might turn out to be wrong.

The sixth original notion that Keynes deployed was liquidity preference, which was a schedule of the resources that an individual wanted to retain as cash, as opposed to resources they held in less liquid forms such as shares, commodities, houses and so on, in various different circumstances. He then defined the interest rate not as the quantity that balanced investments with savings, an idea that had already been rejected in *A Treatise on Money*, but as that quantity which balanced the desire to hold cash against the available quantity of cash.[11] Four basic motives for holding cash were outlined: the income motive, the business motive, the precautionary motive and the speculative motive. Thus, again, what ultimately determined liquidity preference were psychological motives, which could vary across individuals and across nation states.

The seventh original notion that Keynes deployed was the employment function, $N_r = F_r (D_w)$, which assumed that N_r people were employed in industry r when effective demand was D_w, F being the functional relationship involved. The point of this function was to relate the amount of effective demand directed to a given firm or industry with the amount of employment the output of which would compare to this effective demand.[12] Within this function, each industry would exhibit its own elasticity of output or production, which was the rate at which output changed as effective demand varied. In the case of the employment function for all industry as a whole, there was for every level of aggregate effective demand, a unique distribution of demand between the products of the various industries, and thus as aggregate demand varied, demand for each individual industry changed in proportion to the total. Thus, changes in aggregate employment depended not only on the level of aggregate effective demand, but also on how this demand was distributed between different industries at different levels of employment.

Psychology centre-stage

Having outlined the seven original notions that Keynes deployed, it becomes clear that psychological factors were major component parts of at least four of the seven new concepts that were being presented. Expectations, propensities and preferences were all mainly (although not totally) psychological, and as the marginal efficiency of capital itself depended on expected future yields, psychology played a major part here also. Only the multiplier, effective demand and the employment function were (apparently) not at all psychological, although if a role for the propensity to consume was allowed within the multiplier effect, effective demand was connected to entrepreneurial expectations and the employment function contained effective demand and elasticity within it, then even these three concepts had a significant psychological component to them. Thus, the author of *The General Theory* had brought psychology into economic theory to a much greater extent than had previously been accepted.

As he outlined in a related essay published in 1937: 'The theory can be summed up by saying that, given the psychology of the public, the level of output and employment as a whole depends on the amount of investment'.[13] It was true that members of the neoclassical school of economics in the last quarter of the nineteenth century (such as W.S. Jevons) had used psychological motives and subjective feelings to explain aspects of economic behaviour, but only with regard to an individual's choice of purchases in relation to the theory of value and exchange, i.e. within the traditional maximising framework. Keynes used psychology for precisely the opposite reason, to demonstrate why the maximising framework of the classical (and neoclassical) theory was misleading. As the 1936 reviewer of Keynes's book in the *Economic Journal* (J.R. Hicks) duly declared, 'the use of the method of expectations is perhaps the most revolutionary thing about the book'.[14]

Keynes even admitted in private correspondence from August 1936 that 'One of the most important transitions for me', which had enabled him to make the quantum leap in understanding between *A Treatise on Money* of 1930 and *The General Theory* of 1936, was 'suddenly realising' the psychological law governing the propensity to consume, which was a conclusion of 'vast importance to my own thinking'.[15] Significantly, the employment of the concept of 'propensity' in *The General Theory* had some earlier precedents within Keynes's writings. In *A Treatise of Probability* of 1921, he had considered the logical foundations of the concept of probability in some detail, declaring that:

> The judgements of probability, upon which we depend for almost all out beliefs in matters of experience, undoubtedly depend on a strong psychological propensity in us to consider objects in a particular light. But this is no ground for supposing that they are nothing more than 'lively imaginations'.[16]

Here, psychological propensities regarding the natural world were declared as being important and very real, and by 1936, he had come to believe the same about the socio-economic world.

A much earlier use of the word 'propensity' is even more revealing. It occurred in Keynes's notes for the Civil Service entrance examination that he took in psychology in 1906. For this exam he had studied the ideas of two psychologists in significant detail, James Sully (1842–1923) and G.F. Stout (1860–1944), both of whom were authors of major works in various fields of psychology. Stout had even taught at Cambridge, two of his most famous students being G.E. Moore and Bertrand Russell. While discussing the idea of 'habits' in his sixty-five pages of notes on Stout's approach to analytic psychology, Keynes noted that:

> One necessary and omnipresent condition of the formation of habit is the tendency of a mental process to repeat itself simply because it has occurred before, a tendency which becomes stronger with repetition – i.e. i) set in action by a slighter one ii) less liable to disturbance iii) stronger as a propensity...[17]

This 'tendency to habitual repetition' was part of Keynes's account in *The General Theory* of the state of long-term expectations, which relied a great deal on the convention that the existing state of affairs would continue indefinitely.[18]

Stout's work contained another key concept that Keynes employed in his economic theory. As Keynes explained in his notes on Stout, change in a psychical system is analogous to the disturbance of equilibrium within a material system.[19] Keynes also referred to the notion of the disturbance of neural equilibrium while discussing psychical dispositions.[20] This disturbance and restoration of psychical equilibrium was a component part of Keynes's use of psychology in his economic analysis. Few commentators have noted this point, but Keynes obtained his early understanding of psychology from two very explicit sources. Stout's emphasis on mental acts formed part of the later work of Gestalt psychologists, and Sully's approach to applying physiological concepts to psychological analysis can be seen as an early forebear of evolutionary psychology.

As Keynes outlined his new approach to understanding economic equilibrium in the preface to *The General Theory*: 'A monetary economy...is essentially one in which changing views about the future' ultimately influenced the level of employment and trade.[21]

He even declared that 'the rate of interest is a highly psychological phenomenon', and explained in this regard that:

> ...its actual value is largely governed by the prevailing view as to what its value is expected to be. *Any* level of interest which is accepted with sufficient conviction as *likely* to be durable *will* be durable; subject...to fluctuations for all kinds of reasons round the expected normal.[22]

The crucial punch was then extended: the rate of interest could remain 'chronically too high for full employment', if it was the prevailing opinion that the rate of interest, as per the *laissez faire* doctrine, was self-adjusting. Thus, erroneous economic theory itself actually affected the economy through its impact on psychological expectations. This very important emphasis on psychology would turn out to be an underlying strength and also one of the basic weaknesses of the book.

Keynes was so interested in the psychological motivations of economic behaviour that he distinguished fourteen separate aims of saving and spending. The eight motives for saving were: precaution, foresight, calculation, improvement, independence, enterprise, pride and avarice. The six motives for spending were: enjoyment, short-sightedness, generosity, miscalculation, ostentation and extravagance.[23] Other motivations were not excluded. He explained that the strength of these various motives varied enormously according to the institutions and organisation of society, and that they could change over time, but for the purposes of the analysis that he wanted to present in *The General Theory*, they were assumed as being constant. Even so, the nature of these psychological motivations was being placed centre-stage in the economic analysis that was being presented.

The multiplier

It would be wrong to give the impression that Keynes had 'invented' all the components sketched above simultaneously. One of the most significant building blocks of *The General Theory* that had received published dissemination before 1936 was the concept of the multiplier. For a number of years previous to 1933, Keynes had been arguing that increased investment produced 'knock-on effects' that rippled out through the economy, creating additional positive consequences above the initial investment that had been made. For example in August 1930, he spoke of consumer spending in one sector of the economy having 'favourable repercussions on employment' in other sectors.[24] By 1933, he was able to formulate this idea more precisely, and in April he published an article entitled 'The Multiplier' in the *New Statesman*. The fact that it was published in a current affairs outlet rather than in an economics journal was significant: Keynes wanted to reach a wide audience, as the issues being discussed were relevant to current difficulties.

He began 'The Multiplier' by hypothesising that a given amount of additional invested loan-expenditure employed a definite number of additional workers, this increased employment being designated as the 'primary employment' that was created by the extra investment. He then argued that:

> ...this primary employment sets up a series of repercussions leading to what it is convenient to call 'secondary employment'... in my own judgement the secondary employment would be *equal* to the primary employment, i.e., that the multiplier of primary employment to give *total* employment was 2; but, to be on the safe side, I took it as being a half, i.e., a multiplier of $1^1/_2$, and then, as a further precaution against various contingencies reduced it to a third, i.e., a multiplier of $1^1/_3$.[25]

Critics objected to Keynes's judgement by suggesting that much of the 'secondary expenditure' effects were dissipated in unhelpful ways such as increased spending on imports, or on those people not receiving unemployment relief. In order to counter such criticisms, he provided in 1933 a more precise estimate of the magnitudes involved.

In reality around 70 per cent of the extra expenditure accrued to individuals as current income, and around 30 per cent of it was dissipated on expenditure that did not increase income. Furthermore, of that amount which reached the wage-earning classes, around 70 per cent of it would be spent and only 30 per cent saved. On these assumptions what Keynes called 'the first repercussion' would be approximately 49 per cent of the initial expenditure (0.7 multiplied by 0.7 = 0.49), the second repercussion would be one half of the first repercussion (0.5 multiplied by 0.49 ≈ 0.25) and so on. The result was: 1 + 0.5 + 0.25 + ... = 2, meaning that Keynes was correct to assert that the multiplier would approximately be 2. Even so, to cater for various possible contingencies of error, he had then reduced the actual estimate to $1^{1}/_{3}$.

He finally posed the question of why the multiplier effect was for some so difficult to accept. The answer was that the standard ideas about economics held by most ordinary people were 'soaked with theoretical pre-suppositions which are only properly applicable to a society which is in equilibrium, with all of its productive resources already employed'.[26] Multiplier effects would not manifest themselves in conditions of full employment, as by definition, no extra personnel could be brought back into employment in this instance. But the assumption of full employment was not applicable to the UK in the early 1930s. Even in less depressed circumstances, whether full employment had ever existed for a substantial period of time was debatable. Hence, multiplier effects certainly were to be found in times of mass unemployment, and probably in less economically distressing times as well.

Keynes had not been the first to use this concept so named, as R.F. Kahn had published an article in the *Economic Journal* in June 1931 that linked multiplier effects to the case for public works. Keynes readily acknowledged Kahn's prior formalisation of the basic concept, but Keynes was able to deploy it as part of a larger theoretical apparatus used to explain depressions in a more coherent and sophisticated manner than Kahn. Despite Keynes's attempts to further substantiate this idea, by no means all economists even within Cambridge were convinced of its reality. For example, D.H. Robertson argued that the increased investment that would be required to get the multiplier moving would simultaneously require increased savings, which in turn would dampen down the positive effects of heightened investment through an associated degree of reduced consumption. Keynes of course denied that such a 'crowding out' effect would apply, at least in conditions of large-scale unemployment.

The basic analysis

So far Keynes had proposed a set of new concepts that had begun to elucidate more clearly the psychological factors underlying economic behaviour. However, in *The General Theory*, he did more than this, as he related these elements together to form an explanation of how the economy functioned over time. In order to do this, he had to show how the individual elements were linked together to form a structured whole. He began by sorting the various elements into dependent and independent variables, i.e., variables that were themselves caused by others (the dependent), and those that were the 'prime-movers' in economic affairs (the independent). As the independent variables he initially listed the propensity to consume, the schedule of the marginal efficiency of capital and the interest rate. As the dependent variables he listed the volume of employment and the level of national income.[27] Thus, the latter two dependent variables were 'determined' or 'explained' by the former three independent variables in some (as yet) unspecified way.

However, as has already been explained, all three independent variables given so far were at least partially dependent on psychological factors, and hence as 'ultimate' independent variables Keynes listed 'three fundamental psychological factors': the psychological propensity to consume, the psychological attitude to liquidity and the psychological expectation of future yields on capital assets. He then introduced two other 'ultimate' independent variables, these being wages as determined by collective bargaining, and the quantity of money in circulation as set by the central bank. All of these 'ultimate' independent variables together determined the national income of a country and the quantity of employment in it (the dependent variables). Note that all five of the hypothesised 'ultimate' independent variables were entirely in the realm of individual management, i.e., were either psychological conventions (the first three) or were state-controlled policies (the final two). Thus, the capitalist economic system was, it was being tacitly suggested, entirely amenable to human control.

As if to strengthen this claim, Keynes listed various hypothetical 'conditions of stability' that would serve to produce a stable economy over the long-term. Examples of these were: wages that changed only moderately with respect to changes in employment; moderate changes in the prospective yield of capital associated with only moderate changes in the rate of investment; and a multiplier greater than unity but not very large.[28] However, Keynes then outlined the idea for which *The General Theory* was most famous for introducing: the economic system 'could be in equilibrium with less than full employment'.[29]

The controversial nature of this statement becomes apparent when it is explained that previously, mainstream economists had usually only allowed unemployment to be the consequence of a temporary period of disequilibrium or personal choice, so-called frictional and voluntary unemployment, and hence it was assumed for cases of disequilibrium unemployment that forces would be automatically generated that would tend to overcome the unemployment. According to Keynes this idea was fundamentally wrong, it was indeed possible for there to be a less-than-full employment equilibrium; there was no automatic tendency generated to overcome this unemployment by the normal workings of the market system, and hence involuntary unemployment could exist.

One component of Keynes's explanation of why such a position of unemployment equilibrium could come about was that during a period of economic crisis followed by a slump, liquidity preference increased significantly, as individuals became much more psychologically cautious about making long-term investments or buying high-cost items. In such conditions, even a dramatic fall in the interest rate would not necessarily produce a large increase in investment or purchasing, as individuals had become more cautious about borrowing money than they had been previously, preferring to hold cash as an insurance against uncertain times. The propensity to consume was also affected by the onset of a slump, as people chose to save more of their income (in percentage terms) rather than spend it, again because of heightened uncertainty. Thus, these factors all served to act negatively on business confidence, an underlying psychological factor that 'the economists who have put their faith in a "purely monetary" remedy have underestimated'.[30]

So far what has been specified was only a set of components and a structured manner of connecting them together. To obtain a hypothesis providing a 'general theory of employment', an explanation of what determined the actual level of employment throughout the business cycle was required. This Keynes supplied as follows. When the upturn phase of the cycle was beginning, employment increased, and aggregate income also increased, but due to the operation of the psychological propensity to consume, consumption increased but by not as much as income. In order to balance this increased level of saving and decreased level of consumption, increased investment would be required by entrepreneurs, this itself being the result of specific capital asset purchasing decisions in relation to expected future effective demand.

However, the amount of actual investment that would follow an increase in supply and employment depended on the inducement to invest, or the relation between the schedule of the marginal efficiency of capital and the rates of interest offered on various loans. Whether the volume of investment would increase sufficiently to cover the deficit between increased consumer income and decreased spending (in relative terms) was a purely contingent phenomenon. Given a certain propensity to consume and a specific rate of new investment, there was only one level of employment consistent with equilibrium, but there was no necessary reason why this level had to equal full employment. As Keynes explained:

> The effective demand associated with full employment is a special case, only realised when the propensity to consume and the inducement to invest stand in a particular relation to one another…it can only exist when, by accident or design, current investment provides an amount of demand just equal to the excess of the aggregate supply price of the output resulting from full employment over what the community will choose to spend on consumption when it is fully employed.[31]

Hence, the volume of employment in equilibrium depended on the aggregate supply function (or similarly the employment function, the aggregate supply price of the output from employing a given number of employees), on the propensity to consume and the volume of investment. Ultimately it was the propensity to consume and the rate of new investment that, between them, set the actual level of employment. Full employment was only a 'special case' of a more general position of aggregate employment that varied as the determining factors acted out their causal influence across the various phases of the business cycle.

All the content of *The General Theory* has, thus far, been presented only in theoretical terms, but this explanation of a less-than-full employment equilibrium was so obviously linked to the depressed business situation of the Western economies in the mid-1930s, that it could easily be suggested that it had been generated by this situation: the result of a heightened psychological propensity to explain economic crises, which operated in the downturn phase of the cycle. Keynes did not attempt to deny this connection in any way, but would most likely have responded that it was in such periods of acute crisis that the 'real bones' of the economic system could most clearly be seen.

The social philosophy of *The General Theory*

The final chapter of the book, although rather brief, provided an important guide to how Keynes saw his new economic theory sitting within a broader social philosophy. It also contained some powerfully penned passages on the relationship between social justice and wealth creation:

> ...I believe that there is social and psychological justification for significant inequalities of income and wealth, but not for such large disparities as exist today...dangerous human proclivities can be canalised into comparatively harmless channels by the existence of opportunities for money-making and private wealth, which, if they cannot be satisfied in this way, may find their outlet in cruelty, the reckless pursuit of personal power and authority, and other forms of self-aggrandisement. It is better that a man should tyrannise over his bank balance than over his fellow-citizens...[32]

This was not exactly a ringing endorsement of the capitalist spirit as a principle. But at a time of prolonged mass unemployment and international political conflicts of an unprecedented nature (the rise of National Socialism in Germany and the consolidation of Soviet power in the USSR), it should be seen as a bold attempt to hold the liberal democratic fort while simultaneously recognising that capitalism certainly did have a dark *alter ego*, which if allowed to operate unheeded by any moral constraints, would threaten its own existence.

Keynes then provided a clear statement of an underlying dividing line between his own social-democratic type of criticism of free market ideology, and those advanced by socialists: 'The task of transmuting human nature must not be confused with the task of managing it'. The 'wise and prudent statesman' allowed the capitalist game to be played, but only subject to the appropriate legal rules and social constraints. In using the term 'transmuting' human nature, Keynes was alluding to the unattainable medieval goal of transmuting base metal into gold; socialists believed that such a transmutation of base human nature into golden perfection was possible, but for Keynes, this was a dangerous utopian misjudgement that threatened to return humanity back to the dark ages.

On the other hand, his basic criticism of individualist capitalism was that: 'Interest to-day rewards no genuine sacrifice, any more than does the rent of land'.[33] The solution was to reduce the long-term rate of interest significantly. This would help to bring about full employment by harmonising the interest rate with the particular schedule of the marginal efficiency of capital that increased employment, and it would also aid the disappearance of the rentier class who lived solely on their accumulated assets. Thus, *The General Theory* was the supreme abstract expression in economics of the middle way between capitalism and socialism that Keynes had been articulating in varying degrees of sophistication for nearly two decades.

Reception and interpretation

On its first publication, only a few commentators hailed *The General Theory* as the 'powerhouse performance' in pure economics that Keynes had been promising to produce for many years. Joan Robinson described it in private correspondence as making an impression 'of great power and coherence' and as 'the most *readable* book of its weight ever', meaning its intellectual not physical weight.[34] However, instead of offering up great praise, many reviewers were mildly critical of it, despite recognising that it contained various important advances, and some were even overtly hostile. For example, as has been accurately described: 'Professors [Frank] Knight and [Gustav] Cassel joined the mob in the stoning of the revolutionary dissenter'.[35] Knight denied any originality in Keynes's results and Cassel came to the defence of the established doctrines. Perhaps the most widespread criticism was that Keynes's presentation of the classic theory was a straw man set up in order to exaggerate the novelties of his own approach, which especially irked those (like A.C. Pigou) who had been officially designated as inventors of the allegedly failed orthodoxy.

Pigou's own review complained vociferously that the classical economists had been unfairly portrayed as a 'gang of incompetent bunglers', and charged Keynes's own argument as being in places 'so obscure' that it was incomprehensible.[36] To indicate how divisive the book was on its first issue, another reviewer heaped praise on Keynes's book precisely for its 'clarity of style which saves much confusion'.[37] Pigou could even point out that there was a short chapter on expectations in the very book that Keynes had taken as his target, although its significance had evidently been lost.[38] A more positive reviewer hypothesised the existence of a strong 'psychological propensity to resist' Keynes's new arguments, a propensity that was often displayed by classical economists, this being the psychosomatic result of the difficulty of escaping from old ideas.[39] However, its intellectual effect and wider influence quickly overtook any mixed or disappointing reviews.

Certainly in Cambridge it helped to create a generation of 'Keynesian economists' who went forth and multiplied the Keynesian message (and with a knowledge multiplier far greater than unity). One astute observer of the economics scene at Cambridge at this time wrote a little sceptically that:

...subsequent discussion was conducted very much in the atmosphere of the revivalist meeting: "Brother, are you saved?" I am not sure that this may not have been because Keynes himself had found it a severe moral struggle to let go of his old liberal faith in the ultimate automatism of the economic system...The first to be saved seemed to include not only the pure of heart, but a large admixture of the empty of head...The following years provided a most illuminating example of the processes and psychology of conversion, as economists...adjusted their thinking to the new set of ideas that Keynes had put before them...[40]

Internationally *The General Theory* was also hugely influential, and it was so at a very fast pace. As has been explained, the extent and speed of its impact was unparalleled: within two years, the framework it contained was pervasive.[41] If *A Treatise on Money* was both immediately and ultimately a disappointment, then *The General Theory* was the antithesis: it was (arguably) the most important and influential book in economics of the entire twentieth century, and it has rightly taken its place alongside Adam Smith's *Wealth of Nations* and Karl Marx's *Capital* as one of the three most significant books ever written by an economist.

One major part of its speedy success was that there was a 'cohort' of like-minded economists in the UK and the USA, keen to propagate and refine the Keynesian message, and by so doing they made it even more influential. Perhaps the most significant early example of this was an article by J.R. Hicks entitled 'Mr Keynes and the "Classics": A Suggested Interpretation', published in April 1937. Although in *The General Theory*, Keynes had invented major components of what today is understood as macroeconomics, he hadn't quite provided the final step. For example, he illustrated his novel ideas in the form of a simple diagrammatical model of intersecting curves of the basic elements, a form that would be immediately appealing to economists who had been brought up in the neoclassical tradition.

This graph measured the amount of investment (I) on the vertical axis and the rate of interest (r) on the horizontal axis, with various curves being plotted representing different positions of the investment demand-schedule and the amount of saving.[42] In 'Mr Keynes and the "Classics"', Hicks developed this diagrammatical model further – 'a slight extension of Mr. Keynes's similar skeleton' – as intersecting curves illustrating the relation between income and the interest rate (IS) when savings equalled investment, and the demand for and the supply of money (LM), with the rate of interest measured on the vertical axis and income on the horizontal axis. This came to be called the IS-LM model of the economy, and such diagrams (and variations upon them) became a basic feature of numerous textbooks in macroeconomics from the early 1950s to the present day. They were especially useful as the slopes and initial positions of the curves had been set by the determining factors, such as liquidity preference and the amount of saving, but then how any changes in the variables involved (the money supply, the interest rate and so on) would play out in an economy could be determined by reading off the new points of intersection after the curves had been adjusted to the changes. Of course, the accuracy of this type of model depended entirely on the assumptions underlying its structure: if these assumptions were wrong, the model would provide erroneous predictions.

Even so, Hicks was not exactly deferential to Keynes in his 1937 'suggested interpretation'. Hicks began the article by declaring that 'the entertainment value of Mr. Keynes' *General Theory* is considerably enhanced by its satiric aspect'.[43] Here Hicks was being ironic, as Keynes had not meant *The General Theory* to be satirical. What Hicks meant was that Keynes's portrayal of 'the postulates of the classic theory' was in fact a caricature, as many so-called classical economists would 'find it hard to remember that they believed in their unregenerate days the things Mr. Keynes says they believed'.[44] Moreover, Hicks questioned how general *The General Theory* really was, suggesting instead that it was really only 'the Economics of Depression'.[45]

Like all such celebrated texts, *The General Theory* quickly became controversial outside the confines of the economics community. It was attacked from the left as trying to rescue capitalism through state assistance, when revolutionary socialists so desperately wanted it to collapse and then be replaced, and it was attacked from the right for allowing socialism in by the back door, as state-controlled investment and even limited planning were anathema to *laissez faire* supporters. In the USSR it was hailed as further evidence of the impending death throes of capitalism. Other criticisms were more substantial and genuine.

One of the most significant criticisms to emerge was as follows. Keynes had been absolutely correct to emphasise the psychological elements that underlay the economic system to a greater degree than had been done heretofore, but from where exactly had he obtained the particular forms of the psychological laws that were being proposed? It would turn out that, more often than not, he had either invented them out of his own pre-existing beliefs and assumptions, or taken them from the existing literature, instead of discovering them first-hand from any large set of empirical data or representative experiences. Thus, as an example, his 'fundamental psychological law' about the propensity to consume came under critical fire from one Milton Friedman, not as being entirely unimportant to the topic of economics, but as being (in its actual manifestation) quite different to what Keynes had suggested in *The General Theory*.

Friedman investigated this law empirically for his 1957 book *A Theory of the Consumption Function*, and found that Keynes's assumptions about it were incorrect, as the ratio between income and savings was the same for all income levels, and depended on factors other than income such as interest rates and the individual's own wealth/income ratio. Thus Keynes was half right (this type of propensity was indeed crucial to understanding how the economy worked) but half wrong (the propensity to consume did not operate as he had initially supposed).

Paul Samuelson made one of the most famous (or infamous) later judgements of the book ten years after it was published. He declared in riotous mood that:

> It is a badly written book, poorly organised…It is not well suited for classroom use. It is arrogant, bad-tempered, polemical, and not overly generous in its acknowledgements. It abounds in mares' nests and confusions…In it the Keynesian system stands out indistinctly, as if the author was hardly aware of its existence or cognizant of its properties…When it is finally mastered, we find its analysis to be obvious and at the same time new. In short, it is a work of genius.[46]

Despite being amusing and shockingly rude, and apart from the very last sentence, this judgement was entirely questionable. The key to Samuelson's error was in his suggestion that there was something called 'the Keynesian system' that had been cleverly cognised in its entirety by those (like Samuelson) who had finally 'unpacked' Keynes's true message. Certainly, many Keynesian economists thought this to be the case in the 1950s and 1960s, but new developments in the 1970s such as stagflation meant that these economists were forced to re-examine what they had taken as the Keynesian canon. In fact, like the major works of all great thinkers, 'what Keynes really meant' in *The General Theory* has remained perpetually open for dispute and reinterpretation ever since 1936.

And, far from being a badly written book, it was brilliantly and clearly composed, with periodic summaries of the analysis being given along the way; far from being mean, it prominently identified Kahn as first introducing the multiplier, and acknowledged that the marginal efficiency of capital was identical to Irving Fisher's rate of return over cost; far from being bad-tempered, it was supremely measured and moderate in its tone, and inclusive in its general attitude; far from being ill-suited for learning, it is perfect for use in intellectual history and history of economics courses. Another of its strengths was that it clearly articulated the wider policy and philosophical ramifications of its purely theoretical parts.

A much more real (but unacknowledged) issue that Samuelson had with the book was that it represented a major intellectual watershed in the methodological expression of economic ideas, as it marked the high tide and boundary line between what can be called 'literary economics', which had existed for centuries up until 1936, and the birth of a new (and much more technical and exclusive) mathematical economics, which would take almost complete control of the discipline in its mainstream form shortly thereafter. Concepts expressed primarily as flexible phrases – the propensity to consume, the multiplier – began to be replaced by concepts expressed primarily as fixed mathematical equations. In *The General Theory* itself, Keynes complained that it was 'a great fault of symbolic pseudo-mathematical methods' that they assumed strict independence between the factors involved, and did not allow subtle 'reserves and qualifications' to continuously be kept in mind.[47]

Keynes had certainly begun on this controversial path of mathematisation, as even *A Treatise on Money* had contained many sets of equations, but his work had always remained rooted in the literary tradition of conceptual expression in specially phrased terms. As has rightly been explained, he used equations more as symbols of his verbal arguments, not as precise algebraic expressions of mathematical 'concoctions'.[48] But (ironically) the new verbal concepts that he had so brilliantly introduced in *The General Theory* and then developed as basic equations, almost begged to be further refined by expressing them in a more quantitatively rigorous manner, as many of his immediate followers attempted. Samuelson's own 1947 work *The Foundations of Economic Analysis* was much more mathematical than *The General Theory*, and his playful impatience with Keynes was in part an expression of the impatience of the new mathematically-trained economists with the so-called imprecision of verbal expression. Keynes later expressed some grave concerns about the over-mathematisation of economics and the concomitant over-reliance on modelling as exemplified in econometrics, but his criticisms were quickly dismissed by those at the forefront of the new mathematical approach.

The final issue to be considered is that there has been much literature recently devoted to questioning how 'revolutionary' *The General Theory* really was. Thus as an example, it has been argued that 'far from inventing an entirely novel theory to challenge a dead orthodoxy, Keynes fabricated his theory from the ample materials provided by a lively and diverse interwar literature'.[49] In fact both evaluations were partially correct: Keynes did usher in a revolution in understanding of economic analysis, but he did so by drawing upon the existing diverse literature, reinterpreting and then adding to it, and then by recasting it into a novel and more coherent form that better explained the problems that had been identified. It was only Keynes who could have accomplished this mammoth task of adding to, synthesising, recasting and refining the array of existing theory at this particular moment in time, and thus he certainly does deserve the credit (and the blame) for 'inventing' many of the basic elements of macroeconomics.

Conclusion

In May and June 1937, Keynes suffered a series of serious heart and throat problems that resulted in longish periods of hospitalisation following an actual physical collapse. It seems most likely that he had suffered a heart attack of some degree of seriousness, although it was far from being fatal. His punishing work schedule, supreme theoretical efforts and ongoing multitudinous policy advocacies, allied to some unhealthy physical habits (such as smoking), had finally caught up with him. It was the most serious health scare he had encountered thus far in his life by far. As *The General Theory* had placed much greater emphasis on psychological factors, it was unlikely that physical causes alone could have fully accounted for Keynes's dramatically declining health just following its publication. For the next two years or so, until the outbreak of the Second World War in 1939, he was unable to work at anything like his previous degree of effort. But with a massively growing political threat looming on the European horizon, he would soon be called upon once again to serve his country as an applied economist, but now as one of great and long-standing experience and with a glittering worldwide reputation behind him.

15 War finance and the post-war economic order

After the serious heart problems that had developed in 1937, Keynes was never entirely fit again. He was nursed back to relative normality and reasonable health by a combination of medication, substantial rest in a recuperative sanatorium and the love and care of Lydia. By the summer of 1938, he was back at Tilton working on some limited academic contributions, but even before this time he was writing more casually on various topics such as foreign affairs.

One problem that Keynes returned to almost immediately after *The General Theory* had been published was population growth. In 'Some Economic Consequences of a Declining Population' from April 1937, he appeared to accept the idea that the future promised a stationary or slowly declining population level for the UK. In these circumstances, increased individual consumption would be required in order to guarantee the level of effective demand that was required for maintaining full employment. One 'Malthusian devil' had apparently been tamed (population growth) but another one threatened to take its place (unemployment growth). More capital resources per head, resulting from the projected decline in population, would be 'of immense benefit to the standard of life'; it was just that the right balance between saving and consumption had still to be maintained.[1]

Keynes was clearly mistaken with regard to predicting a long-run stable or slowly declining UK population level, but the terms of his underlying economic analysis would still apply. A quickly growing population, allied to capital resources growing at a lower rate, would inevitably produce a declining standard of living. In the early twenty-first century the UK population has been growing substantially, and Keynes would consequently have warned that the potential dangers of the original Malthusian devil had returned.

How to pay for the war

The second half of the 1930s had seen the inexorable rise of National Socialism, against which Keynes initially advocated a variety of 'armed appeasement', something that evidently proved a failure.[2] At the beginning of September 1939 Germany invaded Poland, and as a consequence of the international alliances that were then in existence, Britain almost immediately declared war on Germany. Keynes quickly adjusted his mindset to the necessities of military planning.

He was not initially involved in the official war effort, but in February 1940 he published a substantial pamphlet entitled *How to Pay for the War*, which was a revised version of three articles published in *The Times* in November 1939. Aspects of this topic had also been considered in an article published in the *Economic Journal* in December 1939. The subtitle of the pamphlet – 'a radical plan for the Chancellor of the Exchequer' – indicated that Keynes expected his ideas to be taken seriously by the British government. The pamphlet cost one shilling to buy and was issued in plain red-brown boards, but was bound in quires and did not use the war-economy paper standard that would soon become the norm.

Keynes's argument for the most appropriate means of financing the war was relatively straightforward. The basic task was to divert a percentage of consumer purchasing power away from ordinary civilian goods, in order to use it for military purposes. He calculated that, in addition to the yield of existing taxes and savings that would voluntarily be offered for government use (e.g. through bonds), there remained around £950 million of income in private hands that had to be diverted to war finance ends, in order to fund the military campaign. The question was: what was the best method of doing so? The menu of traditional options was: further taxes, further voluntary savings and inflation. This was the same menu that had been available during the First World War, and that had led to such disastrous consequences for Russia.

Keynes thought that part of the £950 million could legitimately be raised by extra taxation. However, this left around £450 million still to be funded. He believed that inflation as a method should be avoided at all costs because of its detrimental effect on workers, and additional voluntary loans were unlikely to be taken up in anything like enough quantities, so a new method was required. The innovative policy that Keynes proposed was consciously deferred pay, i.e. deferring a given proportion (say 20 per cent) of all personal income until the war was over, with an exemption for those on the very lowest pay scales. This deferred pay would accumulate as a deposit in a financial institution, and become available in instalments at a suitable time after the war was over, for example at the onset of the first post-war slump. Alongside the system of deferred pay, a capital levy would operate after the war in order to pay for it.[3]

Although Keynes did not explicitly say so in the pamphlet, another less-appealing term for compulsory deferred pay might be forced savings. Even so he readily admitted that there were workable alternatives to his scheme, most notably an extra sales tax, a heavier income tax or forced wage cuts. An especially revealing passage then explained that:

> The choice between these drastic and equally effective alternatives must be decided on considerations of public psychology, social justice and administrative convenience.[4]

Considerations of an exclusively economic or theoretical nature were not mentioned. Instead, the grounds of choice were entirely psychological and administrative, given that social justice was a human psychological preference, i.e. selection should be based on which policy would be accepted as reasonable by the public and was easiest to implement. Keynes thought that deferred pay was more likely to be acceptable than further taxes or wage cuts, and hence his basic point of judgement was psychological.

Such a scheme of deferred pay had other advantages too. As he explained in an *Economic Journal* article, it would be fairer to those on lower pay scales than either inflation or extra sales taxes, as these two alternatives would erode the real purchasing power of less wealthy groups. But with deferred pay:

> Instead of the reward due to the working-class for their war effort being just taken away from them, it is at worst merely deferred.

Their sense of security is increased, and, by being given some slight claim on the future resources of the community, they are put in a position a little nearer to that of other classes. This is the only way by which an increased real reward can be given them.[5]

This article was also notable for presenting figures on the 'income potential of the country' for 1938–39, or national income as it is now better known. Keynes called the resulting figure of £5,700 million, which had been estimated by the economic statistician Colin Clark, the 'gross taxable income of the country'.[6] The British government did not yet calculate official national income statistics, and hence Clark's work was pioneering.

Keynes's idea of deferred pay found only an unsympathetic hearing in political circles, calls for voluntary sacrifices being much preferred by various interested parties such as the Trade Unions and Labour politicians. However, his published work on war finance had a definite effect. Not long after Winston Churchill became Prime Minister in May 1940, the new Chancellor of the Exchequer appointed Keynes as an important Treasury adviser in August. He was given his own office and a secretary, and was allowed access to sensitive government information.[7] As has been explained:

He was there to help the Chancellor, and in practice to share some of the heavier burdens with the Second Secretaries, on whom fall the main responsibilities for the ordinary day-by-day business of the Treasury. In the early years he was much concerned with the problem of internal finance, and...the budget speeches of 1941 and 1942 were considerably influenced by Keynes. But increasingly Keynes became concerned with post-war problems... his influence was felt throughout the Treasury...[8]

He spent long hours studying the relevant Treasury papers and worked tirelessly on solving the latest problems of war finance and management. Churchill had evidently forgiven Keynes for writing *The Economic Consequences of Mr Churchill*. Churchill reported that in January 1941, he had instructed the committee responsible for harnessing the economic resources of the nation for military purposes to 'summon economists like Keynes to give their views' personally.[9] Keynes was the only economist whom Churchill had explicitly named.

The other aspect of paying for the war, apart from internal finance, was the international component, or more specifically, the American angle. Just as with the First World War, the role of the USA (both financially and militarily) would turn out to be crucial. As part of his new Treasury duties, in October 1940 Keynes composed a long memorandum entitled 'Notes for U.S.A.' in which he considered the question of the best way for American funds to be employed. He strongly opposed the notion that the US could partially fund the war by 'picking the eyes out of the British Empire and seizing its assets without taking over its liabilities'.[10] Regarding the idea that the US administration should become the owners of (for example) the British Crown Colony assets under the administration of British officials and native Rajahs, Keynes declared stridently that:

> It cannot be a sound proposal to divorce ownership from responsibility to this extent. Divested from the duties and liabilities of management it would be a project of unadulterated... exploitation. For it is a misapprehension to suppose that the British interests in Malaya are those of passive rentiers. They are intensely living and personal enterprises which without the breath of current life would collapse in a very few years. If the United States wish to take over the tin and rubber resources of the British Empire, they must be prepared to take over at the same time the responsibility for the territories in which they are situated.[11]

A clearer statement in support of the 'responsibilities of Empire' thesis, and of the international economic interests underlying the war finance issue, would be difficult to find.

Keynes also argued strongly that for the USA to wait until virtually all of the UK's own financial resources were exhausted, before offering direct assistance, would be a grave error, a mistake that risked repeating the errors of the First World War. If this was allowed to happen, then the US would again have to fund UK expenditure across the world, not only in the USA, and the UK itself would be forced into a 'fire-sale' of its assets at knock-down prices, thus increasing the total amount required from the US in the long run. This argument made perfect sense from both perspectives, but Keynes's most controversial suggestion would make far less sense to the USA: US aid should not be in the form of a loan, either a phoney loan that was later written off or a real loan that proved embarrassing when payments came under pressure: instead it should 'take the form of placing at our disposal without charge' the US aid programme.[12] Whether gift aid was a real possibility is debatable, but even Keynes showed some doubt: 'perhaps it is not for us to ask for, or even to suggest, such a thing'.

Lend-Lease

By December 1940, the UK was in severe financial difficulties in relation to paying for its military supplies. The answer supplied by President Roosevelt was Lend-Lease, or the US supplying some equipment to the UK not in exchange for up-front finance, but in the form of 'lending' or 'leasing' equipment either to be returned after the war was over, or to be recompensed at a later date at terms to be arranged. The UK was to continue to pay for whatever it could, but Lend-Lease provided a crucial extra means by which supplies could be obtained over and above this limit. In effect, it was a lifeline that enabled the UK to function outside the constraints of immediate finance.

That this policy was by no means uncontroversial in the US was clear from a letter Keynes wrote in May 1941 discussing the terms of Lend-Lease:

> After this very general idea had sprung from the brain of Jove, it had to be clothed in detail by the lawyers. Two drafts were prepared...The [US] State Department draft was on the basis of pledging as security almost everything we possess in the world outside the British Empire...The draft prepared in the [US] Treasury...went to the other extreme, kept the $ sign out of the Bill in all contexts and provided for no specific security whatever on our part...There was an acute controversy behind the scenes between the two drafts.[13]

Keynes was relieved that the US Treasury draft was the one eventually adopted, as the other draft would potentially have stripped the UK of many of its assets. However, this did not finally resolve the finance issue, as some reports to the US Congress still spoke of British assets being given as security. Moreover, the precise terms of the Lend-Lease agreement – the so-called 'consideration' of what the US President would deem satisfactory as repayment after the war – were the subject of ongoing negotiations proceeding over a significant period of time.

Keynes was actively involved in these negotiations over the 'consideration', which by June 1941 had him proposing in an unofficial draft that the British government would be liable not only to return all goods received from the USA that had not been destroyed, but also to provide any further facilities for US defence that were desired, hand over information, inventions and secret processes of any description to the US government and provide for any other delivery of goods/property and services 'deemed by the President to have value for the purposes of the defence of the United States'.[14] This could be interpreted to mean that the US could, in the future, demand any goods and services from the UK that they deemed desirable as final settlement. And this was only the 'defence' part of the terms; there were also sections on 'post-war relief' and 'trade', which promised the opening up of all sources of raw materials within British control (i.e. the remaining Empire) to every purchaser on equal terms. This UK draft then spoke, perhaps with a tightly clenched jaw, of the British government being 'deeply appreciative of the magnanimity of these terms'.

The US draft of the 'consideration' came at the end of July 1941. It required, in addition to the return of surviving US defence assets, that the UK would, if circumstances necessitated it, provide 'such articles, services, facilities or information as it may be in a position to supply'. It would also make payments in respect of protecting any US patent rights for defence articles, and 'provide against discrimination in either the United States of America or the United Kingdom against the importation of any produce originating in the other country'.[15] Although this US draft was not quite as explicitly deferential in its terms as some of the previous drafts, the clause promising (basically) any goods and services for defence purposes that the UK was in a position to supply, was still far from providing free funding of the war effort. Although no explicit financial returns were being demanded upfront, some definite strings were being attached.

The most difficult part of the US draft of the 'consideration' for Keynes to accept centred on the word 'discrimination', which was really only a euphemism for protection. A system of imperial trade preferences and import/exchange controls was being deliberately outlawed, which would affect the potential of the British Empire as an active trading bloc. Keynes opposed this anti-discrimination provision strongly on the grounds that it 'saddled upon the future an ironclad formula from the nineteenth century', and would require an Imperial Conference to ratify it.[16] The implication was clear: the 'nineteenth-century formula' was universal free trade, which (as Keynes now recognised) was neither realistic nor beneficial. He labelled the idea of a most-favoured nation clause, i.e. a bilateral free trade agreement between the UK and the USA, as 'the old lumber' that had proved itself 'a notorious failure' in the old pre-war era.[17] Keynes was applying his principled rejection of free trade to his favoured terms for a post-war settlement with the USA.

His answer was not, however, comprehensive protectionism, which after all he had also rejected equally and in principle. Keynes's analysis was rooted in what he believed the concrete reality of the post-war world would be. After the war the UK would require a considerable excess of imports over exports, given the massive structural shifts that had occurred for war production, and for the US this overseas trading position would be reversed. But in such a situation, outlawing exchange controls and all types of protection would be a formula guaranteed to produce disequilibrium in trading relations, not one designed to maintain economies in balance.[18] Another concern was that the shape of the international post-war economic order was highly uncertain. Keynes did not want to burden the UK with a free trade commitment when many other countries and trading blocs (outside the US) might return to some form of trade discrimination. The UK should be able freely to react to circumstances.

In May 1941, Keynes had travelled to the USA to conduct the Lend-Lease discussions face-to-face, returning to the UK at the end of July. He met President Roosevelt twice. However, negotiations about the exact wording of the 'discrimination' phrase continued through to February 1942, when by means of a combination of the added pressure of circumstance and interpretative fudging of the meaning of certain parts, a draft was eventually signed by both sides. Against Keynes's better judgement, it included the commitment to eliminate 'all forms of discriminatory treatment in international commerce'.[19] The US free trade agenda had finally won out.

Post-war arrangements

There were various aspects to the question of devising the international post-war financial system that Keynes was concerned with. The first was the problem of avoiding significant trade imbalances between different countries across the world, such imbalances being seen as a major source of potential future tensions. The second was the more specific question of managing the UK's war debt and its immediate post-war economic needs, both of which must take account of the reality of the UK's fractured economy in 1945 and its uncertain growth prospects immediately after. The third was the issue of devising appropriate international institutions that could accommodate the first two problems, and also provide an appropriate framework for ensuring that pan-European conflicts like those of 1914–18 and 1939–45 would not happen again.

Perhaps the single most important circumstantial factor that Keynes had to deal with in resolving these three interconnected issues was the imbalance of power between the UK and the USA at the end of the war. By 1945, the British economy had been devastated by six years of total war, and the UK's accumulated financial and technological resources had been all but entirely exhausted. The USA, by contrast, had actually benefited economically from the fact that it was a major source of war supplies for the Allied powers, while at the same time it had remained less harmed as a homeland nation, even with Pearl Harbor and US troop losses. Moreover, Keynes's health had been in a precarious state since 1937, and the protracted travel and long periods of negotiating that resolving these issues demanded, meant that he was not in perfect physical fitness as the various contentious solutions were being considered.

The US side had its entirely understandable grumbles. This was the second time in recent memory that the USA had been called upon to 'bail out' a conflict-laden Europe, and in both instances, without US financial and military assistance, it is likely that the UK would have found itself on the losing side. So why shouldn't the USA gain in some way from its decisive efforts in trans-Atlantic solidarity? In the past, the British Empire had been created in part by military victories, and the restrictive trade practices of the Empire bloc had sometimes discriminated against US access. The post-war settlement would be a golden opportunity for the USA to redress the imperialistic imbalance.

That some elements of the US government had been thinking at least abstractly along these lines for some time is evident from War Plan Red, first proposed in 1927 and developed in detail across the 1930s. War Plan Red was a top-secret 'war games' outline of US military strategy in the event of a full-scale war between the USA and the British Empire. Active updates to this plan had only been halted in 1939, when Germany had stepped in to assume the actual adversarial role. Although the US government never believed the outbreak of a US–UK war to be imminent, nor very likely, it was evidently not entirely inconceivable.

Keynes's own plan for the post-war monetary system was called the 'International Currency Union' or the 'International Clearing Union', and involved the issuing of an international reserve currency called 'bancor'. The key elements of this plan were facilitating flexibility between economies and helping to maintain balance of payments equilibrium. In the proposed plan, each country's transactions between central banks would be undertaken through an international clearing union denominated in a special international currency. Each country's reserves of this international currency would be set in relation to the country's own assets. The aim would be for any developing bilateral imbalances in the holdings of this international currency to be managed by means of a combination of transfers of reserves and exchange rate modifications (i.e. devaluations), so as to maintain balance of payments equilibrium. The reason why this was so important to maintain was that disequilibrium in this area had been a major cause of previous social discontent and war.[20]

The US side, however, were not convinced by Keynes's idea for the creation of a new international currency. Far better for them if the dollar were to take on an increased international role, as the pound sterling had done in relation to trade within the British

Empire up until this time. The counter-posed American plan devised by Harry Dexter White, a mid-ranking economist and administrator of nowhere near Keynes's status, proposed the creation of a Bank for Reconstruction and Development and an associated Stabilisation Fund. The Fund would help to stabilise exchange rates and maintain international equilibrium through a system of pegged currency regimes, and the Bank would provide funding for post-war reconstruction and to overcome crises. Although contributing members to the Bank and the Fund would pay in their stakes in gold and local funds, and there was a special Bank unit of account, loans and interventions would be linked to gold and US dollars more explicitly than in Keynes's plan. In addition, White's Stabilisation Fund had a more restricted remit, both in size and scope, than Keynes's Clearing Union.

The final round of negotiations over these (and other variant) proposals occurred at Bretton Woods in New Hampshire, USA, in July 1944. Keynes led the British delegation, but the resulting agreement reflected the reality of American power. An International Monetary Fund (IMF) was created (a variant of White's Stabilisation Fund) alongside the World Bank (a variant of White's Bank for Reconstruction) and also a General Agreement for Tariffs and Trade (GATT) that would promote the free trade agenda that the US side so desired. Sometime later it was revealed that Harry Dexter White, if not an official Soviet spy, was informally passing some restricted information on to Soviet intelligence. He probably believed that by doing so he was facilitating US interests, in that the USSR had not (by 1945) become the mortal enemy of the USA that it had by the mid-1950s, but a decade later White would have been jailed and vilified for his pro-Soviet attitude.

Keynes had no idea that, during his negotiations over establishing the post-war financial architecture, he was actually dealing with a part-time Soviet sympathiser: Lydia would have been shocked. In this context, White's concern not to follow a British-inspired plan acquires new overtones, as Stalinist ideology at this time was far more hostile to the British Empire than it was to American 'bourgeois' democracy. Given the existence of (the albeit purely hypothetical) War Plan Red, that some in the US government saw an element of overlap between US and Soviet interests at this time is more understandable. The Bretton Woods system of international monetary institutions, as the IMF and World Bank became known, lasted in operation from the end of the Second World War until the early 1970s. Although Keynes had only exerted moderate and mediated impact on its design, this was one of his most obvious economic policy legacies.

Lord Keynes of Tilton

In June 1942 Keynes was named in the Honours List as a Baron, at Churchill's recommendation, and he decided to adopt the geographical designation Lord Keynes of Tilton. In the House of Lords he chose appropriately to sit on the Liberal benches.[21] At first sight this haughty Lord-ability was a long way from the youthful rebellion and social daring of Bloomsbury – by the early 1940s the title Lord Keynes of Bloomsbury would have been anachronistic – but he only ever had one foot fixed in juvenile artistic revolt. The other foot was always striving for something more real and substantial, which by this time he had achieved.

The main policy issues that Keynes was concerned with immediately after the war had ended were managing the UK's war debt, and arranging post-war finance for the reconstruction of its domestic economy. In August 1945, Keynes again travelled to North America to arrange the remaining details of the UK's settlement with the USA. In negotiations in Washington, he asked for the not insignificant sum of $5 billion as the amount of additional funding that the UK would need outside of the Lend-Lease arrangement, in order to rebuild its economy.

Perhaps understandably, the US side suggested a lower figure of $3.5 billion, offered at repayment terms of 2 per cent. Keynes received instruction from UK ministers to the effect of reducing the repayment terms to between 1 per cent and zero over fifty years. Detailed and substantial negotiations then proceeded, during which Keynes became increasingly frustrated both with UK ministers and US negotiators. Four billion dollars at 2 per cent was the best the US side would then offer, repayable over fifty years and commencing after five. Major sticking points were the terms of temporary waivers of repayments if circumstances demanded, the level of related sterling balances and possible discrimination in relation to imports into the UK.

Eventually a deal was forthcoming, with $3.75 billion offered plus some extra funding for resolving Lend-Lease, and the precise details of the terms were finally settled. On the US side, there had been no formal obligation to lend the UK a cent after the war, so $3.75 billion was not a negligible commitment. On the UK side, the fact that the US appeared to want semi-commercial terms and other strings attached in terms of setting trade policy and institutions, grated with the reality that it had been the UK standing virtually alone in 1940 that had initially provided the platform to defeat the global Nazi threat. But the UK had no choice other than to accept the US terms on offer, as there was simply no other option available. When the Marshall Plan was launched in 1948, the idea of US gift aid for Europe was finally accepted, but Keynes would not live to see it in action.

When he eventually returned from the protracted negotiations in the USA in December 1945, Keynes was physically and intellectually exhausted. During the Christmas holiday he met up again with Leonard Woolf, Virginia having tragically committed suicide by drowning in March 1941. In the first few months of 1946, Keynes worked intermittently on various post-war financial issues, and he even visited the USA again in February and March. But he died on the morning of 21 April 1946, a Sunday, around a month after his return to the UK. After Lydia had made some tea, he collapsed from the same type of heart attack that he had endured and survived previously, but which now proved fatal.[22] He was only 63 years old. His father (J.N. Keynes) did not die until 1949, and his mother survived until 1958. Lydia outlived her husband by many decades, finally passing away in 1981.

A memorial service was held at Westminster Abbey a few days after Keynes's funeral. Attending were the British Prime Minister, leading staff of the Bank of England and the Treasury, key members of King's College and the remaining Bloomsbury members (including Vanessa Bell, Duncan Grant and Leonard Woolf). Keynes's legacy across many areas of British life was very significant, and will be considered in more detail in the conclusion. But in the UK at least, the era of epoch-defining giants in the field of economics was over.

Conclusion

No one could doubt Keynes's very significant influence on economic theory and world affairs, but how brilliant was he as a thinker? The philosopher Bertrand Russell has provided a concise and accurate evaluation of his fellow Cambridge don:

> Keynes's intellect was the sharpest and clearest that I have ever known. When I argued with him I felt that I took my life in my hands, and I seldom emerged without feeling something of a fool. I was sometimes inclined to feel that so much cleverness must be incompatible with depth, but I do not think this feeling was justified.[1]

What would Keynes the biographer have made of Keynes the economist? It could be argued that he would have placed himself some way between the other-worldly and aloof natural-scientific type of genius as represented by Isaac Newton, and the worldly and more socially engaged artistic type of genius as represented by some of his Bloomsbury friends (e.g. Virginia Woolf). Having a foot in both camps, he was perfectly positioned to excel in the social scientific work that was an essential component of economics.

Like the high artistic genius, he excelled at writing and at understanding ephemeral things that cannot easily be quantified; like the lone scientific genius, he excelled at focusing his intellect on finding the solution to a single strictly quantifiable problem. But in addition to these two opposite qualities, he also possessed a profound understanding of human beings as social animals, and the nexus of natural, social and individual elements that must be comprehended by the philosopher-economist, if they are to be relevant to real-world issues.

He was not without faults. The conflict with David Lloyd George over war finance has been documented. Having a superior academic intellect does not necessarily guarantee ownership of the superior policy argument. Lloyd George's characterisation of Keynes as 'mercurial' (eloquent and ingenious but changeable) was not entirely inaccurate. And even though, in his wisdom of intellect, Keynes profoundly transcended his privileged class position, there were still echoes of condescension towards the 'boorish proletariat'. Why did workers fail to appreciate the beauty of fine ballet or of vellum-bound incunabula? Probably because they were too busy earning near-subsistence wages. But if he did not fully understand the individual limitations of class background, he certainly supported general improvements to universal social welfare, qualifying as a classic English liberal within the proud tradition that he had explicitly outlined. However, just as there were tinges of socialism in his concern for social welfare, there were also tinges of conservatism in his concern for the future prospects of the UK as a nation.

Keynes and the UK

Keynes was very clear that British economic policy should be framed solely in terms of British national interest, and felt no need to make any apologies for this entirely natural goal. Even if, today, many desire to adopt a Rawlsian perspective and give added weight to the needs of less fortunate groups across the world ('the welfare of worst-off groups should be of primary consideration'), it is not always as clear as it used to be exactly who these groups might be taken to be, or where they are located. The BRIC economies (Brazil, Russia, India and China) are in the early twenty-first century growing at a much faster rate than they did previously, and the expansion of the industrial sectors of these countries (especially the latter two) is providing serious competition for some sluggish West-European economies. The 2008 financial crisis in the Eurozone has only exacerbated this problem, bringing massive levels of unemployment to countries like Spain and Greece, and high unemployment to the UK. Some Europeans are now being forced to migrate to so-called less-developed countries in order to find work, just as economic migration into Europe continues.

In the case of India, arguments from an anti-imperialist perspective ask the question of whether nineteenth-century colonial rule 'exploited' the economic resources of India. But the situation in the early twenty-first century has (in some ways) come full-circle, as it is wealthy Indian companies (like Tata Steel) that are buying up ailing British companies. Is this not taking advantage of Britain's long-term industrial decline? Those historians who argue in favour of the 'drain' thesis – that Britain drained resources out of India and thus exploited it by means of investments made by British companies before 1914 – must, to be consistent, allow the logical possibility that Indian companies who buy struggling British industries today might similarly be 'draining' resources out of the UK, especially as foreign workers in Britain often send a part of their earnings back to their country of origin. In the early twenty-first century India has its own space programme, but still receives some humanitarian aid from the UK.

The author of *Indian Currency and Finance* would certainly have had something important to say on these issues, especially as he had emphasised the 'responsibilities of colonial rule' contention, and argued against the idea that British rule only ever operated in British interests: the concept of *noblesse oblige* was seen to apply to nations as well as individuals. There was undoubtedly an element of condescension operating here, and Keynes was not fully aware of the sometimes very negative side to colonial rule, but this does not mean that there had never been a positive side to British involvement in India, as he had emphasised. What Keynes wrote in 1913 about the Indian financial system might be seen to have wider relevance: 'the complexity and the coherence of the system require the constant attention of anyone who would criticise the parts'.[2] In 1933, Keynes called for a 'moderate and statesman-like demeanour' in dealing with the controversial topic of the future form of government for India.[3] In 1943, he even highlighted the 'very large' contribution that India had made 'on the physical and man-power plane' to the Second World War.[4]

As has been shown throughout this book, Keynes always looked for a balanced and multi-sided approach to any issue, including economic development policy. Rigidly following any abstract principle in its most extreme form across all circumstances was precisely the type of doctrinaire approach that was anathema to him. Thus, always following Rawls's maxim about targeting policy to the least fortunate, if applied in every circumstance, would undoubtedly produce some undesirable outcomes even for those who were the target, partly due to the law of unintended consequences, and partly because Rawls failed to consider the complexity of the link between moral belief and real interest.

Evolutionary biologists suggest that the emotive thirst for justice is an offspring of the gene-survival strategy of reciprocal altruism (providing benefits to non-relatives in anticipation of future reciprocity), and hence the indiscriminate use of Rawls's maxim might encourage the eventual receipt of a sucker's payoff.[5] Consequently, the wise Keynesian statesman should know when to follow and when not to follow such an approach, as with any other abstract principle. As Keynes declared in *The General Theory*, *contra* Rawls: 'there is social and psychological justification for significant inequalities of income and wealth', these being that 'dangerous human proclivities can be canalised' into more socially useful channels by allowing the individual pursuit of profit within properly regulated constraints.[6] Consequently, those who take *The General Theory* as inspiration for an extensive redistribution agenda are confusing full employment with full uniformity.

Consequences for economic theory

One of the most immediate results of Keynes's 'new economics' was the invention of the IS-LM model of the economy that quickly became a central component of macroeconomic analysis. But beyond this and at a more fundamental level, *The General Theory* made a convincing case that economic theory should not only be concerned with prices, interest rates, profits and so on in their empirical manifestation, but should look more deeply into the psychological drives, motivations and behaviours that underpinned them. In order to understand how the economy operates, economists have to understand the human behaviour that generates the variables that they have conventionally studied. This aspect of *The General Theory* was sometimes lost on those who first created the early manifestations of 'Keynesian economics'. Part of the problem here was the profound (but mistaken) belief that existed for a very long time amongst many mainstream economists, that economics should use mechanistic models, methodologies and techniques that had been developed in the natural sciences.

A classic example was Léon Walras's mathematical model of general equilibrium in an economy constructed as a system of simultaneous equations, which has been celebrated by some as the most significant achievement of pure economics, and criticised by others as entirely irrelevant to understanding real-world issues. As the latter group would maintain, fixed mechanical laws (such as Force equals Mass multiplied by Acceleration) might be very appropriate to describe the physical universe, but they are often very inappropriate to describe the social universe. Individual human beings do not behave like inanimate particles subject to gravitational fields. People can (usually) choose what they want to do, their behaviour is not deterministic and they can even decide to do things that go wilfully against their apparent self-interest (e.g. commit suicide). Suicides are more convincingly explained by psychological factors linked to social context, not as the result of universal mechanistic laws expressed by mathematical equations.

Keynes absolutely and explicitly emphasised this point in his writings, most clearly in a letter he wrote in July 1938 about the inappropriateness of econometric modelling:

> I want to emphasise strongly the point about economics being a moral science. I mentioned before that it deals with introspection and with values. I might have added that it deals with motives, expectations, psychological uncertainties...It is as though the fall of the apple to the ground depended on the apple's motives, on whether it is worth while falling to the ground, and whether the ground wanted the apple to fall, and on mistaken calculations on the part of the apple as to how far it was from the centre of the earth.[7]

In the physical universe, the apple has no choice on whether to fall or not, given certain mechanistic regularities and its position in space and time; in the social universe, apples (human beings) must decide for themselves whether to fall or not, even given any set of physical realities that they might find themselves in. The methodology of understanding the former type of system cannot, therefore, be applied simply and analogously to the latter type. If it is, grave errors will undoubtedly be made. It could be argued that the most recent example of such errors in the financial arena is the 2008 credit crunch.

2008 versus 1929: a comparative anatomy

The main reason why Keynes has been 'resurrected' in the press and other media at the end of the first decade of the twenty-first century, a phenomenon not unreasonably promoted by some as 'the return of the master', is the outbreak of the international financial crisis that occurred in 2008, which then produced a worldwide economic slump that has reasonably been compared to the depression that followed the Wall Street crash in 1929. There are indeed some notable similarities between 2008 and 1929, but there are also some important differences.

Firstly, the similarities: both started off in the financial and banking sector but quickly spread to many other parts of the 'real' economy; both followed a long period of boom in which it was declared that 'the good times would never end', or that a 'Goldilocks economy' had been created in which the balance of growth factors was 'just right'; both involved a 'flight to cash' that put severe strain upon the prices of many capital assets; both showed similarities of progression and effect across various different nation states; both included (in some instances) countries attempting desperately to maintain existing fixed exchange rate regimes (the gold standard in 1929 and the Euro in 2008); and both had a serious dampening effect on overall levels of employment and business confidence.

However, there were also some notable differences: whereas, following 1929, many banks in profound crisis in America were allowed to go bust, following 2008 some banks (for example those in the UK) were rescued and bailed out by the government; whereas in America after 1929, the government only tentatively and after a period of time had elapsed began a programme to stimulate the economy, in 2008, a fiscal stimulus programme was much quicker to emerge; and whereas after 1929, much of the poverty that was seen in advanced Western states was shocking in absolute terms, after 2008, many people have been very seriously affected by the global meltdown, but mass poverty has not re-emerged in the West on the same scale as it did after 1929.

But perhaps the single biggest intellectual difference between 2008 and 1929 was that in 2008 there was a set of recognised 'Keynesian policies' in existence to deal with an economic depression, whereas in 1929 Keynes had only began to outline some aspects of these policies, and by no means were they accepted by governments as being useful. Policies that are characterised as Keynesian have been used following 2008. The main elements are: fiscal stimulus packages (a combination of increased government spending and some tax cuts to encourage consumer spending), an attempt to counter global trade imbalances, some measure of control on international capital flows and so-called quantitative easing of the money supply. The first three do have some definite basis in Keynes's own thinking of the 1930s, but he had only recommended quantitative easing (i.e. the creation of additional money) as a means of war finance during the First World War. Sometime after 1918 he recognised that this method had been a very dangerous one, and during the Second World War he was much more cautious about using it.

A basic problem faced by those advocating increased government expenditure as a means to stimulate demand following 2008 is that, over a number of years, many Western governments have accumulated large budget deficits, which means that their capacity for financing such expenditure from extra borrowing is limited. Thus, some governments have been faced with the contradictory tasks of having to increase their expenditure in order to stimulate economic growth, while simultaneously trying to reduce their expenditure in order to bolster their creditworthiness and diminish the interest rates paid on debt. Having to make some tax cuts in order to stimulate growth further exacerbates this problem, as falling tax revenue is a common feature of economic downturns even without cutting tax rates. Raising taxes might be seen as part of an easy solution to the government debt problem, but this would have its own consequences, such as reduced consumer and/or business expenditure, and might generate additional political and international effects such as capital flight, company relocation and government unpopularity.

The underlying problem causing the large government deficits is that some Western countries have been living above their means, but the political will to make the changes necessary to counteract this has been noticeably absent. The international component of this is that as less-developed countries grow and become more prosperous, this inevitably means that in relative terms, developed Western economies become less comparatively advanced. If Western states want to increase their standards of living, then they must maintain their competitiveness in the global marketplace, but this is much easier said than done. One way of influencing global trade flows is of course customs tariffs, which Keynes for a while at least in the early 1930s did advocate. But free trade ideology is so prevalent today that anyone caught suggesting that tariffs might have even a small role to play in certain limited areas is invariably dismissed as economically illiterate. It is true that Keynes only promoted tariffs in certain specific instances, and he did not see increased protectionism as an ultimate solution to global economic problems, but neither did he dismiss national trade safeguards entirely. His cautious brand of internationalist nationalism is something that should have great resonance in today's world of increased globalisation in some areas and heightened national awakenings in others.

Whether the overall policy response to 2008 will, in years to come, be judged as being more successful than it was to 1929, is (in 2012) rather difficult to tell. Certainly, the rescue of the banks in the UK has prevented some of the worst immediate knock-on effects of individuals and companies actually losing their deposits, but the ultimate cost of this to the taxpayer is not at all certain. Socialising the debt certainly helped in the short-term; whether in the long-term the judgement will be as clear-cut is unknown. But, from the opposite perspective, the fact that the long-term consequences of something might not totally be clear is not a compelling reason to do nothing at all. It can with reasonable certainly be stated that, if he were alive today, Keynes would have supported the idea of rescuing troubled high-street banks as a principle, although he might have outlined some different means of doing so and some dissimilar precise objectives.

However, one much less frequently discussed but very relevant parallel consequence that Keynes would have been concerned with was that between the disastrous effects of attempting to maintain the traditional form of the gold standard, as occurred for example in the UK in the second half of the 1920s, and the damaging effects of attempting to preserve the existing form of the Euro in countries like Greece and Portugal in the period after 2008. Both the gold standard and the Euro forcibly lock nation states into rigid and inappropriate exchange rate levels, preventing them from undergoing natural devaluations that should take place as a consequence of relative changes in economic structure and performance. Thus they create additional social, political and economic problems in a crisis period that would have been at least partially avoidable in a flexible exchange rate system.

It should be noted that the underlying cause of the inappropriate adherence in both cases was exactly the same: dogmatic belief in an abstract principle that, it was erroneously thought, had to be maintained in all circumstances. The abstract principles themselves were different in the two cases – the anchor of gold versus the need for pan-European currency union – but the fact of ideological belief trampling over common-sense pragmatism was identical in both cases. Many of Keynes's own economic arguments were directed against precisely such inappropriate doctrinal beliefs that had little relation to reality.

Later development of Keynes's ideas

Although Keynes's influence has, by the early twenty-first century, been declared at an end and then resurrected many times, and hence it can be assumed that (like Schrödinger's cat) in the long run Keynes's legacy is both dead and alive, it is worth briefly considering some of the more notable twentieth-century currents in economics that have claimed to be founded on aspects of his thought. The most significant in theoretical terms have been: the old Keynesianism of the neoclassical synthesis, post-Keynesian economics and the new Keynesian economics of the 1980s.

The neoclassical synthesis aimed to integrate the insights of *The General Theory* (taken as being sticky or inflexible wages and imperfect competition), and the IS-LM approach, with some of the existing ideas of the neoclassical school (such as the rational maximising behaviour of individuals). Across the 1950s and the 1960s, the mixing of these two currents duly occurred, based on the assumption that in the long-run prices and wages were flexible but in the short-run they were not, resulting in what some called (rather unflatteringly) Bastard Keynesianism. However, the veracity of this approach came under severe fire in the 1970s when stagflation (significant inflation combined with stagnant growth) began to develop, something that had not been considered within the framework of the neoclassical synthesis.

Out of a fundamental disagreement with the notion that the neoclassical synthesis truly represented Keynes's vision, post-Keynesian economists went back to *The General Theory* and adopted a more radical approach. They stressed the idea that what Keynes had called 'animal spirits' determined the behaviour of entrepreneurs, rather than the rational maximising assumption taken from the neoclassical tradition, and highlighted that uncertainty was the essential backdrop to all economic decision-making. The new Keynesian economics of the 1980s went further than the neoclassical synthesis in explaining why wages might actually be inflexible: all participants in the economy were not price-takers, as had been tacitly assumed by the neoclassical school; instead some agents were price-makers with market power. Prices were sticky because of menu costs, i.e. there were costs involved in changing prices, and hence the assumption that wages and prices would automatically and instantaneously adjust to changes in the wider economy was false.

There are also some more eclectic interpretations of *The General Theory*. Hyman Minsky proposed that its essential feature was that money was conceived as a financing veil between real assets on the one hand, and their values as expressed in equivalent units at any given time on the other. What caused financial instability were disequilibrium forces that affected the valuations of assets relative to the value of current output and wages. As this ratio changed, prospects for future investment also changed, producing the fluctuation in investment activity that was the essential feature of a capitalist economy. Minsky's financial instability hypothesis was offered as an explanation of the financial turmoil of the early 1970s, but might equally be applicable to the more recent events of 2008.

It can accurately be said that, between them, the various currents of Keynesian economics have not been entirely free of the factionalism and internecine disputes that have also affected more obviously political movements like Marxism. What they all lacked was a towering figure (like Keynes) who had the authority to convincingly arbitrate what the 'true' interpretation of the doctrine should be.

The rarest of birds

Finally, it is worth considering what Keynes's life and work tell us about the nature and requirements of being an economist. The subject of this book was very clear in providing an answer to this question. In his biographical study of Alfred Marshall, Keynes explained that:

> The study of economics does not seem to require any specialised gifts of an unusually high order. Is it not, intellectually regarded, a very easy subject compared with the higher branches of philosophy and pure science? Yet good, or even competent, economists are the rarest of birds. An easy subject, at which very few excel! The paradox finds its explanation, perhaps, in that the master-economist must possess a rare *combination* of gifts...and must combine talents not often found together. He must be mathematician, historian, statesman, philosopher – in some degree. He must understand symbols and speak in words. He must contemplate the particular in terms of the general...He must study the present in the light of the past for the purposes of the future.[8]

As this book has tried hard to illustrate, Keynes was indeed a mathematician, historian, statesman and philosopher – and even a nascent psychologist – of the very highest calibre. In his own biographical studies, such intellectual boundary crossing was especially noted and highly praised.

The physicist Isaac Newton, for example, 'possessed in exceptional degree almost every kind of intellectual aptitude – lawyer, historian, theologian, not less than mathematician, physicist, astronomer'.[9] The classical economist T.R. Malthus exhibited an 'unusual combination of keeping an open mind to the shifting picture of experience and of constantly applying to its interpretation the principles of formal thought'.[10] The neoclassical economist W.S. Jevons was 'certainly a notable example of this' many-sidedness of talent, possessing scientific and experimental training, a logical and analytical bent, plus significant historical and antiquarian interests.[11] And the financial journalist Walter Bagehot, author of a classic study of the London money market entitled *Lombard Street*, was really a psychologist whose 'main strength lay in his characterisation of the psychology of the City, of the springs of motive and the practical behaviour of bankers'.[12]

If only all economists (and financial experts) today had the same multifarious conception of their professions as Keynes promulgated, alongside the same concern with what can be called the social function of business investment, then the financial crisis of 2008 might well have been mitigated to a large degree, or even avoided entirely. But, unfortunately, as Keynes would undoubtedly have warned, the baby (an understanding of market failure) was often thrown out with the bathwater (central planning) when the various Soviet-type economies collapsed after 1989.

That Keynes's conception of the economist differed from the accepted view even in the 1930s, was clear from his 'target' in publishing *The General Theory*, A.C. Pigou. In *The Theory of Unemployment* of 1933, Pigou declared that while 'many economists' sought to play a part in guiding conduct, 'that is not their primary business. They are physiologists, not clinical practitioners; engineers, not engine-drivers'.[13] For Pigou, the 'real' economist was a pure theorist concerned primarily with abstract cognition. However, the danger of this purist view is that understanding the consequences of adopting theories is relegated to second place. Having discovered the 'correct' theory to explain the economy, Pigou-type economists then wash their hands of the practical consequences: any problems must be due to bad implementation or misunderstandings. Surely, pure theory cannot be wrong? But for Keynes, pure theory was *invariably* wrong, if it did not attempt to engage with the reality of engine-driving or clinical practice. After all, there is no universal 'pure economy' in existence, only historically specific national economies, as they exist in any given country at any given time.

The financial crisis of 2008 can thus be conceived as merely the latest disastrous expression of the various extremist doctrinal certainties that Keynes had devoted a major part of his life to arguing against. As was often erroneously suggested immediately after 1989, the collapse of the USSR had 'proved' that Adam Smith was right and Karl Marx was wrong, whereas, in fact, the reality was much more complicated and much less reassuring than this. Both Smith and Marx had *always* been wrong: free markets and centralised plans not only did not function as their advocates had claimed, but in fact were governed by forces operating at an ontological level much more fundamental than either individual maximisation or the social good, neither of which actually existed in a pure or universal form. In fact, human behaviour is really determined by psychological, physiological and institutional habits and customs, which are historically, socially and genetically grounded. In *The General Theory*, Keynes tentatively called such behaviour 'habits of psychological response', and they must be studied scientifically, without any *a priori* assumptions about their absolute rationality (or utter irrationality).[14]

Psychological reckoning

Consequently, the international economic downturn following 2008 provoked not only the return of Keynesian economics, but also illustrated the inevitable revenge of 'illogical' psychology over 'rational' maximising behaviour. The human mind invented the maximising approach to economics (and later rational-choice theory) to explain its own activities, but by doing so it had perpetuated a 'grand illusion' against itself, partly as the result of its own autistic inability to perceive the complexities and realities of the social universe as it really is. According to the eminent historian E.H. Carr, it was Sigmund Freud who drove 'the last nail into the coffin of the ancient illusion that the motives from which men allege or believe themselves to have acted are in fact adequate to explain their action'.[15] But in much of economic theory, this illusion was still widespread at least up until the 1930s, when Keynes began his assault on the mechanistic postulates of the classical school.

As he explained in *The General Theory* with regard to the evaluation of stock market investments, 'the outcome of the mass psychology of a large number of ignorant individuals is liable to change violently as the result of a sudden fluctuation of opinion'.[16] This mass or crowd psychology was the subject of an entire book by Freud entitled *Group Psychology and the Analysis of the Ego*, the

English translation of which (published in 1922) was made by none other than James Strachey, Keynes's Bloomsbury friend.[17] In *The General Theory*, Keynes added this type of collective herd behaviour to financial speculation and obtained 'the psychology of the market'.[18] There was often a definite and explicable logic to this type of economic behaviour, but it was certainly not always and entirely 'rational' in the narrow sense meant by neoclassical theory.

That Keynes had been attuned to the importance of psychology to economics well before *The General Theory* is apparent from *A Treatise on Money* of 1930. Here he had explained that, with regard to setting short-term stock and bond investment strategy, 'it may often profit the wisest to anticipate mob psychology rather than the real trend of events, and to ape unreason proleptically'.[19] He even suggested the application by management of a 'homeopathic cure' to the 'half-unreasonable' psychological characteristics of the market. Still earlier, in *A Tract on Monetary Reform* of 1923, Keynes had outlined the idea that there was a 'psychological equilibrium' in operation within capitalism in relation to the acceptance of unequal rewards between classes, which could be disturbed and then re-established just like the more conventional economic equilibrium itself.[20] This type of psychical equilibrium was a concept that the young Keynes had first encountered in the work of the psychologist G.F. Stout.[21]

Thus, Keynes had begun on the path of seeing beyond the thin veil of pseudo-rationalism that had encompassed much of mainstream economics until 1936 – what Joan Robinson called Freud's uncovering of the psychological 'propensity to rationalization' – but given the nature of the human mind itself, this is a struggle that is ongoing and easy to overlook.[22] As Keynes explained in February 1937:

> ...false rationalisation follows the lines of the Benthamite calculus. The hypothesis of a calculable future leads to a wrong interpretation of the principles of behaviour...and to an underestimation of the concealed factors of utter doubt, precariousness, hope and fear.[23]

Moving beyond this type of false rationalisation requires that economists should master other disciplines (like psychology) that they have sometimes frowned upon, and thus for individuals to use the rational part of their minds to document the organic and animalistic behaviour of their own selves. This latter part of behaviour is steeped in foggy and complex mechanisms of camouflage, primarily for evolutionary biological reasons.

It was certainly true that, even by 1936, Keynes had only glimpsed the need for economists to 'get the psychology right' as far as it underpinned economic behaviour, and he provided no fully-developed treatise along these lines, but this does not mean that he did not accept that such an approach was absolutely necessary. He even characterised it as 'that exciting, dangerous subject, psychology'.[24] And what was Keynes's account of 'the method of modern statesmen', if not a part-psychological analysis of how the political class within capitalism operated?

Part of the answer to the question of where Keynes had obtained his early knowledge of psychology from is a matter of record: he had formally studied it as a special subject for the Civil Servant entrance examinations in 1906. He had unexpectedly topped the class in the psychology exam, whilst coming 'unaccountably low' in political economy. At the time this discrepancy in performance seemed entirely incongruous, but it was much less so by 1936. His substantial notes on the work of two psychologists (Stout and James Sully) showed clearly that he had a definite talent for understanding this subject.[25]

Even apart from Keynes's direct study of psychology for the Civil Service exams, there was another more personal link between Stout and Keynes: G.E. Moore. When Keynes admitted in his autobiographical memoir entitled 'My Early Beliefs' that under Moore's spell, 'Nothing mattered except states of mind', what springs directly to mind is Stout's definition of psychology as was noted by the young Keynes: 'the positive science of mental process'.[26] Stout's philosophical emphasis on mental acts was something that Moore had obtained at least in part from his Cambridge teachers. Although today known as a specialist in psychology, Stout had also lectured at Cambridge on the history of philosophy. Another of his students (in addition to Moore) was Bertrand Russell.[27]

Moreover, as Keynes argued in March 1926 with respect to the quickly-discarded late nineteenth-century idea of combining mathematics with social psychics, to form a hybrid type of 'mathematico-economics':

> The atomic hypothesis which has worked so splendidly in physics breaks down in psychics. We are faced at every turn with the problems of organic unity, of discreteness, of discontinuity... comparisons of quantity fail us, small changes produce large effects, the assumptions of a uniform and homogeneous continuum are not satisfied.[28]

The answer is what might boldly be called 'discontinuity economics' in analogy with discontinuity physics, or perhaps more obviously 'psychological economics', 'behavioural economics' and even 'neuro-economics'. These three fields have recently received a great deal of attention from scholars, and it can be argued that these relatively new disciplines are the real methodological grandchildren of *The General Theory*, not IS-LM-style macroeconomic modelling.

As has been outlined, economic psychology explains business behaviour 'by learning and decision processes, motivation, personality factors, perception, preferences' and other basic motivators.[29] Behavioural economics employs methods from other fields such as game theory to model human action. Neuro-economics studies the neurological and physiological bases of economic choices in brain activity. Indicatively and rightly, a psychologist (Daniel Kahneman) was recently awarded the Nobel Prize for economics: Keynes would have felt both delighted and vindicated.

There was actually a definite, if usually unrecognised, link between Keynes and an early US-based pioneer of economic psychology, George Katona. In 1942, Katona published a book entitled *War Without Inflation: A Psychological Approach to Problems of War Economy*. In this book the author used (among other things) both Keynes's work on war finance, and his work on entrepreneurial expectations as found in *The General Theory*, to analyse the psychological factors contributing to price inflation. Katona argued that behavioural responses to situations depended on how they were viewed by subjects, i.e. on psychological perceptions. Price rises only became inflationary when further rises were expected, and hence inflation was not the automatic effect of purely economic factors, as was suggested by the mechanical quantity theory of money.[30] Here Katona was being even more radical than Keynes by fully embracing the psychological expectations agenda that the author of *The General Theory* had only partially initiated. But some economists even today still dismiss the psychological underpinnings of human behaviour as either irrelevant to their subject, or as fully explained by the rational-choice approach.

A major problem here is not necessarily completely intellectual in nature, but institutional as well, as economists are part of social groups that define their status and validity by the accuracy and relevance of their ideas. Anything that questions the veracity of their long-received ideas and methodology might also question their accepted status. But as Keynes rightly declared, economists should also be mathematicians, historians, statesmen, philosophers (and by extension of *The General Theory* also psychologists): if they are not, then they may be condemned to repeat the same pseudo-rationalist errors of 1917 (for the left), 1929 (for the right) and now 2008 (for both the right and the left) for generations to come.

Notes

Introduction

1. J.M. Keynes, *CW* (London: Macmillan, 1972), vol.X, p.363.
2. Milo Keynes (ed.), *Essays on John Maynard Keynes* (Cambridge: CUP, 1975), p.xiv.
3. Vincent Barnett, *Kondratiev and the Dynamics of Economic Development* (London: Macmillan, 1998) and Vincent Barnett, *E.E. Slutsky as Economist and Mathematician* (London: Routledge, 2011).
4. L.R. Klein, *The Keynesian Revolution* (London: Macmillan, 1952); R.E. Lucas and T.J. Sargent, 'After Keynesian Macroeconomics', in *After the Phillips Curve* (Boston: Federal Reserve, 1978).
5. David Laidler, *Fabricating the Keynesian Revolution* (Cambridge: CUP, 1999); R.E. Backhouse and B.W. Bateman, *Capitalist Revolutionary* (Harvard: Cambridge, MA, 2011).
6. Michael Stewart, *Keynes and After* (Harmondsworth: Penguin, 1967), p.254.
7. Keynes, *CW*, vol.X, pp.363–64.
8. J.M. Keynes, *CW* (London: Macmillan, 1971), vol.II, p.26.
9. Some of Keynes's fellow Bloomsbury members were interested in Jung. See Gilles Dostaler, *Keynes and his Battles* (Cheltenham: Elgar, 2007), p.50.
10. R.S. Lazarus and E.M. Opton (eds), *Personality* (Harmondsworth: Penguin, 1967), p.18.
11. Keynes Papers, King's College, UA/4/3/4. J.M. Keynes, *The General Theory of Employment, Interest and Money*, (London: Macmillan, 1973), p.150.
12. Keynes, *CW*, vol.X, p.86.
13. Ibid, p.98.
14. Adam Smith, *Essays on Philosophical Subjects* (Indianapolis: Liberty, 1982), p.265.
15. Keynes, *CW*, vol.X, p.388.
16. J.M. Keynes, *Essays in Persuasion* (London: Hart-Davies, 1952), p.vi.
17. Ibid, p.450.
18. Keynes, *CW*, vol.II, p.23.
19. J.M. Keynes, *A Treatise on Money* (London: Macmillan, 1930), vol.2, p.290.

20. William James, *The Principles of Psychology* (London: Macmillan, 1891), vol.2, p.424.

21. Robert Skidelsky, *John Maynard Keynes: The Economist as Saviour 1920–37* (London: Macmillan, 1992), p.234 and p.414.

22. J.M. Keynes, *CW* (London: Macmillan, 1973), vol.VIII, p.332. Keynes Papers, UA/4/3/8.

23. Sigmund Freud, *The Ego and the Id* (London: Hogarth Press, 1927).

24. Keynes, *Essays in Persuasion*, p.366.

25. Sigmund Freud, *Beyond the Pleasure Principle* (London: Psycho-Analytic Press, 1922), p.1.

1 A most indescribable and extraordinary game

1. Robert Skidelsky, *John Maynard Keynes: Hopes Betrayed* (London: Macmillan, 1983), p.74.

2. D.E. Moggridge, *Maynard Keynes* (London: Routledge, 1992), p.33.

3. Eton school website.

4. Thorstein Veblen, *The Theory of the Leisure Class* (London: Unwin, 1925), pp.35–67.

5. Skidelsky, *John Maynard Keynes: Hopes Betrayed*, pp.51–57.

6. Moggridge, *Maynard Keynes*, p.35.

7. J.M. Keynes, *Two Memoirs* (London: Hart-Davies, 1949), p.81.

8. Ibid, pp.81–82.

9. A.J. Ayer, *Philosophy in the Twentieth Century* (London: Counterpoint, 1982), p.40.

10. Skidelsky, *John Maynard Keynes: Hopes Betrayed*, p.124.

11. Keynes Papers, King's College, PP/53/0.

12. Moggridge, *Maynard Keynes*, p.59.

13. Keynes, *Two Memoirs*, p.81.

14. Skidelsky, *John Maynard Keynes: Hopes Betrayed*, p.177.

15. Keynes Papers, King's College, TP/A/1–2.

2 Early writings

1. Keynes Papers, King's College, PP/31/9/1.

2. Keynes Papers, PP/31/9/1–2.

3. Keynes Papers, PP/31/4/1.

4. Keynes Papers, PP/31/4/3.

5. Keynes Papers, PP/31/15/9.

6. Keynes Papers, PP/31/15/10.

7. Robert Skidelsky, *John Maynard Keynes: Hopes Betrayed* (London: Macmillan, 1983), p.91.

8. Keynes Papers, PP/31/15/5.

9. G.E. Moore, *Principia Ethica* (Cambridge: CUP, 1903), p.181.

10. Skidelsky, *John Maynard Keynes: Hopes Betrayed*, p.148.

11. J.M. Keynes, *Two Memoirs* (London: Hart-Davis, 1949), p.82.
12. Ibid, p.83.
13. Ibid, pp.86–87.
14. Keynes Papers, TP/A/1/5.
15. J.M. Keynes, *CW* (London: Macmillan, 1973), vol.VIII, p.342.
16. Keynes Papers, TP/A/2/180–82.
17. Keynes, *CW*, vol.VIII, pp.342–44.
18. Ibid, pp.345–47.
19. J.M. Keynes, *CW* (London: Macmillan, 1971), vol.XV, p.48.
20. Ibid, p.56.
21. Ibid, p.55.
22. Ibid, p.59.
23. Skidelsky, *John Maynard Keynes: Hopes Betrayed*, p.228.

3 Selling economics by the hour and on the Q.T. (of M.)

1. J.M. Keynes, 'Early Lectures', in *CW* (London: Macmillan, 1983), vol.XII, p.688.
2. A.F.W. Plumptre, 'Keynes in Cambridge', in *Keynes: Critical Assessments* (London: Routledge, 1990), vol.1, p.148.
3. A. Robinson, 'John Maynard Keynes', in *Keynes: Critical Assessments* (London: Routledge, 1990), vol.1, p.97.
4. J.A. Schumpeter, 'J.M. Keynes', in *Keynes: Critical Assessments* (London: Routledge, 1990), vol.1, p.53.
5. Ibid, p.97.
6. Keynes, *CW*, vol.XII, p.695.
7. D.E. Moggridge, *Maynard Keynes* (London: Routledge, 1992), p.202.
8. Keynes, *CW*, vol.XII, p.698 & p.756.
9. Robert Skidelsky, *John Maynard Keynes: Hopes Betrayed* (London: Macmillan, 1983), pp.273–74.
10. *The Times*, 1 November 1912, p.17.
11. Skidelsky, *John Maynard Keynes: Hopes Betrayed*, p.273.
12. *The Times*, 14 November 1912, p.17.
13. J.M. Keynes, *CW* (London: Macmillan, 1971), vol.I, p.24.
14. J.M. Keynes, *CW* (London: Macmillan, 1972), vol.X, p.41.
15. Keynes, *CW*, vol.I, p.101.
16. Ibid, p.136.
17. Moggridge, *Maynard Keynes*, pp.838–39.
18. Ibid, p.214.
19. Ibid, p.215.
20. Ibid, p.203.
21. Vincent Barnett, *Marx* (London: Routledge, 2009), p.110.
22. Carlo Cristiano, 'Keynes and India, 1909–13', in *European Journal of the History of Economic Thought*, 16 (2), p.313.
23. John Toye, *Keynes on Population* (Oxford: OUP, 2000), p.64.
24. Cristiano, 'Keynes and India, 1909–13', p.313.

25. Keynes, *CW*, vol.X, p.264.
26. J.R. Hicks, 'Mr Keynes' Theory of Employment', *Economic Journal*, XLVI, pp.238–53.
27. Moggridge, *Maynard Keynes*, p.210.
28. Keynes, *CW*, vol.XII, p.4.
29. Piero Mini, 'Keynes' Investments', *American Journal of Economics and Sociology*, 54 (1), p.48.
30. Skidelsky, *John Maynard Keynes: Hopes Betrayed*, p.242.
31. Ibid, pp.240–41.

4 Early economics

1. J.M. Keynes, *CW* (London: Macmillan, 1983), vol.XII, p.695.
2. Ibid, pp.696–98.
3. Ibid, p.706.
4. *The Economist*, 20 September 1913, p.554.
5. J.M. Keynes, *CW* (London: Macmillan, 1971), vol.I, pp.166–68.
6. Keynes Papers, King's College, ID/4/240.
7. J.M. Keynes, *CW* (London: Macmillan, 1973), vol.XIII, p.2.
8. Ibid, p.4.
9. Keynes, *CW*, vol.XII, p.717.
10. Keynes, *CW*, vol.XIII, p.11.
11. Keynes, *CW*, vol.XII, p.717.
12. J.M. Keynes, 'Tables Showing for Each of the Years 1900–11 the Estimated Value of the Imports and Exports of the UK at the Prices Prevailing in 1900', *Economic Journal*, December 1912, p.631.
13. John Toye, *Keynes on Population* (Oxford: OUP, 2000), p.66.
14. Ibid, p.71.
15. Ibid, p.42.
16. Ibid, pp.70–71.
17. Ibid, p.40.

5 Killing Germans as cheaply as possible

1. J.M. Keynes, *CW* (London: Macmillan, 1972), vol.X, p.24.
2. J.M. Keynes, *CW* (London: Macmillan, 1971), vol.XVI, pp.208–9.
3. Robert Skidelsky, *John Maynard Keynes: Hopes Betrayed* (London: Macmillan, 1983), p.335.
4. D.E. Moggridge, *Maynard Keynes* (London: Routledge, 1992), p.267.
5. Skidelsky, *John Maynard Keynes: Hopes Betrayed*, p.350.
6. Ibid, pp.317–18.
7. Moggridge, *Maynard Keynes*, p.255.
8. Keynes, *CW*, vol.XVI, p.159.
9. Ibid, p.160.
10. Skidelsky, *John Maynard Keynes: Hopes Betrayed*, p.349.

11. Ibid, p.352.
12. Keynes, *CW*, vol.XVI, p.194.
13. Ibid, p.193.
14. Ibid, p.194.
15. D.C. Rielage, *Russian Supply Efforts During the First World War* (Jefferson, N.C.: McFarland, 2002), p.52.
16. J.M. Keynes, *CW* (London: Macmillan, 1971), vol.II, p.148.
17. Rielage, *Russian Supply Efforts During the First World War*, p.55.
18. Ibid, p.72.
19. David Lloyd George, *The Truth About Reparations and War-Debts* (London: Heinemann, 1932), p.98.
20. For the financial and economic effects of the war on Russia see Vincent Barnett, 'Calling up the Reserves: Keynes, Tugan-Baranovsky and Russian War Finance', *Europe-Asia Studies*, 2001, 53 (1), pp.151–69.
21. Moggridge, *Maynard Keynes*, p.280.
22. *War Memoirs of David Lloyd George* (London: Odhams, 1938), vol.1, p.410.
23. Keynes, *CW*, vol.XVI, p.265.
24. Skidelsky, *John Maynard Keynes: Hopes Betrayed*, p.345.
25. Niall Ferguson, *The Pity of War* (New York: Basic, 1999), p.327.
26. Moggridge, *Maynard Keynes*, p.296.
27. Keynes, *CW*, vol.XVI, p.425.
28. Ibid, p.418.
29. Skidelsky, *John Maynard Keynes: Hopes Betrayed*, p.372.
30. Moggridge, *Maynard Keynes*, p.312.
31. Keynes, *CW*, vol.XVI, p.460.

6 The economic consequences of war

1. J.M. Keynes, *CW* (London: Macmillan, 1971), vol.II, pp.148–9.
2. J.M. Keynes, *A Treatise on Money* (London: Macmillan, 1930), vol.2, pp.170–72.
3. J.M. Keynes, *CW* (London: Macmillan, 1981), vol.XIX, p.786.
4. Keynes, *A Treatise on Money*, vol.2, p.175.
5. Vincent Barnett, 'Keynes and the Non-neutrality of Russian War Finance during World War One', *Europe-Asia Studies*, 61 (5), July 2009, pp.797–812.
6. Peter Gatrell, *Russia's First World War* (Harlow: Pearson, 2005), p.137.
7. A.C. Pigou, *The Economy and Finance of the War* (London: Dent, 1916), pp.82–3.
8. Ibid, p.66.
9. J.M. Keynes, *How to Pay for the War* (London: Macmillan, 1940), p.73.
10. Robert Skidelsky, *John Maynard Keynes: Hopes Betrayed* (London: Macmillan, 1983), p.376.
11. Keynes, *CW*, vol.II, p.92.
12. Ibid, p.101 and p.105.
13. Ibid, p.117.

14. Ibid, p.126.
15. Ibid, p.166.
16. Ibid, p.142.
17. Ibid, p.171.
18. Ibid, p.178.
19. Ibid, p.188.
20. Keynes, *CW*, vol.XVI, p.342.
21. Ibid, pp.374–5.
22. Skidelsky, *John Maynard Keynes: Hopes Betrayed*, p.392.
23. Quoted in the publisher's advertising catalogue at the end of J.M. Keynes, *A Revision of the Treaty* (London: Macmillan, 1922), p.3.
24. Ibid, p.5.
25. Niall Ferguson, *The Pity of War* (New York: Basic, 1999), pp.411–19.
26. Quoted in A.P. Thirlwall (ed.), *Keynes as a Policy Adviser* (London: Macmillan, 1982), p.81
27. Keynes, *CW*, vol.II, p.18.
28. J.M. Keynes, *CW*, (London: Macmillan, 1972), vol.X, pp.24–6.

7 Cycling for Britain's national interest

1. Robert Skidelsky, *John Maynard Keynes: The Economist as Saviour 1920–37* (London: Macmillan, 1992), p.19.
2. D.E. Moggridge, *Maynard Keynes* (London: Routledge, 1992), p.352.
3. Skidelsky, *John Maynard Keynes: The Economist as Saviour 1920–37*, p.41.
4. J.M. Keynes, *CW* (London: Macmillan, 1983), vol.XII, p.8.
5. Ibid, pp.260–1.
6. Ibid, p.12.
7. Skidelsky, *John Maynard Keynes: The Economist as Saviour 1920–37*, p.26.
8. Keynes, *CW*, vol.XII, pp.100–1.
9. Moggridge, *Maynard Keynes*, p.409.
10. Keynes, *CW*, vol.XII, p.241 and p.244.
11. Ibid, p.9.
12. Ibid, p.100.
13. Skidelsky, *John Maynard Keynes: The Economist as Saviour 1920–37*, p.93.
14. Moggridge, *Maynard Keynes*, p.398.
15. Ibid, p.396.
16. Ibid, p.395.
17. J.M. Keynes, *CW* (London: Macmillan, 1981), vol.XIX, p.146
18. J.M. Keynes, *CW* (London: Macmillan, 1971), vol.II, p.5.
19. J.M. Keynes, *Economic Journal*, December 1912, p.631.
20. Keynes, *CW*, vol.XIX, p.132.
21. Ibid, p.133.
22. Ibid, p.134.
23. John Toye, *Keynes on Population* (Oxford: OUP, 2000), p.175.
24. William Beveridge, 'Population and Employment', *Economic Journal*, December 1923, pp.463–4.

25. Ibid, p.466.
26. Keynes, *CW*, vol.XIX, p.141.
27. Ibid, p.283.
28. Ibid, p.284.
29. Keynes, *CW*, vol.XII, p.14.
30. Ibid, p.12.
31. Keynes, *CW*, vol.XIX, p.227.
32. Ibid, p.329.
33. Ibid, pp.221–22
34. Ibid, p.223.
35. R.F. Harrod, *The Life of John Maynard Keynes* (London: Macmillan, 1951), p.349.
36. Keynes, *CW*, vol.XIX, p.318.
37. Harrod, *The Life of John Maynard Keynes*, p.349.
38. Skidelsky, *John Maynard Keynes: The Economist as Saviour 1920–37*, p.184.

8 The method of modern statesmen

1. J.M. Keynes, *CW* (London: Macmillan, 1973), vol.VIII, p.3.
2. Ibid, pp.3–4.
3. Ibid, p.121.
4. Ibid, p.339.
5. J.M. Keynes, *CW* (London: Macmillan, 1983), vol.XII, p.248.
6. Keynes, *CW*, vol.VIII, pp.445–58.
7. Ibid, p.23.
8. Ibid, p.353.
9. Robert Skidelsky, *John Maynard Keynes: The Economist as Saviour 1920–37* (London: Macmillan, 1992), p.59
10. Alessandro Roncaglia, 'Keynes and Probability', *European Journal of the History of Economic Thought*, 2009, 16 (3), p.494.
11. C.D. Broad, *Mind*, January 1922, XXXI, p.72, p.79, and p.85.
12. F.Y.E., 'Review', *Journal of the Royal Statistical Society*, 85 (1), 1922, p.110.
13. J.M. Keynes, *A Revision of the Treaty* (London: Macmillan, 1922), list of advertisements, p.5.
14. J.M. Keynes, *A Revision of the Treaty* (London: Macmillan, 1922), pp.1–3.
15. Ibid, p.168.
16. Ibid, pp.4–5.
17. Ibid, pp.154–7.
18. Ibid, pp.163–5.
19. Ibid, p.164.
20. Ibid, p.167.
21. Ibid, p.187.

9 The fool's gold standard and *laissez faire*

1. P. Hill and R. Keynes (eds), *Lydia and Maynard* (London: Macmillan, 1989), p.234.
2. J.M. Keynes, *CW* (Cambridge: CUP, 1981), vol.XIX, p.271
3. J.M. Keynes, 'The Economic Consequences of Mr Churchill', *Essays in Persuasion* (London: Hart-Davis, 1952), p.246.
4. Ibid, p.257.
5. Ibid, p.268.
6. Ibid, p.248.
7. R.F. Harrod, *The Life of John Maynard Keynes* (London: Macmillan, 1951), p.361.
8. Keynes, *CW*, vol.XIX, p.432.
9. Ibid, p.528.
10. Ibid, pp.532–33.
11. Ibid, p.530.
12. J.M. Keynes, *CW* (Cambridge: CUP, 1983), vol.XI, pp.445–46.
13. Keynes, *CW*, vol.XIX, p.554.
14. Ibid, pp.555–56.
15. Hill and Keynes (eds), *Lydia and Maynard*, p.323.
16. J.M. Keynes, *CW* (Cambridge: CUP, 1973), vol.X, p.57.
17. Hill and Keynes (eds), *Lydia and Maynard*, p.110.
18. J.M. Keynes, 'A Short View of Russia', *Essays in Persuasion* (London: Hart-Davis, 1952), p.298.
19. Ibid, p.300.
20. Ibid, p.306–7.
21. Ibid, p.311.
22. Robert Skidelsky, *John Maynard Keynes: Hopes Betrayed* (London: Macmillan, 1983), p.337.
23. J.M. Keynes, *CW* (Cambridge: CUP, 1971), vol.II, p.150.
24. Keynes Papers, King's College, RV/1/38.
25. J.M. Keynes, 'Am I a Liberal?', *Essays in Persuasion* (London: Hart-Davis, 1952), p.329.
26. Ibid, p.335.
27. Hill and Keynes (eds), *Lydia and Maynard*, p.293.
28. Ibid, p.35.
29. Ibid, p.115.
30. Ibid, p.300.
31. Ibid, p.307.
32. Ibid, p.324.
33. Ibid, p.326.
34. Ibid, p.323.
35. Ibid, p.294.
36. J.M. Keynes, 'The End of Laissez-Faire', *Essays in Persuasion* (London: Hart-Davis, 1952), p.312.
37. Ibid, pp.316–17.
38. Ibid, p.314.

39. Ibid, p.318.
40. Robert Skidelsky, *John Maynard Keynes: The Economist as Saviour 1920–37* (London: Macmillan, 1992), pp.225–26.
41. D.E. Moggridge, *Maynard Keynes* (London: Routledge, 1992), p.452.
42. Keynes, 'The End of Laissez-Faire', p.321.

10 The fluctuating value of monetary reform

1. R.F. Harrod, *The Life of John Maynard Keynes* (London: Macmillan, 1951), p.339.
2. J.M. Keynes, *A Tract on Monetary Reform* (London: Macmillan, 1923), pp.30–31.
3. Harrod, *The Life of John Maynard Keynes*, p.325.
4. Keynes, *A Tract on Monetary Reform*, p.58.
5. Ibid, p.145.
6. Ibid, p.185.
7. Ibid, p.183.
8. Ibid, p.204.
9. Ibid, p.197.
10. Ibid, pp.76–77.
11. Ibid, p.80.
12. Ibid, p.84.
13. Ibid, pp.84–85.
14. Harrod, *The Life of John Maynard Keynes*, p.339.
15. D.E. Moggridge, *Maynard Keynes* (London: Routledge, 1992), p.434.
16. Irving Fisher, *Stabilizing the Dollar* (New York: Macmillan, 1925), p.81.
17. Ibid, p.104.
18. J.M. Keynes, *CW* (London: Macmillan, 1983), vol.XI, pp.416–18.
19. Robert Skidelsky, *John Maynard Keynes: The Economist as Saviour 1920–37* (London: Macmillan, 1992), p.164.

11 Organising prosperity

1. J.M. Keynes, *A Treatise on Money* (London: Macmillan, 1930), vol.2, p.195.
2. R.F. Harrod, *The Life of John Maynard Keynes* (London: Macmillan, 1951), pp.399–400.
3. Robert Skidelsky, *John Maynard Keynes: The Economist as Saviour 1920–37* (London: Macmillan, 1992), p.295.
4. Ibid, p.291.
5. J.M. Keynes, 'Am I a Liberal?', *Essays in Persuasion* (London: Hart-Davis, 1952), p.327.
6. J.M. Keynes, *CW* (London: Macmillan, 1981), vol.XIX, p.578.
7. Ibid, pp.580–81.
8. Ibid, p.585.
9. Ibid, p.591.

10. Skidelsky, *John Maynard Keynes: The Economist as Saviour 1920–37*, p.262.
11. Keynes, *CW*, vol.XIX, p.592.
12. Ibid, p.598.
13. Ibid, p.599.
14. Ibid, pp.603–5.
15. Harrod, *The Life of John Maynard Keynes*, p.382.
16. Keynes, *CW*, vol.XIX, p.613.
17. Ibid, p.626.
18. Ibid, pp.626–27.
19. Ibid, p.632.
20. Ibid, p.636.
21. Ibid, pp.641–42.
22. Ibid, p.643.
23. Ibid, pp.644–46.
24. Ibid, p.647.
25. Ibid, p.540.
26. Skidelsky, *John Maynard Keynes: The Economist as Saviour 1920–37*, p.265.
27. Keynes, *CW*, vol.XIX, p.754.
28. Skidelsky, *John Maynard Keynes: The Economist as Saviour 1920–37*, p.284.
29. A. Robinson, 'John Maynard Keynes, 1883–1946', in *Critical Assessments* (London; Routledge, 1983), vol.1, p.119.
30. Keynes, *CW*, vol.XIX, p.764.
31. Ibid, p.765.
32. Donald Markwell, *John Maynard Keynes and International Relations* (Oxford: OUP, 2006), p.144.
33. D.E. Moggridge and S. Howson, 'Keynes on Monetary Policy, 1910–46', in *Keynes: Critical Assessments* (London: Routledge, 1990), vol.1, p.457.
34. Keynes, *CW*, vol.XIX, p.568.
35. Ibid, p.573.
36. J.M. Keynes, *CW* (London: Macmillan, 1981), vol.XX, p.383.
37. Keynes, *CW*, vol.XIX, p.721.
38. J.M. Keynes, The German Transfer Problem', *Economic Journal*, March 1929, p.6.
39. Keynes, *CW*, vol.XIX, p.811.
40. Robinson, 'John Maynard Keynes, 1883–1946', p.117.
41. J.M. Keynes, 'A Programme of Expansion', *Essays in Persuasion* (London: Hart-Davis, 1952), p.127.
42. Keynes, *CW*, vol.XIX, p.838.
43. Skidelsky, *John Maynard Keynes: The Economist as Saviour 1920–37*, p.298.
44. Peter Clarke, *The Keynesian Revolution in the Making, 1924–36* (Oxford: Clarendon, 1988), p.86 and p.92.
45. Ibid, p.164.
46. Keynes, *A Treatise on Money*, vol.2, p.189.
47. *Minutes of Evidence Taken Before the Committee on Finance and Industry* (London: HMSO, 1931), vol.1, p.257.
48. Keynes, *CW*, vol.XIX, p.803.

49. Clarke, *The Keynesian Revolution in the Making*, p.89.
50. *Report of the Committee on Finance and Industry* (London: HMSO, 1931), p.82.
51. Keynes, *CW*, vol.XIX, p.821.
52. Skidelsky, *John Maynard Keynes: The Economist as Saviour 1920–37*, p.303.
53. *Minutes of Evidence Taken Before the Committee on Finance and Industry*, vol.1. p.345
54. Ibid, p.326.
55. Ibid, vol.2, p.318.
56. Keynes, *CW*, vol.XIX, p.808.
57. Ibid, p.810.
58. Keynes, *CW*, vol.XX, pp.350–51.
59. Keynes, *CW*, vol.XIX, p.829.

12 It all comes out in the wash

1. J.M. Keynes, *A Treatise on Money* (London: Macmillan, 1930), vol.2, p.408.
2. Ibid, vol.1, p.153.
3. Ibid, p.153.
4. Ibid, p.184.
5. Ibid, p.154.
6. Keynes, *A Treatise on Money*, vol.1, p.200 (quotation), p.189; vol.2, p.203.
7. Keynes, *A Treatise on Money*, vol.1, p.131 and p.162.
8. Ibid, p.330.
9. Ibid, p.163.
10. Ibid, p.346.
11. Ibid, p.347.
12. Ibid, p.345.
13. Ibid, vol.2, p.307.
14. Ibid, p.303.
15. Ibid, p.304.
16. Ibid, p.187.
17. J.M. Keynes, *CW* (London: Macmillan, 1981), vol.XX, pp.354–55.
18. J.M. Keynes, 'Economic Possibilities for our Grandchildren', *Essays in Persuasion* (London: Hart-Davis, 1952), p.358.
19. Ibid, p.369.
20. Keynes, *A Treatise on Money*, vol.2, p.361.
21. Ibid, pp.360–61.
22. David Laidler, *Fabricating the Keynesian Revolution* (Cambridge: CUP, 1999), pp.84–85.
23. Keynes, *A Treatise on Money*, vol.2, p.365.
24. Ibid, vol.1, p.vi.
25. A. Robinson, 'John Maynard Keynes, 1883–1946', in *Critical Assessments* (London; Routledge, 1983), vol.1, p.118.
26. Keynes, *A Treatise on Money*, vol.1, p.viii.

13 Multiplying (un)employment by expectations

1. A. Robinson, 'John Maynard Keynes', in *Keynes: Critical Assessments* (London: Routledge, 1990), vol.1, p.119.
2. A.F.W. Plumptre, 'Maynard Keynes as Teacher', in Milo Keynes (ed.), *Essays on John Maynard Keynes* (Cambridge: CUP, 1975), p.250.
3. Robert Skidelsky, *John Maynard Keynes: The Economist as Saviour 1920–37* (London: Macmillan, 1992), p.526.
4. Milo Keynes, 'Maynard and Lydia Keynes', in Milo Keynes (ed.), *Essays on John Maynard Keynes* (Cambridge: CUP, 1975), p.1.
5. R.F. Harrod, *The Life of John Maynard Keynes* (London: Macmillan, 1951), p.402.
6. R.E. Backhouse and B.W. Bateman, *Capitalist Revolutionary* (Harvard: Cambridge, MA, 2011), p.72.
7. Harrod, *The Life of John Maynard Keynes*, p.474.
8. Ibid, p.476.
9. J.M. Keynes, *Essays in Persuasion* (London: Hart-Davis, 1952), p.300.
10. Backhouse and Bateman, *Capitalist Revolutionary*, pp.66–67.
11. J.K. Galbraith, *The Great Crash* (London: Hamilton, 1955), p.152.
12. J.M. Keynes, *CW* (London: Macmillan, 1982), vol.XXI, pp.39–40.
13. Ibid, pp.43–44.
14. Ibid, pp.46–47.
15. Ibid, p.214.
16. Michael Stewart, *Keynes and After* (Harmondsworth: Penguin, 1967), p.17.
17. Keynes, *CW*, vol.XXI, p.57.
18. Ibid, p.60.
19. Ibid, p.124.
20. Ibid, p.136.
21. Skidelsky, *John Maynard Keynes: The Economist as Saviour 1920–37*, p.470.
22. J.M. Keynes, *CW* (London: Macmillan, 1973), vol.IX, p.352.
23. Ibid, p.352.
24. Ibid, p.335.
25. Skidelsky, *John Maynard Keynes: The Economist as Saviour 1920–37*, p.475.
26. D.E. Moggridge, *Maynard Keynes* (London: Routledge, 1992), p.573.
27. Keynes, *CW*, vol.XXI, pp.194–97.
28. *Minutes of Evidence taken before the Committee on Finance and Industry* (London: HMSO, 1931), vol.2, p.81.
29. J.M. Keynes, *CW* (London: Macmillan, 1973), vol.XIII, pp.190–92.
30. J.M. Keynes, *CW* (London: Macmillan, 1981), vol. XIX, p.551.
31. Keynes, *CW*, vol.XXI, p.204.
32. Ibid, pp.206–7.
33. Ibid, pp.208–10.
34. Joan Robinson, *Economic Philosophy* (London: Watts, 1962), p.88.
35. Lionel Robbins, *The Great Depression* (London: Macmillan, 1934), p.67.
36. Lord Kaldor, 'Keynes as a Policy Adviser', in *Keynes as a Policy Adviser* (Houndmills: Macmillan, 1982), p.21.
37. Robbins, *The Great Depression*, p.158.

38. Keynes, *CW*, vol.XXI, pp.87–88.
39. Ibid, p.137.
40. Ibid, p.92.
41. J.M. Keynes, *CW* (London: Macmillan, 1983), vol.XII, p.12.
42. Ibid, p.2.
43. Ibid, p.65.
44. Ibid, p.57.
45. J.M. Keynes, *The General Theory of Employment, Interest and Money*, (London: Macmillan, 1973), p.158.
46. Keynes Papers, King's College, Cambridge, PP/56/8/7.
47. Ibid, PP/56/9/1.
48. A.N.L. Munby, 'The Book Collector', in Milo Keynes (ed.), *Essays on John Maynard Keynes* (Cambridge: CUP, 1975), p.293.
49. Derek Gjerktsen, *The Newton Handbook* (London: RKP, 1986), p.289.
50. Ben Seligman, *Main Currents in Modern Economics* (New York: FP, 1962), p.731.
51. Harrod, *The Life of John Maynard Keynes*, p.446.
52. Skidelsky, *John Maynard Keynes: The Economist as Saviour 1920–37*, p.476.
53. Moggridge, *Maynard Keynes*, p.573.
54. J.M. Keynes, *CW* (London: Macmillan, 1981), vol.XX, p.379.
55. Keynes, *CW*, vol.XXI, p.235.
56. Ibid, p.236.
57. Ibid, pp.241–42.
58. Ibid, p.244.
59. Ibid, p.238.
60. Keynes, *The General Theory of Employment, Interest and Money*, p.382.
61. Ibid, p.349.
62. Moggridge, *Maynard Keynes*, p.518.
63. Keynes, *CW*, vol.XXI, p.293.
64. Ibid, p.295.
65. Ibid, p.305.
66. Ibid, pp.308–9.
67. Harrod, *The Life of John Maynard Keynes*, p.20.
68. Moggridge, *Maynard Keynes*, p.582.
69. J.K. Galbraith, 'How Keynes came to America', in Milo Keynes (ed.), *Essays on John Maynard Keynes* (Cambridge: CUP, 1975), p.134.
70. Harrod, *The Life of John Maynard Keynes*, p.449.
71. Keynes, *CW*, vol.XXI, pp.321–22.
72. Ibid, p.337.
73. Ibid, p.325.
74. Galbraith, 'How Keynes came to America', p.135.
75. Keynes, *CW*, vol.IX,, pp.358–59.
76. Keynes, *CW*, vol.XXI, p.281.
77. Harrod, *The Life of John Maynard Keynes*, p.443; Skidelsky, *John Maynard Keynes: The Economist as Saviour 1920–37*, p.472.
78. Keynes, *CW*, vol.XIII, pp.492–93.

79. Moggridge, *Maynard Keynes*, pp.562–66.
80. Keynes, *CW*, vol.XIII, p.422.
81. Ibid, p.488.

14 Liquidising the classical theory

1. J.M. Keynes, *The General Theory of Employment, Interest and Money*, (London: Macmillan, 1973), p.292.
2. J.M. Keynes, *CW* (London: Macmillan, 1973), vol.XIII, p.406.
3. Keynes, *The General Theory of Employment, Interest and Money*, p.3.
4. Ibid, p.55.
5. Ibid, pp.25–26.
6. Ibid, p.46 and p.50.
7. Ibid, p.96.
8. Keynes, *CW*, vol.XIII, p.445.
9. Keynes, *The General Theory of Employment, Interest and Money*, p.118.
10. Ibid, pp.135–36.
11. Ibid, pp.166–67.
12. Ibid, p.280.
13. J.M. Keynes, *CW* (London: Macmillan, 1973), vol.XIV, p.121.
14. J.R. Hicks, 'Mr. Keynes's Theory of Employment, *Economic Journal*, vol.XLVI, p.240.
15. Peter Clarke, *The Keynesian Revolution in the Making, 1924–36* (Oxford: Clarendon, 1988), p.260.
16. J.M. Keynes, *CW* (London: Macmillan, 1973), vol.VIII, p.56.
17. Keynes Papers, King's College, UA/4/3/34.
18. Keynes, *The General Theory of Employment, Interest and Money*, p.152.
19. Keynes Papers, UA/4/3/24.
20. Ibid, UA/4/3/19 and UA/4/3/27.
21. Keynes, *The General Theory of Employment, Interest and Money*, p.xxii.
22. Ibid, p.203.
23. Ibid, p.108.
24. Peter Clarke, *The Keynesian Revolution in the Making, 1924–36* (Oxford: Clarendon, 1988), p.197.
25. J.M. Keynes, *CW* (London: Macmillan, 1982), vol.XXI, pp.171–72.
26. Ibid, p.178.
27. Keynes, *The General Theory of Employment, Interest and Money*, p.245.
28. Ibid, pp.250–51.
29. Ibid, p.243.
30. Ibid, p.317.
31. Ibid, p.28.
32. Ibid, p.374.
33. Ibid, p.376.
34. Keynes, *CW*, vol.XIII, p.638.
35. L.R. Klein, *The Keynesian Revolution* (London: Macmillan, 1952) p.96.

36. A.C. Pigou, 'Mr J.M. Keynes' *General Theory of Employment, Interest and Money'*, in *Keynes: Critical Assessments* (London: Routledge, 1990), vol.2, p.18, p.21.

37. W.B. Reddaway, 'The General Theory of Employment, Interest and Money', in *Keynes: Critical Assessments* (London: Routledge, 1990), vol.2, p.38.

38. A.C. Pigou, *The Theory of Unemployment* (London: Macmillan, 1933), pp.241–43.

39. A.P. Lerner, 'Mr Keynes' 'General Theory of Employment, Interest and Money'', in *Keynes: Critical Assessments* (London: Routledge, 1990), vol.2, p.56.

40. A. Robinson, 'John Maynard Keynes', in *Keynes: Critical Assessments* (London: Routledge, 1990), vol.1, p.120.

41. Roger Backhouse, *A History of Modern Economic Analysis* (Oxford: Blackwell, 1985), p.333.

42. Keynes, *The General Theory of Employment, Interest and Money*, p.180.

43. J.R. Hicks, 'Mr Keynes and the "Classics"', in *Keynes: Critical Assessments* (London: Routledge, 1990), vol.2, p.162.

44. Ibid, p.162.

45. Ibid, p.169.

46. Robert Skidelsky, *John Maynard Keynes: The Economist as Saviour 1920–37* (London: Macmillan, 1992), p.548.

47. Keynes, *The General Theory of Employment, Interest and Money*, p.297.

48. R.E. Backhouse and B.W. Bateman, *Capitalist Revolutionary* (Harvard: Cambridge, MA, 2011), p.122.

49. David Laidler, *Fabricating the Keynesian Revolution* (Cambridge: CUP, 1999), back cover quotation.

15   War finance and the post-war economic order

1. J.M. Keynes, *CW* (London: Macmillan, 1973), vol.XIV, p.131.

2. Robert Skidelsky, *John Maynard Keynes: Fighting for Britain 1937–46* (London: Macmillan, 2000), p.29.

3. J.M. Keynes *How to Pay for the War* (London: Macmillan, 1940), p.10, p.28, p.46.

4. Ibid, p.58.

5. J.M. Keynes, 'The Income and Fiscal Potential of Great Britain', *Economic Journal*, vol.XLIX, December 1939, p.631.

6. Ibid, p.626.

7. Skidelsky, *John Maynard Keynes: Fighting for Britain 1937–46*, p.79.

8. A. Robinson, 'John Maynard Keynes', in *Keynes: Critical Assessments* (London: Routledge: 1990), vol.1, p.129.

9. Winston Churchill, *The Second World War: The Grand Alliance* (London: Cassell, 1950), p.102.

10. J.M. Keynes, *CW* (London: Macmillan, 1989), vol.XXIII, p.16.

11. Ibid, p.15.

12. Ibid, p.25.

13. Ibid, p.88.

14. Ibid, p.139.

15. Ibid, p.175.
16. Ibid, p.176.
17. Ibid, p.178.
18. Ibid, p.176.
19. D.E. Moggridge, *Maynard Keynes* (London: Routledge, 1992), p.668.
20. Donald Markwell, *John Maynard Keynes and International Relations* (Oxford: OUP, 2006), p.257.
21. Skidelsky, *John Maynard Keynes: Fighting for Britain 1937–46*, p.265.
22. Ibid, p.471.

Conclusion

1. A.P. Thirlwall (ed.), *Keynes as a Policy Adviser* (Houndmills: Macmillan, 1982), p.25.
2. J.M. Keynes, *CW* (London: Macmillan, 1971), vol.I, p.181.
3. J.M. Keynes, *CW* (London: Macmillan, 1982), vol. XXVIII, p.18.
4. J.M. Keynes, *CW* (London: Macmillan, 1979), vol.XXIII, p.337.
5. D.M. Buss, *Evolutionary Psychology* (Boston: Pearson, 2004), p.388.
6. J.M. Keynes, *The General Theory of Employment, Interest and Money* (London: Macmillan, 1973), p.374.
7. J.M. Keynes, *CW* (London: Macmillan, 1973), vol.XIV, p.300.
8. J.M. Keynes, *CW* (London: Macmillan, 1973), vol.X, p.174.
9. Ibid, p.371.
10. Ibid, p.108.
11. Ibid, p.139.
12. J.M. Keynes, *CW* (London: Macmillan, 1981), vol.XIX, p.471.
13. A.C. Pigou, *The Theory of Unemployment* (London: Macmillan, 1933), p.v.
14. Keynes, *The General Theory of Employment, Interest and Money*, p.64.
15. E.H. Carr, *What is History?* (Harmondsworth: Penguin, 1964), p.139.
16. Keynes, *The General Theory of Employment, Interest and Money*, p.154.
17. E.G. Winslow, 'Organic Interdependence, Uncertainty and Economic Analysis', *Economic Journal*, December 1989, p.1180.
18. Keynes, *The General Theory of Employment, Interest and Money*, p.158.
19. J.M. Keynes, *A Treatise on Money* (London: Macmillan, 1930), vol.2, p.361.
20. J.M. Keynes, *A Tract on Monetary Reform* (London: Macmillan, 1923), pp.25–26.
21. Keynes Papers, King's College, UA/4/3/24.
22. Joan Robinson, *Economic Philosophy* (London: Watts, 1962), p.1
23. Keynes, *CW*, vol.XIV, p.122.
24. J.M. Keynes, *CW* (London: Macmillan, 1981), vol.XXVIII, p.333.
25. In total, Keynes's surviving notes for the psychology exam occupy over one hundred pages of detailed study. See Keynes Papers, UA/4/2 (37 pages) and UA/4/3 (65 pages).
26. J.M. Keynes, *Two Memoirs* (London: Hart-Davis, 1949), p.83. Keynes Papers, UA/4/3/2.
27. Ray Monk, *Bertrand Russell: The Spirit of Solitude* (London: Cape, 1996), p.63.

28. Keynes, *CW*, vol.X, p.262.
29. W.F. van Raaij, 'Economics and Psychology', in *Companion to Contemporary Economic Thought* (London: Routledge, 1991), p.800.
30. George Katona, *War Without Inflation: A Psychological Approach to Problems of War Economy* (New York: Columbia, 1942).

Index

Allport, Gordon 7
art 70, 71, 201, 202
Asquith, Herbert Henry 68,
    102

backwardation 95, 96
Bagehot, Walter 22, 76, 89,
    272
balance of payments 257
balance of trade 175, 176
Baldwin, Stanley 128
ballet 38, 99, 100, 101, 200,
    201, 262
Bank of England 54, 55, 65,
    67, 130, 151, 152,
    165, 172, 174, 181,
    198, 260
Bank rate 151, 153, 176, 177,
    188
bankers 41, 42, 56, 57
Barocchi, Randolfo 71, 100
Bell, Clive 18, 69, 100, 101,
    102
Bell, Vanessa 101, 201, 260
Bentham, Jeremy 21, 274
Beveridge, William 104–8
biography 3–4, 6–10

Bloomsbury group 19, 20, 22,
    38, 62, 89, 100, 101,
    102, 141
Blunt, Anthony 20, 160
Boer War 17, 35
Bolshevik revolution 90, 146
Bolshevism 136–39
books 49, 214
Bretton Woods 223, 258
Britain's Industrial Future 167,
    168
British Empire 12, 24, 36, 45,
    46, 109, 252, 253, 254,
    255, 257
Burke, Edmund 21, 33, 36, 89,
    124
business cycle 52, 97, 183,
    195, 238

Camargo Society 200, 201
Cambridge 12, 14, 17, 22, 23,
    25, 37, 51, 62, 64, 94,
    143, 160, 168, 199, 241,
    275
Cambridge Apostles 18, 19,
    22, 160
Cambridge Circus 168–71, 196

capital 23, 34, 57, 112, 113, 114, 195, 201, 229, 230, 237, 238, 248
capitalism 1, 138, 139, 145, 146, 166, 240, 275
Carr, E.H. 273
cartels 162, 164, 165
Chamberlain, Austen 44, 50, 95
Chamberlain, Neville 207
Christianity 29, 137, 138, 142
Churchill, Winston 127, 128, 131, 132, 135, 136, 168, 251, 259
Civil Service 17, 23, 24–26, 275
Clark, Colin 251
Clemenceau, Georges 92
coal 107, 131, 133, 135, 160, 174
communism 138, 139, 211
conservatism 36, 115, 139
Copernicus, Nicolaus 214
cotton 160–66, 200
credit 35, 37, 57, 72, 73, 98, 132, 151, 186, 195
credit cycling 97–98
Currie, Lauchlin 222

deferred pay 249, 250, 251
deflation 112, 129, 150, 172, 199
depression 57, 166, 171, 187, 196, 198, 199, 202, 210, 215, 243
Diaghilev, Serge 38, 71, 142
dollar 66, 67, 111, 127, 129, 132, 155, 257

Eagleton, Terry 5
Economic Consequences of Mr Churchill, The 12, 131, 133, 251
Economic Consequences of the Peace, The 9, 81, 86–92, 93, 94, 104–5, 108, 136, 184, 204
Economic Journal 34, 47–49, 70, 104, 105, 134, 156
Edgeworth, F.Y. 22, 47, 48, 121
effective demand 227–28, 230, 238
employment function 230, 238
End of Laissez-Faire, The 143–46, 167
England 12, 27, 28, 210, 215
equilibrium 54, 132, 185, 188, 232, 237
Essays in Biography 9
ethics 31, 32, 33, 202
Eton 15–18
Eton Wall Game 15–16
Euro 266, 269
expectations 228, 230, 231
exports 59, 106, 111, 112, 125, 178

First World War 37, 63–81, 82–93, 134, 150, 216
Fisher, Irving 155, 245
foreign investment 34, 35, 108, 109, 111, 174–80, 189, 190, 192, 205
France 37, 42, 65, 67, 70, 80, 92, 94, 126, 161, 205
free trade 23, 35, 51, 115, 143,

178, 207, 209, 210, 216,
217, 218, 255, 256
Freud, Sigmund 10, 273, 274
Friedman, Milton 154, 244
Fry, Roger 201

Garnett, David 69, 102
General Strike (1926) 133,
134, 135, 199
*General Theory of Employment,
Interest and Money, The* 6,
10, 11, 13, 48, 98, 111,
200, 202, 206, 213, 221,
224, 226–47, 264, 273
Genoa conference 103
Germany 24, 70, 79, 80,
86–88, 90, 124, 150,
161, 249
gold 10, 43, 54, 67, 75, 152,
157, 177, 198, 222
gold standard 39, 40, 43, 54,
64, 67, 127, 128, 129,
131, 135, 154, 191, 199,
203, 204, 266, 268
gold-exchange standard 40, 43
Gordon Square 38, 100, 101,
142
Grant, Duncan 26, 32, 37, 45,
69, 71, 201, 260
Great Britain 12–13, 34–36,
54, 87, 205
Great Depression 166, 171,
187, 196, 198, 199, 210
Greece 28, 37, 262, 269

Harrod, Roy 113, 114, 154,
215, 225
Hawtrey, R.G. 18, 180, 225
Hayek, F.A. 195, 196, 200

Hegel, G.W.F. 19
Henderson, Hubert 102, 167,
176, 223
Hicks, J.R. 48, 242, 243
Hitler, Adolf 91
Hogarth Press 131

imports 59, 106, 125
India 24, 25, 35, 37, 39–45,
46, 47, 55–56, 61, 262,
263
Indian Currency and Finance 42,
43, 55, 148
inflation 82, 83, 86, 112, 149,
150, 249, 250, 276
interest rate 54, 187, 188,
192, 193, 219, 220, 229,
233, 236, 237, 238, 240,
242
International Monetary Fund
223, 258, 259
investment 47, 49, 57, 95, 96,
97, 109, 110, 185,
212–14, 229, 237, 242,
243, 270, 274
Islam 29
IS-LM model 242–43, 264,
276,
Italy 37, 65, 70, 161

James, William 10
Jevons, W.S. 22, 89, 231, 271
Jung, Carl 7, 278

Kahn, R.F. 169, 170, 225,
229, 235, 245
Kahneman, Daniel 276
Katona, George 276, 277
Keynes, Florence 14, 101

Keynes, Geoffrey 101, 201
Keynes, J.N. 14, 21, 101, 260
Keynesian revolution 4–5, 206, 210, 225, 246
King's College, Cambridge 17, 20, 25, 26, 32, 37, 94, 96, 215, 260
Kolmogorov, A.N. 121

laissez faire 111, 112, 113, 115, 138, 163, 166, 167, 174, 191, 202, 212, 225
Lancashire 160–66
Law, Andrew Bonar 68, 76, 102
Lend Lease 253–56, 259
Lenin, V.I. 82
Leninism 137
Liberal Party 102, 140, 158, 167, 179
liberalism 28, 50, 102, 103, 115, 139, 140, 145, 166, 167
liquidity preference 229, 237, 243
Lloyd George, David 9, 20, 63–64, 65, 66, 69, 72–77, 79, 81, 90, 92, 93, 102, 114, 122, 124, 136, 158, 167, 176, 262
London 2, 23, 35, 38, 40, 62, 65, 66, 77, 94, 130, 179, 191
Lopokova, Lydia 71, 99–102, 127, 137, 138, 139, 140–42, 159, 200, 248, 260

Macmillan Committee on Finance and Industry 180, 196
Malthus, T.H. 8, 58, 59, 60, 64, 89, 271
marginal efficiency of capital 229, 236, 238, 240, 245
Marshall, Alfred 9, 18, 19, 22, 23, 25, 47, 53, 169, 195, 271
Marx, Karl 1, 2, 3, 8, 20, 46, 59, 89, 137, 147, 273
Marxism 224, 225
mathematics 32, 245, 246, 276
McKenna, Reginald 66, 68, 72
McTaggart, J.E. 18, 19, 20, 33
Meade, James 170
Means to Prosperity, The 205–7, 222
Milton Keynes 2
Minsky, Hyman 270
Moggridge, Donald 45, 216
monetary theory 39, 42, 52–55, 148–56, 185–88
money 37, 52, 53, 54, 97, 149, 187, 194, 203, 226, 236, 237, 270
Montagu, Edwin 42, 43, 50, 65, 69
Montagu, Samuel 42, 43, 44
Moore, G.E. 18, 19, 20, 27, 30–33, 36, 51, 62, 232, 275
morality 32, 33, 193
multiplier 172, 229, 233–35, 237, 241, 245

Nation and Athenaeum, The 102, 103, 105, 108

national self-sufficiency 215–18
nationalism 60, 114, 206,
    215–18
Net National Gain 190
New Deal 219, 222
New York 77, 125, 130, 191
Newton, Isaac 6–7, 214, 261,
    271

Paish, George 65
Paris Peace Conference 9, 79,
    86, 91, 92
Peace Treaty, 86, 90
Pigou, A.C. 18, 19, 25, 85,
    169, 195, 224, 241,
    272
planning 163, 211–12, 243
population 58–61, 91, 104,
    248
prices 37, 46, 53, 54, 86, 95,
    96, 97, 163, 164, 185,
    186, 189, 192, 208, 215,
    228, 270
Principia Ethica 19, 20, 30
probability theory 24, 25, 32,
    116–21
propensity to consume 228–29,
    231, 236, 237, 244, 245
protectionism 23, 35, 51,
    207–11, 216, 255, 268
psychology 7, 9–10, 23, 182,
    194, 206, 230–33, 274,
    275, 276
public works 112, 114, 173,
    219, 221

quantity theory of money 11,
    39, 52–55, 152–54,
    155–56, 276

Rawls, John 262, 264
reparations 78–81, 204
Revision of the Treaty, A 98, 99,
    121–26
Ricardo, David 8, 22, 89, 160,
    227
Robbins, Lionel 210
Robertson, D.H. 141, 167,
    169, 180, 225, 235
Robinson, Austin 169, 170,
    176
Robinson, Joan 169, 210, 225,
    240, 274
Roosevelt, F.D. 219, 220, 222,
    253, 255
Russell, Bertrand 18, 19, 120,
    121, 232, 261, 275
Russia 24, 30, 42, 65, 67, 70,
    71, 72, 73, 74, 75, 78,
    84, 137, 138, 161, 262

Samuelson, Paul 244, 245,
    246
Sarkar, B.K. 44, 45
savings 57, 110, 112, 173,
    175, 181, 185, 228, 235,
    238, 249, 250
Say's Law 228, 229
Second World War 5, 39, 86,
    247, 248–59, 263
sexual orientation 17, 22, 45,
    50, 100
shares 49, 50, 97, 178, 213,
    229
Short View of Russia, A 137,
    138, 144
Shove, Gerald 45, 50, 69
Sidgwick, Henry 21, 33
silver 39, 41, 42, 44, 54

silver standard 39
Skidelsky, Robert 30, 35, 144, 206, 216
Smith, Adam 1, 2, 8, 143, 147, 227, 273
socialism 2, 51, 115, 139, 146, 240
Sraffa, Piero 159, 160, 225
Stalin, Joseph 91
statesmen 93, 121–24, 206, 240
sterling 39, 40, 43, 65, 66, 67, 75, 110, 127, 129, 132, 133, 151, 198
Stout, G.F. 232, 274, 275
Strachey, James 10, 38, 274
Strachey, Lytton 18, 22, 26, 38, 69, 102, 142
Sully, James 232, 275

tariffs 34, 165, 190, 207–11, 268
taxation 83, 249
terms of trade 59, 104, 105, 106
Tilton 141, 142, 159, 200, 248, 259
Tract on Monetary Reform, A 103, 131, 148–57, 184
trade cycle 56–58, 97, 98, 185, 186
Trade Unions 113, 251
Treasury (UK) 65, 68, 72, 73, 74, 75, 76, 78, 80, 83, 85, 95
Treasury view 180, 181, 182
Treatise on Money, A 83, 170, 178, 184–97, 206, 219, 231

Treatise on Probability, A 98, 99, 116–21, 123, 231
truth 124

unemployment 104, 105, 112, 132, 173, 175, 202, 219, 224, 235, 237
Union of Soviet Socialist Republics 136, 137, 140, 199, 243, 258
United Kingdom 12, 13, 29, 66, 67, 70, 104, 108, 109, 110, 112, 114, 124, 127, 129, 177, 179, 191, 198, 205, 206, 208, 217, 248, 252, 254, 255, 262–64
United States of America 71, 77–78, 79, 87, 88, 90, 91, 94, 124, 125, 126, 158, 219, 221, 252, 256

Veblen, Thorstein 16
Versailles 79, 81, 91, 126, 131

wages 34, 107, 132, 150, 207, 227, 236, 269, 270
Walras, Leon 265
war finance 83–86, 249–53, 267, 276
War Plan Red 257, 258
Washington 219, 259
White, Harry Dexter 258
Whitehall 24, 25, 42
Whitehead, A.N. 18, 19
Wicksell, Knut 196
Wilson, Woodrow 7, 10, 78, 80, 91, 92

Wittgenstein, Ludwig 20, 159
Woolf, Leonard 10, 22, 102,
     131, 260

Woolf, Virginia 10, 22, 131,
     260, 261
World Bank 258, 259

A Political History
7ᵗʰ Edition
David Childs

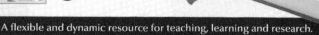